XAVIER
TALES

MICHAEL PERRY

FOREWORD BY U.S. SENATOR JIM BUNNING

PONE
PRESS

WWW.XAVIERTALES.COM

ISBN: 978-0-615-21073-5

Publisher: Michael Perry
Dust jacket design: Kelly Cassidy
Inside page design: Kelly Cassidy
Editors: Jennifer Scroggins, Sadie Browning Johnson, Rory Glynn
Cover and dust jacket photography: Greg Rust, Xavier University
Editorial assistant: Beth Hesse

Printed in the United States of America
Pone Press
P.O. Box 24068
Cincinnati, OH 45224
Web site: www.xaviertales.com
Email address: xaviertales@aol.com

CONTENTS

Jim Bunning...
the Xavier student

Jim Bunning...
the U.S. Senator

FOREWORD

I graduated from St. Xavier High School in Cincinnati in 1949 and had four opportunities to go to college on a scholarship: Louisville, Oregon State, Holy Cross and Xavier. Holy Cross was for baseball, and the other three were for basketball. I thought I was better at basketball than baseball in high school.

I chose Xavier because I was familiar with the school and I didn't really want to leave town. I was in love with the woman who would become my wife, Mary, and I also thought it would be a perfect opportunity to continue my Jesuit education.

At Xavier, I played freshman basketball in 1949–50 for coach Ned Wulk, and I started every game I played in. At 6 feet 4, I was one of the taller guys on the team, but I played guard. That was a little unusual. Our biggest guy, I think, was Huck Budde, and he was only an inch taller than I was. I did most of my scoring on the fast break or driving to the basket. Wulk installed a run-run-run offense, which was different from the style the varsity played under coach Lew Hirt.

I also played baseball for Ned as a freshman. It was after that season that I signed a professional baseball contract with the Detroit Tigers. Ned was instrumental in me going into baseball. I went in and told him I had a really good offer from Detroit. He said: "Jim you're probably going to be a regular (basketball) player at Xavier for two years when you get to be a junior and senior. You'll probably be a starter. But you've got a chance to be a major-league baseball player." He was very supportive.

I actually had worked out with three or four baseball teams after high school. The best offers I had were from Cleveland and Detroit, but my father, Lou, insisted I go to college. After my freshman year at Xavier, I told my father that I had an offer from Detroit and I wanted to take it. He said, "I won't sign your contract until you promise me you'll finish school." I was under-age, so I had to promise I would finish college. The Tigers worked with me so I could attend school each spring, then I would spend the summers in the minor leagues.

I got a signing bonus of $4,000. Because I was now considered a pro and I could not be on scholarship, I had to work. During my sophomore year at Xavier, I coached the varsity and reserve basketball teams at St. Thomas High School in Fort Thomas. Ned became Xavier's varsity coach in 1951 and invited me back to coach the freshman basketball team in 1951–52 and 1952–53. I coached against another Hall of Fame pitcher, Sandy Koufax, who played at the University of Cincinnati.

I scouted opponents for Ned. I can remember going to watch Branch McCracken's Indiana team in 1951 and handing in the scouting report to Ned and saying, "Boy, we have our hands full." We lost 92–69. As a coach, I was kind of a Ned Wulk junior, ranting and raving. My job on the varsity team was to try to keep Ned in the game because he was up and down and all over the place. I remember him falling backward off the bench one game, and I was trying to get him back on board. I remember getting kicked in the shins really hard one other game when he was running up and down and I was trying to keep him from getting thrown out. He was a pretty active coach.

I loved coaching basketball. In fact, I went back and coached grammar-school basketball at St. Catherine of Siena in Fort Thomas while I was a professional pitcher. I coached two years of seventh and eighth grade.

It was all great at Xavier when I was playing. It wasn't so great when I was trying to get through classes and fulfill the promise I made my father. I was taking 20 to 22 hours of classes. It was a heavy load, *and* I was working on the side. It was not easy. But I graduated in 3½ years, in January 1953.

Between 1950 and 1955, I played minor-league ball in Richmond, Ind., Davenport, Iowa, Williamsport, Pa., Buffalo and Little Rock, Ark. I finally got my chance with the Tigers, making my major-league debut on July 20, 1955. I was 23 years old at the time.

I follow Xavier's basketball program very closely. They've had a very proud tradition of doing extremely well in getting into the NCAA Tournament and advancing. I think of my time at Xavier pleasantly. I thank God every day for my education because I can walk and chew gum at the same time now. My background in economics has helped me in every phase of my service in Congress, both on the Ways and Means Committee and now on the Senate Finance Committee. I don't feel behind the curve because of the education I had at Xavier.

My father was absolutely right. I told him that more than once.

Jim Bunning

Bunning is a former Xavier University basketball and baseball player and freshman basketball coach. He retired in 1971 after a 17-year Major League Baseball career as a pitcher and was inducted into the Baseball Hall of Fame in 1996. A Republican from Kentucky, Bunning has served in the U.S. Senate since 1998.

ACKNOWLEDGMENTS

There were a lot of messages left and calls returned. There were endless late nights and weekends on the telephone and in front of the computer.

The real thanks for this book coming to life belongs to all those who were willing to share their stories with me between January 2007 and May 2008. This anecdotal history of sorts is the result of these fine folks spending time reminiscing.

The calls came and went from more than 15 states. Two correspondences were from Italy (one by phone, one by e-mail).

It was a sometimes frustrating, often exhausting but overall rewarding experience to track down so many people from Xavier's basketball history, many of whom I had written about in the past and many of whom I had only read about in media guides.

My deepest appreciation to:

Sherwin Anderson, Tay Baker, Jeff Battle, Mike Bobinski, Jim Boothe, Alvin Brown, Lenny Brown, Jim Bunning, Stanley Burrell, Bill Cady, Justin Cage, Lionel Chalmers, Bill Daily, Nick Daniels, Michael Davenport, Justin Doellman, Josh Duncan, Dave Fazioli, Rose Ann Fleming, Jeff Fogelson, David Fluker, Kevin Frey, Dino Gaudio, Joe Geiger, Steve Gentry, Pete Gillen, Brian Grant, Richie Harris, Jerry Helmers, Tyrone Hill, Keith Jackson, Eddie Johnson, Pat Kelsey, Stan Kimbrough, Bill Kirvin, Bob Kohlhepp, Byron Larkin, Drew Lavender, Ralph Lee, Gary Lumpkin, Andy MacWilliams, Gary Massa, Thad Matta, Maurice McAfee, Walt McBride, Joe McNeil, Sean Miller, Joe Pangrazio, Bob Pelkington, Mike Plunkett, James Posey, Skip Prosser, Bob Quick, Luther Rackley, Jerry Robinson, Dawn Rogers, Jay Ross, Don Ruberg, Romain Sato, Gene Smith, Bob Staak, Hank Stein, Derek Strong, Joe Sunderman, Larry Sykes, Frank Tartaron, Matt Terpening, Jack Thobe, Steve Thomas, Brian Thornton, Ray Tomlin, Joe Viviano, Jamal Walker, Tyrice Walker, David West, Aaron Williams, Darnell Williams and Steve Wolf.

That's only the beginning.

I could not have finished this — perhaps ever — without Beth Hesse, a 2008 Xavier graduate who helped me sort through 70-some interviews on tape. Beth and I would meet periodically at the Musketeer statue outside Cintas Center to exchange microcassettes, which she would transcribe between classes, internships and her senior year of college. Her dedication to this project was extraordinary.

Kelly Cassidy is the talented designer who created the striking cover and laid out the entire book. Sadie Browning Johnson and Jennifer Scroggins did a fantastic job editing, providing excellent suggestions and game-saving fixes.

My thanks also to Tom Callinan, *The Enquirer's* vice president for content and audience development; Xavier sports information director Tom Eiser; Xavier's director for photography Greg Rust; Dustin Dow, the newspaper's outstanding Xavier beat reporter and blogger; Jeff Suess, an Enquirer library technician; Rory Glynn, also a former Xavier beat reporter; Pat Latham at CJK; Brad and Chris Fenison at Pediment Publishing; and Mike DeCourcy from the Sporting News for his kind words on the back of the book.

Marilyn Seebohm, my mother-in-law, used to clip stories from the paper when I covered Xavier from 1996–2000, and after the season I'd file them away by subject. Who knew how valuable her efforts would become more than 10 years after she started that process? I appreciated what she did then, but even more so as I worked on this book.

I can't say enough about so many at Xavier University who embraced this project and have been supportive since I first explained what I planned to do: Bobinski, Eiser, Brian Hicks, Massa, Dan Cloran, D.J. Hodge, Joe Ventura and Skip Tate. I am grateful for all they have done.

When I conducted my final interview, Lionel Chalmers said to me: "I bet you'll be glad when this is over." I replied: "Yes, but my wife and kids will *really* be glad."

Eiser has been telling me how I "overachieved" in the marriage department from the first time he met my wife, Valerie. I've never been able to dispute that. Valerie and my children, Ben, Olivia and Dan, have been as patient as possible during the past 18 months. Saying "thanks" to them doesn't seem like enough. Suffice it to say, I am one fortunate man.

Please enjoy the book.

Michael

Michael Perry

1

FIVE UNFORGETTABLE GAMES

XAVIER 78, NO. 11 DAYTON 74 (OT)
March 22, 1958
National Invitation Tournament final, New York City

IT WAS THE TOURNAMENT Xavier did not belong in. That's what everyone said.

The Musketeers had lost seven of their last eight regular-season games, and National Invitation Tournament officials actually asked XU to give up its bid, which had been awarded Feb. 27 — the day after a victory over Western Kentucky halted a five-game losing streak and improved XU's record to 15-9.

"You invited us, so we'll be showing up," first-year Xavier coach Jim McCafferty told the NIT.

XU had started the 1957—58 season with a 10-1 record, but Cornelius "Corny" Freeman, the team's leading rebounder and a double-digit scorer, was declared academically ineligible for the second semester.

"When you lose a player like that, you're just kind of defeated," former Musketeer Hank Stein said. "Nobody really stepped up to fill what he gave to the team. It didn't happen until we hit the NIT."

National Invitation Tournament MVP Hank Stein is carried by his teammates after the Musketeers captured the 1958 title.

After receiving the tournament bid, Xavier lost its final regular-season games to Miami and Cincinnati, and the NIT selection committee was taking a beating for including the Musketeers, who were the No. 12 seed in the 12-team tournament.

Stein readily admits to packing only two days worth of clothing.

"Based on the way we were playing, I felt that we weren't going to be around too long," he said.

"We probably all had one change of clothes," teammate Joe Viviano agreed. "We thought we'd be up there for one game."

Newspaper articles called Xavier "unheralded and unwanted" and "the laughingstock of New York."

It was XU, however, that got the last laugh.

The Musketeers defeated Niagara, No. 2 seed Bradley

and No. 3 seed St. Bonaventure to set up a meeting with 11th-ranked and top-seeded Dayton in the NIT championship game. The Flyers already had defeated Xavier twice that season, 74-59 at Dayton and 64-58 at Cincinnati Gardens.

Dayton had lost in the NIT finals in 1951, '52, '55 and '56 and was heavily favored over Xavier.

"Here it was, New York, Madison Square Garden and sure enough we play the school, other than Cincinnati, that's right down the street from us," Viviano said.

"All four (NIT) games we were the underdog," Stein said.

This time, Xavier prevailed 78-74 in overtime.

Stein scored six points in the extra period, including the go-ahead basket, finished with 23 points and was named the tournament's MVP. He averaged 22.5 points over four games.

"I did not have a bad game in any game," he said. "It's very difficult to describe the feeling, the jubilation that you have when you win a tournament like that. It was a national tournament, and back then it was just as prestigious as the NCAA. It's the greatest feeling in the world to win a major tournament."

It was the first NIT final to go into overtime.

Sport magazine once called it "one of the greatest upsets in basketball history."

"The championship game between Dayton and Xavier was the best in the 21-year history of the NIT," Madison Square Garden executive director of basketball John Goldner said at the 1958 trophy presentation.

"It just happened to be that those four games were the best ones we played all year," Stein said.

NO. 25 XAVIER 74, NO. 5 GEORGETOWN 71
March 18, 1990
NCAA Tournament, second round, Indianapolis

In a world of college basketball storylines, this was the ultimate David vs. Goliath battle. At least in the minds of everyone outside of Cincinnati.

After defeating Kansas State in the opening round of the 1990 NCAA Tournament, seventh-seeded Xavier was set to face mighty Georgetown, a No. 3 seed in the tourney and just six years removed from winning the national championship.

"I just knew we were going to win and I think the kids knew," then-Xavier coach Pete Gillen said. "I just felt it. Why? I can't tell you."

The Hoyas had a reputation as one of the big, bad programs in college basketball, boasting a physically intimidating coach in John Thompson and two future pros in 6-foot-10 Alonzo Mourning and 7-2 Dikembe Mutombo. "The two best big men in the country," Gillen called them. The Twin Towers combined to average 27.2 points and 18.7 rebounds a game with 194 total blocked shots.

The Musketeers knew Mourning and Mutombo were big and physical. They also didn't much care. Especially not XU's frontline players, Tyrone Hill, Derek Strong and Aaron Williams.

"We've got some big fellows, too," forward Maurice Brantley was quoted as saying. "... Right now, they're beatable."

"The biggest thing I remember is the coaches putting together this lowlight film, which was the bloopers of Georgetown, missed passes and all that sort of stuff," Michael Davenport said. "When we watched that, I remember thinking: *You know what? We're not losing this game.*"

PHOTO BY BRIAN SPURLOCK

Jamal Walker drives to the basket and splits Georgetown's Alonzo Mourning (33) and Anthony Allen during the 1990 NCAA Tournament.

The matchup was shown live on CBS. The Musketeers were center stage. They had never advanced to the Sweet 16 before.

"A lot of people are going to know where Xavier University is by the time this telecast is over," a CBS producer told *The Cincinnati Enquirer* before the game.

How prophetic.

Xavier's goal was to get off to a good start and not be intimidated.

"I told our guys we're going to go right at them," Hill said. "If we lose, let's lose playing hard, playing together and we're going to have our heads up."

"They were making fun of us before the game … They gave us a hard time," Gillen said.

Then came the game.

The Musketeers never trailed. They built an 18-point lead late in the first half.

The offense took the ball right at Georgetown's big men. The full-court defensive pressure caused the Hoyas to turn the ball over repeatedly.

"As underdogs, sometimes you're kind of under the radar," Hill said. "I think the first four or five minutes, a couple guys from Georgetown were like, *these guys play hard*. That set them back. I think they kind of expected us to lie back a little bit and be intimidated."

It got close before it ended. Georgetown rallied with an 11-3 run to tie the game with about three minutes left.

In the final minutes, XU's Williams, a freshman, played a big role, filling in for Hill, who had fouled out with six minutes remaining. Williams sank a fade-away jumper off an offensive rebound to put Xavier ahead 72-70 with 1:36 to go. And with 12 seconds left, he blocked a 3-point attempt by Georgetown's Mark Tillmon.

"No one gave us a chance in hell to beat them. *Nobody*," Strong said. "They were bigger than us, but we were more agile. Our basic strategy was to get them in an up-and-down game. We wanted to get them running. That was the only way to get them out of their comfort zone. If we played halfcourt, I don't think we would've had as much of a chance to be victorious."

"That was really a mega-win," Gillen said. "It was something that kind of put us in a different class, like these guys are for real at Xavier now. That really got us some recognition. That was a special win for sure."

NO. 1 MASSACHUSETTS 78, XAVIER 74 (OT)
Feb. 4, 1996
Cincinnati Gardens

This was the Musketeers' first season in the Atlantic 10 Conference after years of dominating the lower-level Midwestern Collegiate Conference. Now Xavier would be regularly facing coaches such as Temple's John Chaney and John Calipari of Massachusetts, not to mention George Washington, Virginia Tech, St. Joseph's and Miami Valley rival Dayton.

"The question early on was: Can Xavier compete in the Atlantic 10?" then-XU coach Skip Prosser would say later.

UMass was ranked No. 1 in the country and came to town with 6-foot-11 Marcus Camby, who would go on to be named the National Player of the Year. In addition, the Minutemen had one of the country's best backcourts with Carmelo Travieso and Edgar Padilla.

Xavier, meanwhile, was starting three freshmen, Lenny Brown, Gary Lumpkin and Darnell Williams, and a sophomore, T.J. Johnson.

"I loved the big-game buzz," Prosser said. "It was electric that game."

UMass came into Cincinnati Gardens with a 20-0 record and was a 13½-point favorite. Xavier was 9-8.

"We know we've got to give a super effort," Johnson said the day before the game. "We can't be concerned about making mistakes. Everybody expects us to lose anyway. So we've just got to come out loose and aggressive and do the job."

That's what happened. Xavier took it right to the Minutemen and was ahead 68-65 with 23.6 seconds remaining. Padilla then came down the floor and hit a 3-pointer with 15 seconds to go.

Prosser would regret not fouling before Padilla could shoot.

"When I was guarding him, I was kind of relaxed," Lumpkin said. "He was at the half-court line and he looked real lazy, and next thing you know he made a crossover and took two dribbles to the 3-point line and just let it go. I always remember Coach Prosser telling us, 'Make sure you contest a shot.' And I contested it. I was right in his face, and he made a tough shot."

Brown then missed a jumper, Lumpkin and Johnson each missed follow-ups, and the game went into overtime. "I thought we had 'em," Xavier center Kevin Carr said afterward. "We let it slip through our fingers."

Johnson fouled out on the Minutemen's first possession of the second half. Carr and Terrance Payne, XU's other top frontline players, already had fouled out.

Massachusetts took a 71-68 lead. The Musketeers stayed close but could not catch up.

Camby had 26 points and 11 rebounds. Brown and Lumpkin, XU's guards, outscored Padilla and Travieso 28-10, but UMass forward Donta Bright pitched in 21.

UMass went 35-2 and lost in the Final Four to Kentucky, which won the national championship.

"Because we should have actually won the game, we were really distraught," Lumpkin said. "But I would say it let us know that we could play with anybody, not just in the league, but in the country."

XAVIER 71, NO. 1 CINCINNATI 69
Nov. 26, 1996
Shoemaker Center, Cincinnati

Going into the 64th Crosstown Shootout, the University of Cincinnati was ranked No. 1 in the country and was a 17½-point favorite to beat Xavier.

The game was at UC's Shoemaker Center with a sellout crowd of 13,176. Both teams were 1-0. The Musketeers started three sophomores and were coming off a 13-15 season. They had never won before in The Shoe.

"It would be a breakthrough game," Prosser said beforehand. "It would catch people's eyes."

The previous season, UC had won 99-90 at Cincinnati Gardens with Danny Fortson finishing with 40 points and 17 rebounds. But Prosser recalled that "even though we lost, we went right at them."

He thought that if Xavier

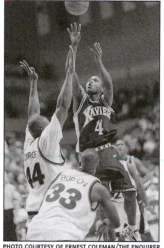

PHOTO COURTESY OF ERNEST COLEMAN/THE ENQUIRER

Lenny Brown scored 1,885 career points at Xavier, but none were bigger than the two that came on this last-second shot that beat No. 1-ranked UC in November 1996.

brought the same will, the same effort, it had a chance for the upset.

"We never realized how determined we were to win that game until we got into that locker room," former Musketeer Sherwin Anderson said. "I remember leading the team out (to the court). The crowd was going crazy, and I ran over to the guys and said: 'We're going to win this game. This is something you are going to tell your kids about.' "

It was a sloppy first half; the teams combined for 25 turn-overs. Xavier's James Posey, playing his second college game, threw up an air ball on his first shot.

But most of the night, the game was close.

Then came one of the greatest finishes in the history of the heated rivalry.

Posey scored on an inbounds play near the Musketeers' basket to tie the game at 69 with 6.7 seconds left. UC guard Charles Williams raced up the court but dribbled the ball off his foot and out of bounds, giving XU possession and a chance to win it.

Time out, Xavier.

Prosser drew up a play called "Army." It was not for Lenny Brown. But assistant coach Jeff Battle realized Brown did not know where he was supposed to be.

"As we broke the huddle, Lenny had kind of a confused look on his face," Battle said. "He looked right at me eye to eye. I just told him, 'Lenny, go get the ball and make a play.' One thing I know about him: He's good with the ball in his hands. And if we're going to go down, I want to go down with him with the ball in his hands. In a chaotic situation like that ... I was trying to simplify things for him."

Lumpkin inbounded the ball. Brown took the pass.

"I looked up and saw (UC's) Darnell Burton," Brown said. "He plays pretty good 'D.' I knew he wasn't just going to let me go by him. I saw the big guy (UC's Roderick Monroe) come off the baseline like he was going to block it, so I had to pull up at the free-throw line. I got enough separation and let it go. It looked good when I let it go. I felt good about it. I was just watching it like everybody else.

"When it went in, the place got quiet. I looked at the Xavier bench and saw (assistant) Coach (Mark) Schmidt jump the highest I ever saw him jump."

After they won, the Xavier players ran over and celebrated in front of Bob Huggins and the UC bench.

"We just screamed and screamed at Huggins," Anderson said. "What an amazing experience that game was. That game exemplifies everything about Xavier."

During the celebration, Prosser walked to the locker room, letting the players bask in the glow of victory.

"I'll never forget the looks on the guys' faces when we beat them," Prosser said.

In the locker room, he told the players: "For the rest of your life, you'll always be able to reference this game as doing something people said you had no chance of doing."

"That was special," Prosser said. "We worked hard, we were unselfish, and we worked together."

It never gets old. More than 11 years later, Brown said he could talk about that night forever.

"I think about that shot at least once or twice a week," Brown said. "That was probably the highlight of my basketball career."

NO. 6 DUKE 66, XAVIER 63
March 28, 2004
NCAA Tournament, regional final, Atlanta

Making its first appearance in the Elite Eight of the NCAA Tournament, Xavier was as hot as any team in the country.

The Musketeers, seeded seventh, came in to this game having won nine in a row and 16 of 17 games. They won their first three NCAA games over Louisville, No. 8-ranked Mississippi State and No. 12 Texas by an average of 11 points.

All that stood in the way of a remarkable Final Four berth was No. 1 seed Duke, perhaps the model program for all of college basketball.

"It's just a name," Dedrick Finn told *The Enquirer's* Dustin Dow. "They might be the best team the last 20 years, but they still have to get through us."

"At that point, we weren't scared to play anybody," Lionel Chalmers said. "Teams were scared to play *us*. I think they had a little fear in their eyes; they knew that we could win."

Such is the mentality the Musketeers took into the game against a program that had been to 17 regional finals.

"We were excited because we were the underdogs and we believed that we could win," Justin Doellman said. "And everyone's kind of like, 'Oh, they shouldn't even be here, they're a Cinderella team.' That gave us even more confidence in ourselves. We had nothing to lose."

"At that point, I wasn't changing anything," then-coach Thad Matta said. "We had been the underdog for about a month and a half."

Here's what's hard to forget: Xavier and Duke were tied 56-56 with three minutes to play. Only 180 seconds to a Final Four berth.

And then, in the blink of an eye, J.J. Redick nailed a 3-pointer for Duke and Luol Deng scored on a rebound basket, and — *poof* — it was all but over.

The Blue Devils won 66-63.

"Luol Deng made a couple of plays that I didn't have an answer for," Matta said. "I remember walking off the floor of the Georgia Dome saying to myself, 'What just happened?'"

"We felt we were going to win it the entire time and then … just like that, you lose," Doellman said. "It was shocking."

Xavier did not play a great game:

• Romain Sato, who would finish his career as the No. 3 scorer in Xavier history, was held to 10 points;

• Chalmers, the team's leading scorer, had just four points the entire second half;

• The Musketeers were only 3-of-15 from 3-point range;

• Starting center Anthony Myles fouled out with 12:27 remaining; he had 16 points and 10 rebounds in 23 minutes and was playing one of the best games of his career.

"Looking back on it, and as you continue to study the NCAA Tournament, anything is possible," Matta said. "We beat some great basketball teams to get there. Nobody had a harder road than we did to get to that point. It just goes to show you the parity across college basketball."

"Still, to this day, I think about it," Chalmers said. "That three points. That three minutes. If Anthony Myles doesn't foul out ... I think we win that game."

"We were three minutes away from going to the Final Four," Doellman said. "It's something I'll never forget. It was a good starting point for me just being a freshman. It kind of raised the bar pretty high ... and it set the tone for the seniors that I graduated with to try to leave a legacy behind."

2

SIX NAMES TO KNOW

IF YOU FOLLOW Xavier University basketball, then names like Larkin, West, Hill and Grant come easily to the mind. Points and rebounds are tangible. It's not hard to look in the record book and find those players' contributions.

Same with coaches: Bob Staak, Pete Gillen, Skip Prosser, Thad Matta, Sean Miller. Not a losing record among them.

And then there are people whose roles in the rise of Xavier basketball are known only to those close to the program. Here are six whose contributions, ideas, passion, generosity, vision and courage make them critical figures in XU history.

RAY TOMLIN: PROGRAM PIONEER

Xavier did not recruit Ray Tomlin when he was at Lockland Wayne High School in the early 1950s. Neither did the University of Cincinnati. But Ohio State offered him a scholarship, so Tomlin was off to Columbus.

He and the legendary Robin Freeman from Cincinnati's Hughes High School made up the starting backcourt of the Buckeyes' freshman team. But ...

"I didn't get very good guidance counseling," Tomlin said. "I wound up taking courses I shouldn't have taken and my grades were suffering. I had to work, go to practice. It was a little bit too much for me."

Tomlin returned to Cincinnati in June 1953 and worked at Stearns & Foster, a mattress company in Lockland.

In January 1954, he enrolled at Xavier.

"I decided working in a factory wasn't for me," Tomlin said. "It was a little bit too tough. I came over to talk to (Xavier coach) Ned Wulk. He said I'd have to pay my way my first semester and get my grades up. He said he had four starters coming back on varsity with three good freshmen and one guy coming out of the Army named Frannie Stahl. I enrolled anyway.

"I walked on and got a full ride the next semester."

So it came to pass that in 1954—right around the beginning of the Civil Rights Movement in the United States—Xavier's basketball program had its first African-American player.

"I'm very proud of that," Tomlin said.

Tomlin was 6 feet 1 and quick, a run-and-gun type player. He says he shot mostly from outside beyond what is now the 3-point arc. "That was routine for me," he said.

He didn't realize at the time he was breaking a racial barrier, but as he got closer to joining the varsity team, the media started to play up that fact.

"I was kind of indifferent," Tomlin said. "I didn't think of it in those terms. I love the game of basketball and I wanted to play Division I ball. That was my goal. Very few blacks were getting a Division I education back then. And that's what I wanted and what motivated me more than being the first black (player)."

No matter the motivation, Tomlin vividly recalls details of Jan. 30, 1955.

It was Xavier vs. 15th-ranked Dayton at Cincinnati Gardens, and he was going to dress with the XU varsity for the first time.

"When I walked into the locker room, there was my uniform hanging there in the locker," Tomlin said. "My warm-ups were neatly folded. My warm-up jersey had X-A-V-I-E-R across the front and my last name on the back. There was a brand new pair of Chuck Taylor All-Star gym shoes right out of the box. And I looked at that stuff and I thought, *I made it to the big time.*

"When I put the jersey on, I looked around because I just knew everybody in there could hear my heart beating. That was quite a thing for me. That was 53 years ago, and I can still see me putting that jersey on right now — No. 21."

Even though Tomlin did not get in the game and Dayton won 91-80, none of that mattered.

It was a night he would never forget.

BILL DAILY: RAISING THE BAR

Bill Daily's Xavier basketball playing career ended the day he was cut by freshman coach Jim Bunning, who would go on to be a National Baseball Hall of Fame pitcher and a U.S. senator.

"I obviously didn't have the talent," Daily said.

He would return later as an assistant coach for three years under Don Ruberg (1964–68) and freshman coach under George Krajack.

But Daily's impact on the men's basketball program came as chairman of the university's Athletic Board on which he served from 1975–84.

Over a 16-year period, from 1962–79, XU had only two winning seasons.

"I was tired of losing, and everybody else was tired of losing," Daily said. "So I started setting some goals."

A Feb. 3, 1979, press release from Sports Information Director Dan Weber carried the headline: "Xavier Athletic Board calls for strong, winning program." In that release, Daily outlined specific goals for the program:

1. There is a definite commitment to winning at the Division I level. By "winning," the committee means a program that, at the end of three years, is winning 75% of its games.

2. The schedule should be a national one, with exposure in the East, South and occasionally the West, as well as the Midwest. This goal is to be accomplished as soon as possible.

3. At the end of four years, the goal is participation in a postseason tourney. And from that time on, the aim is for a postseason tourney appearance at least once every four years.

4. Financially, the basketball program will be expected to break even within three years, with the aim of making money by the fourth year.

5. By the end of a five-year period, the goal is for Xavier to appear on regional and/or national TV.

6. Keeping in mind all of the above goals, Xavier is seeking a suitable conference affiliation as soon as possible.

"Most people thought I was nuts," Daily said. "I figured if Marquette can do it, and if Villanova can do it, why couldn't we do it? I was really convinced."

It was Daily's charge to find the next men's basketball coach. First, he consulted with legendary UCLA coach John Wooden. He talked to Marquette coach Al McGuire and Dayton's Don Donoher. Dailey made up a list with more than 100 questions that he asked each candidate.

It was Daily who drove his Volkswagen to pick up University of Pennsylvania assistant coach Bob Staak for his interview on an icy day in Cincinnati.

Staak was offered the job as coach and athletic director.

"I think I was the motivator," Daily said. "It just took a long time to convince people that we could get this done. When Staak came in, I had to spend a day teaching him how to pronounce Xavier. That was kind of funny. He had a good interview, he was very positive, and he had a plan. I think there's no question, I had the vision. But I think he's the real hero."

PHOTO COURTESY OF XAVIER UNIVERSITY

In a letter nominating Bill Daily (pictured) for Xavier's Athletic Hall of Fame, former Musketeer Kevin Carr was quoted as saying: "Dr. Daily did not only take an interest in Xavier athletes when they were in school, but continued to make you feel a part of his family well after you had graduated."

Xavier acknowledged Daily's contributions by inducting him into the Athletic Hall of Fame in 2007.

"He realized what basketball could do for your visibility and your exposure," former player Gary Massa said of Daily. "I don't know if he dreamed that it could be what it is today, but at least he had the guts to stand up and say, 'Let's give it a chance here, let's make the investments, let's get a good coach and try to make a run of it.' "

JERRY ROBINSON: XU'S HOME-MAKER

When Kenco Corp. bought the Cincinnati Gardens in 1979, the plan was to turn the red brick building in Roselawn into an industrial warehouse. Kenco President Jerry Robinson wanted to tear out the seats.

Before that happened, Robinson said, the building had to live up to a previous commitment and host a closed-circuit telecast of a 1980 boxing match between Roberto Duran and Sugar Ray Leonard. Robinson loved the electricity of the event, loved the atmosphere with people actually in the Gardens.

So much for the industrial warehouse.

What he needed was a full-time resident to give the Gardens an identity.

Xavier could be a perfect match, he thought. The Musketeers had no real home. They played most of their games on campus in Schmidt Fieldhouse, which seated 2,900. The Midwestern City Conference required seating of at least 5,000. Xavier had played some games at Riverfront Coliseum, but there it was—at best—the No. 2 tenant behind the University of Cincinnati.

"I don't remember who approached who," said Robinson, who grew up an XU fan. "But I was able to assure them they'd have their first choice of dates, and I think that made the big difference."

In 1983, Robinson gave Xavier what former athletic director Jeff Fogelson once called "a sweetheart deal."

"We had to have our own place and we had to have a place we could afford," Fogelson said. "Jerry made it so favorable to us. He was charging us a flat rent. He wasn't participating in ticket sales. He was very generous on the parking.

"It was very important because the rent was so low that we were making enough money to also stay competitive as far as the team and travel, and it helped all the other sports."

From his point of view, Robinson thought having a regular

tenant gave the Gardens credibility. "Xavier dignified our presence and sent the message that this was a good place," he told *The Cincinnati Enquirer* in March 2000.

The Gardens bought a basketball floor — previously owned by UC — from a Westwood warehouse. Robinson got an old scoreboard that had belonged to the University of Louisville. Xavier coach Bob Staak brought in some personal furniture for the locker room.

It was a rewarding scenario for both parties for 16 years.

"I think it was important because it made Xavier a first-class citizen, not a third-class citizen," Robinson said.

The Musketeers played their home games at the Gardens from 1983–2000. XU was 215-25 after moving into the Gardens full time. In their last four seasons there, the Musketeers were 55-3.

"No university team playing in an arena that they don't own has a better deal than what Xavier had at the Gardens," Fogelson told *The Enquirer* in 2000. "Jerry Robinson made it possible for us to grow that program."

ROSE ANN FLEMING: ACADEMICS FIRST

In nine years as Xavier's coach, Pete Gillen named only one most valuable player at the team's postseason banquet. Same with Skip Prosser, who succeeded Gillen.

Both honored the same person: Sister Rose Ann Fleming, academic advisor for Xavier's student-athletes.

Players standing 6 feet 9 and weighing 250 pounds cower when a call comes from Sister asking about a missed class, late assignment or bad grade.

"Coach Gillen had a lot to do with that tradition at Xavier of graduating every single senior," Prosser said in May 2007. "I think Coach Gillen empowered her, and the guys knew that. They knew that if they didn't do what she said, she had the power to take them off the floor — practice, game or whatever."

"I think that's very much the key," Fleming said.

Fogelson previously had worked at Georgetown, where Mary Fenlon was the team's academic advisor from 1972–99. Fogelson wanted to have a similar position at Xavier, where officials already had discussed the idea.

"He felt very strongly we needed to separate someone taking care of the academics from someone who was reporting to the basketball coach or even to the athletic director," Fleming said.

In August 1985, Fogelson offered the newly created position to Fleming, who was teaching at XU at the time. Since then, every senior men's basketball player has received his degree.

"I have to build a trusting relationship with them," Fleming said. "You can't do anything with people who don't trust you. They (have to) understand

PHOTO BY GREG RUST/XAVIER UNIVERSITY

Tyrone Hill, XU's all-time leading rebounder who graduated in 1990, said of Sister Rose Ann Fleming (pictured): "Sister loved the students. She acted like we were her sons. And the only way you were going to fail was if you didn't care."

that I'm not getting anything personal out of it; I have nothing to gain. I'm just asking them to do something for their own success, academically. Once they believe that, then they buy into it."

Originally, she spent most of her time with men's basketball. Now, she works with all student-athletes. She may talk to coaches three or four times a day. She lives on campus in Manor House residence hall.

"I knew that a lot of players needed help to balance their academic programs with their athletic requirements," she said. "I had no way of knowing what the range of abilities was and what some of the challenges were."

Fleming holds a master's degree in business administration, a Ph.D. in educational administration and a law degree. She was president of Summit Country Day School in Cincinnati (1975–76) and president of Trinity College in Washington, D.C. (1976–82).

She has been the subject of stories in Readers Digest and Women's Day magazine and was honored as one of *The Cincinnati Enquirer's* Women of the Year in 1992.

"She played a big part in my college academic career," said former player Aaron Williams, who graduated in 1993. "She was great for me. She had us in line, that's for sure. I probably wouldn't have graduated without her guidance."

The creation of the Sister Rose Ann Fleming Endowment for Student-Athlete Academic Advising was announced in November 2007.

"I don't really look at it as my success," she said. "I look at it as their achievements and the fact that the program is working. We've built a structure that includes those players having to live in an academic environment in order to succeed."

Fleming says she asks every recruit she meets: Do you really want to go to Xavier and why? Do you want to work for this degree? Do you realize how challenging the Jesuit motive education is?

"Of course, they all say, 'Yes,' " she laughs. "They don't have a clue what that really means."

BOB KOHLHEPP & FATHER HOFF: THE CINTAS STORY

Bob Kohlhepp's involvement with Xavier University started simply enough. He received a master's degree from XU in 1971 and began buying season tickets to men's basketball games in 1976.

He later became a member of the school's Business Advisory Board. He was asked to join the Board of Trustees in 1989. His three children graduated from Xavier.

But his lasting contribution to the athletic department will be his vision for what would become Cintas Center.

The Rev. James E. Hoff, Xavier's president from 1991–2000, was also a key in making Cintas a reality, but even Hoff used to refer to Kohlhepp as "the go-to guy" for the facility.

Kohlhepp, vice chairman of Cintas Corp., traces the roots of the idea to a loss at Dayton shortly after Hoff became Xavier's president. After the game, Xavier held a reception in the Dayton area. It was there Kohlhepp approached Hoff and Mike Conaton, then-chairman of Xavier's Board of Trustees.

"I walked up to them and said: 'You know what? We need to have an arena like Dayton has. That's the reason we lost this game.' I was so impressed with the attendance and the enthusiasm of the Dayton fans," Kohlhepp said.

He continued: "If you guys will get behind that, I'll give you the first million dollars."

"They sort of looked at me like I had three heads," Kohlhepp said.

He believed the men's basketball program was "a center of

The Rev. James E. Hoff, Xavier's president from 1991–2000, was a strong presence around the team. "There weren't two days that went by without him being at practice," former player Pat Kelsey said.

excellence" for the university, that a good program brought free publicity to the school and helped attract students, faculty and staff from all over. "One thing I realized is how many people I talked to learned about Xavier through the men's basketball program," he said. "It is one of the things that Xavier University is known for."

Kohlhepp kept talking about the idea. As it became more closely considered, there was some negative reaction in the Xavier community. Some faculty, students and administrators did not believe a new basketball arena was the way Xavier should spend its money.

"We sort of backed off at that point and let it cool down," Kohlhepp said. "One of the things we realized was that we had to quit calling it an arena. If we were going to get this thing built, it was going to have to be more than just an arena.

"Father Hoff then came up with the label: The Convocation Center. And he kept describing it as a living room."

It would be a multipurpose facility, conference facility, banquet center and dining hall. Oh, and by the way, there would be an arena attached.

"We began down that road," Kohlhepp said.

There was still negative feedback. And Father Hoff was on the fence.

Kohlhepp said he called Hoff one day and offered to take him to dinner at one of his favorite restaurants, China Gourmet in Hyde Park.

He looked Hoff in the eye and said: "Jim, on any football team, there's only one quarterback. The quarterback has to call all the plays. As far as I'm concerned, you're the quarterback and you call the plays. But I want you to know I'm going to keep pushing for this on-campus facility until you tell me to keep my mouth shut. And if you tell me to keep my mouth shut, I'll never say another word about it."

"Thank God he never told me to keep my mouth shut," Kohlhepp said.

Hoff and Kohlhepp are largely credited with building the $46 million on-campus facility, which opened in 2000. The building is now host to as many as 1,500 events a year, including civic events, weddings, receptions, high school tournaments, business conferences and board meetings.

Kohlhepp personally contributed the most money to the project. Dick Farmer, Cintas CEO, and Jim Gardner, Farmer's brother-in-law, were the other top contributors. No money came from the Cintas company, but the deal was made with

Hoff and Xavier that the Cintas name would go on the building if those three collectively produced the biggest financial commitment.

As for Hoff, at the men's basketball banquet in April 2004, XU officials surprised him with an induction into the Athletic Hall of Fame.

Hoff had been diagnosed with cancer a month earlier. In July 2004, he died at age 72 at his campus residence.

"He raised the bar for the entire university and got us over it," the Rev. Michael Graham, who succeeded Hoff as XU's president, said the night of that basketball banquet.

"I remember being in on those preliminary discussions about how they were going to get Cintas Center done, and he never wavered in his belief that it would happen," former coach Skip Prosser told *The Enquirer* after Hoff died.

Hoff had great expectations for Xavier, wanting the Jesuit University to be second to none academically, spiritually and athletically. Hoff's "jersey" hangs in Cintas Center, alongside those of Byron Larkin, Tyrone Hill and David West.

"If he wasn't convinced (Cintas Center) was the right thing to do, it wasn't going to happen," Kohlhepp said. "He played a key role in recognizing we had to quit calling it an arena and he had the guts to stand up and say, 'We need to do this,' even though there were some dissenters."

3

LEW HIRT
(1946–51)

XAVIER FIRST SENT A BASKETBALL TEAM onto the court Feb. 20, 1920, in what would be a 24-18 loss to Dayton at the Fenwick Club in Cincinnati. Harry Gilligan's coaching tenure at XU began and ended with that game.

Coaches Joe Meyer (94-52, 13 seasons), Clem Crowe (96-79, 10 seasons) and Ed Burns (3-16, one season) followed.

Through all those years, the Musketeers never won more than 14 games and never played in a postseason tournament. That changed during Lew Hirt's five seasons as Xavier's coach. He led Xavier to its first 20-win season (24-8 in 1947–48) and first national postseason tournament (1948 NAIB Tournament).

We now begin the journey through 12 coaching eras of Xavier basketball.

WHERE DID HE GO?

Hirt, a DePauw University graduate, took over as Xavier's fifth head coach in 1946, inheriting a team that had gone 3-16 the season before.

"He was really a character," said Gene Smith, Xavier's first 1,000-point scorer, who played for Hirt. "You could write a whole book about him. He was really funny.

"I would say Lew was very fundamental, especially on the defensive end. He insisted that you play good defense. We practiced in Schmidt Fieldhouse. Lou would sit up in the last row of the bleachers and look down at the floor, and he would let the assistant coach pretty much run the practice. He wanted to see how the flow of the game was going.

"He would never say, 'OK, boys, that's the end of practice.' You would just look up there and he'd be gone. He would just get up and go out the back door and leave everybody standing there. He did this almost every day."

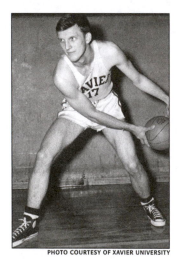

PHOTO COURTESY OF XAVIER UNIVERSITY

Gene Smith played in 66 career games and was Xavier's leading scorer three consecutive years.

SCORING LEADER

Smith, known as "Middie" because he was from Middletown, was recruited by XU out of Hamilton Catholic High School — where Hirt had coached before Smith played there — and arrived at Xavier in 1948. Freshmen were ineligible, so Smith's career numbers came in three seasons in which he averaged 15.8, 13.9 and 20.6 points a game.

"He was a fine ballplayer," teammate Bill Cady said. "He would invent shots as he went along. He was loose as a goose. His body was very flexible and he utilized it."

Smith's high game of 45 points against Georgetown, Ky., at Schmidt Fieldhouse in January 1952 remains tied for the third-best single-game performance in Xavier history.

He finished his career with 1,109 points, which made him the school's all-time leader at that time. Smith remained No. 1 until Dave Piontek broke the record in 1956.

HEY, MY TEETH!

Smith recalls a game at Evansville — he doesn't remember which year — when Hirt jumped up to protest an official's call, and when he started hollering, "His false teeth popped out on the floor and the referee slipped on them and fell.

"All the players went crazy; we knew exactly what happened," Smith said. "Then he's scrambling around trying to pick up the teeth. He was a funny character."

DEFENSIVE STOPPER

Cady, an all-state basketball and football player from St. Xavier High School, decided to attend Xavier University in the fall of 1947. He played both sports as an XU freshman, but in spring 1948 he had to choose because there were spring practices for basketball and football.

"I picked basketball," Cady said. He was the leading scorer on Xavier's 1947–48 freshman team and then started three years whenever he was healthy.

At 6 feet 4, the Park Hills, Ky., native scored plenty, but he also became known as the team's defensive stopper. This became evident midway through the 1948–49 season when Hirt asked Cady to guard Indiana State All-America forward Duane Klueh in a matchup at Schmidt Fieldhouse.

Cady not only led XU with 13 points in the 66-43 victory, but he held Klueh to just two baskets, both coming in the final minutes. "I just tried my hardest with him," Cady said.

GARDENS DEBUT

Xavier's first basketball game at Cincinnati Gardens came Feb. 24, 1949, against No. 1-ranked Kentucky (23-1) and coach Adolph Rupp. The Musketeers were 13-8 and had lost to the Wildcats by 46 points two weeks earlier in Lexington.

The crowd was 13,200 strong, a building record at the time. Fans came to see the Gardens *and* the defending national champion Wildcats.

"It was jammed," Cady said. "I'm sure they turned people away. (Hirt) made a big deal out of it. Actually, we were all pretty excited about it."

The game went back and forth much of the night, and the Musketeers led 34-30 with 10 minutes remaining. It was tied at 36, but from then on, XU had trouble scoring and ended up losing 51-40.

A *Louisville Courier-Journal* reporter wrote that it would have been "the most fantastic upset of the decade."

The Cincinnati Enquirer's Bill Ford wrote: "To say the game was great would be a gross understatement. It was more than that. It was basketball at its best."

Xavier held Kentucky All-American Alex Groza to just seven points and another All-American, Ralph Beard, to eight.

"There was so much emotion in that game," said Cady, who scored a game-high 17 points. "It was fantastic. It was nip-and-tuck, and at the very end they got some free throws (to win the game). You know how that goes. That night was quite a thrill."

HEARSAY

Later, Cady heard this story about Kentucky's visit to the Gardens:

"I don't know if it's the truth or not, but rumor had it that Adolph Rupp came in (to the Gardens) at noon or so and…

looked around and said to the guard: 'Do you see those rims up there? They're black now, and if they're not orange by 8 o'clock, we're not having a ballgame!' The rims were supposed to be officially orange, I guess. They were black when they bought them from the store because they were for outdoors. "They made sure they did a quick job painting, I guess."

NOW THAT'S SOLID 'D'

The 1948–49 team gave up an average of just 54.7 points a game. Only one opponent scored more than 75 points against the Musketeers, and that was top-ranked Kentucky. In 10 games, XU's opponents scored fewer than 50 points.

"I don't know if we ever played zone (defense)," Cady said. "It was always man–to–man. We had scrappy guards defensively. We just had some kids who worked real hard at it."

Cady went on to become the first basketball coach at La Salle High School, where he guided the Lancers for 28 seasons.

NO HARD FEELINGS

Xavier had a date with No. 1-ranked Kentucky in February 1951. The Musketeers' bus was scheduled to leave at 11 a.m. for the drive to Lexington, and when it was time to go, one player, Bill Donovan, was not there.

"He was a sub, so nobody got too excited about it," Smith said.

Coach Hirt said: "If he's not here, the hell with him. Let's go. We don't need him anyways."

The bus started down toward Dana Avenue, and there was Donovan, jumping out of a car and waving his arms for the bus to stop, which it did. When Donovan got on the bus, Hirt chewed him out for not being on time.

Just before the UK game started, Hirt announced a surprise starting lineup — and Donovan was in it. Regular starters Cady and Don Ruberg did not enter the game until late in the first half. Neither scored that night.

"Nobody could believe it," Smith said. "The players were amazed. Donovan was amazed. He hardly played at all before that and here he's starting against one of the best teams in the country. (Hirt) just had a hunch, I guess. He had hunches all the time."

Didn't matter. Kentucky won 78-51.

PHOTO COURTESY OF XAVIER UNIVERSITY

Lew Hirt lettered in basketball at DePauw University in Greencastle, Ind., in 1923, '24 and '25.

It was Xavier's 16th straight loss to the Wildcats. The Musketeers are 2-37 all-time vs. UK; the teams have not met since Nov. 30, 1968.

CHANGE AHEAD

After five years and a 76-61 record, Hirt resigned as Xavier's coach just before the start of the 1951–52 season. He had led Xavier to three winning seasons.

"I'm not really sure why (Hirt left)," Smith said. "He was getting old, too, and I think he had his fill of coaching. He was very much a disciplinarian. He wanted the game run the way he wanted it and if you didn't want to do it, you didn't play."

Named for him is the Lew Hirt Society, a non-university affiliated group of Xavier men's basketball fanatics founded in 1986 in Toledo by alum Jim Valiton, a 1969 graduate. It's for fans living more than 100 miles from the Xavier campus.

"In an old press guide, we saw a picture of him," said Valiton, explaining why the group is named for Hirt. "He had a great big smile. We found out he had a good record. When we saw he was 1-0 against North Carolina, he was our man."

Ned Wulk was hired in the fall of 1951 — one week before practices started — as Hirt's replacement. A native of Marion, Wis., Wulk originally was hired at Xavier to be the freshman football coach, freshman basketball coach and varsity baseball coach. At first, Xavier made him head basketball coach for only one year.

Wulk had a different approach than Hirt.

"He was a very, very young-looking guy," Smith said. "A lot of times when we played on the road, people would confuse him as a player because he was so young-looking. He didn't have a lot of experience in coaching; he started at Xavier when I did. He was my freshman coach. He was there three years as an assistant and became the head coach. He was a very good coach.

"He was the exact opposite from Lew. He played the fast break, beat the other team down the floor and tried to outscore them. He was not a stickler on defense or ball control like Hirt was. It was two different styles entirely."

Wulk's style eventually would help guide the Musketeers to the National Invitation Tournament for the first time.

4

NED WULK
(1951–57)

RAY TOMLIN, Xavier's first African-American men's basketball player, dressed with the varsity team for the first time in January 1955. Soon after, Xavier left on a road trip to the South for games at Memphis State, Loyola (La.) and Spring Hill in Mobile, Ala. Tomlin couldn't go with the team because the university had yet to make housing arrangements for him.

This was less than a year after the Supreme Court ruled that segregation in public schools was unconstitutional (Brown vs. Board of Education of Topeka, Kan.) and 11 months before Rosa Parks would refuse to give up her seat on a bus to a white passenger. It was a challenging time for an African-American athlete traveling to the South.

A year later, in January 1956, Xavier played at Loyola (La.), Spring Hill and Miami. In Mobile, Tomlin stayed with a black dentist and his family. In New Orleans, he stayed on the Xavier University of Louisiana campus. In Miami, he stayed in the Booker T. Washington Hotel, the largest black hotel in town.

"I remember I had a walk-in closet that was bigger than my room back home," Tomlin said. "That's the only way the school could take the pressure off me. I was separated from the team. I knew it was coming. From that aspect, I was comfortable. But sometimes you're sitting around there by yourself and you wonder *why*?"

At the New Orleans airport, the team's flight was delayed. The Xavier administration decided the team would have a quick lunch in an airport restaurant.

"They had round tables, table clothes, beautiful silverware," Tomlin said. "At my table was the athletic director, the publicity director, an assistant coach and the team chaplain. A young girl comes up and takes our order. She leaves. She's back in about a minute. She had two guys with her. These two guys were helping her put these two dressing screens — like the ladies use — around that table. That was a moment I will never forget."

The restaurant wanted Tomlin separated from its white customers.

"I looked at the athletic director and he didn't know what to do or what to say," Tomlin said. "The publicity director was the same way. The Catholic priest, he reached over and grabbed my hand and just looked at me and nodded his head. The message he was sending was: *We're behind you, don't worry about it.* One of the assistant coaches … got up and just walked out. I thought about joining him out on the concourse. But after I thought about it, if you go out there, you can't even sit with him. You'll have to go over and sit in the black section. You might as well stay where you are."

Most of Tomlin's teammates did not know what to say to him when these incidents occurred.

"I couldn't see what the rest of the guys' reactions were when they put that screen up," Tomlin said. "But you could kind of see it in their faces (later). It was awkward for everybody."

Tomlin's poised and calm demeanor served him well during those years.

"(Ray) handled it extremely well," teammate Jim Boothe said. "(The players) had ambiguous feelings about it. We didn't know what to do. I can't speak for everybody. We were all uncomfortable. We just tried to make basketball the thing."

"I handled it as best I could at that time," Tomlin said. "That's the way it was. I wasn't angry about it because I had been subjected to that stuff just about all of my life. I had been steeled against it."

When Corny Freeman arrived in 1956, he at least gave Tomlin an African-American teammate to talk to. But Freeman was high-strung — the opposite of Tomlin.

One player who became close friends with Tomlin was Frannie Stahl, from Maysville, Ky. They were both backup guards.

After a game in Louisville in 1957, Stahl and Tomlin decided to go out for some hamburgers and bring them back to the hotel. On their way out, they noticed the hotel's bar and grill was still open.

"We go in," Tomlin said, "and Frannie jumps up on the stool and sits down, and he looks at me and I'm still standing. He said, 'Sit down.' I hesitated. He said, 'Sit down, Ray.' So I sit down. I knew better.

"Up comes this big kid, about 6 feet 4, 250 pounds. He tapped me on the shoulder and said, 'Sir, we don't serve Negroes here.' Before I could say anything, before I could do anything, Frannie is off that stool and in this guy's face. Now Frannie was only 5-9, about 160 pounds. Frannie, however, was a Korean War vet. He was in an elite paratrooper outfit when he was over there, and he's in this guy's face. And the expletives that came out of his mouth we can't repeat in the paper. But he really showed his loyalty to me. I wound up having to grab *him* and take him out of the restaurant."

HELLO, SENATOR

Tomlin remembers being on his way to his first practice in Schmidt Fieldhouse. It was the fall of 1954, and as he climbed the stairs to get to the gym, he kept hearing a loud popping sound. *Pow!* A few seconds later, again. *Pow!* Pause. *Pow!*

"It was like somebody was beating a rug," Tomlin said. "I thought, *what in the world is that?*

"So I go in the door and into the gym and I look over on the side, and there's now-Senator Jim Bunning warming up on the sideline. He was the assistant freshman basketball coach then, and he was popping that (catcher's) glove with that 95-mile-an-hour fastball of his. I had followed him in high school. I went over and shook his hand, and he welcomed me. He took me off to the side and talked to me about going to school, doing what's right. I'll never forget that."

Bunning doesn't recall doing anything more than reaching out to a new player.

"I remember meeting him," Bunning said. "I did that with a lot of people I met at that time."

A LONG TIME COMING

Perhaps the most inspiring story related to Tomlin did not materialize until five decades after he left the university without a degree when he got drafted into the U.S. Army.

He got out of the military in 1960 and went to work for Procter & Gamble. He got married and started a family. He worked until retiring in 2000.

In 2004, Tomlin was called upon by the All For One booster club to speak about being XU's first African-American player. His talk received rave reviews, and he was invited to speak again, this time to a larger audience. Then Tomlin was asked to be the keynote speaker at a banquet honoring all Xavier athletes.

"I was kind of hesitant because I didn't have my degree, but I decided to go ahead and do it," Tomlin said. "I'm sitting there waiting my turn and I'm looking down the row on the stage at all of these people, and I'm thinking, *Do people know that I don't have my degree yet?* And *I'm* standing up here telling kids the importance of education. I decided right then and there (to go back to school)."

Tomlin researched what he needed to earn a degree and found out he had to take 18 hours of classes. He went back to school on Saturdays. In May 2006 — 52 years after he first enrolled at Xavier — he received his diploma.

"I went over and got my cap and gown," Tomlin said. "I came home and went into my restroom and tried my cap and gown on, and I swear to God, it felt like 1957. I felt like I had gone back in time.

"And when I marched in there to get my degree that day, there was a calm that came over me. It was as though I had reached back in time and done something that I should have done years ago. It was just a wonderful feeling. And when I went up and hugged (Xavier President) Father (Michael) Graham and got my degree, I almost blurted out crying on stage. Some of those same people were on the stage who were there at the honors award ceremony, and one of them yelled out to me, 'You're my hero.' That made me feel so great."

'THE WASP'

Ned Wulk was the right coach for Boothe, a product of Dayton (Ky.) High School, where John Wooden began his coaching career after graduating from Purdue University. Boothe's only scholarship offers were from XU and the University of Cincinnati. He wasn't sure he'd get a chance to play much for the Bearcats, so he opted for Xavier.

His freshman coach in 1953 — only briefly — was Bunning, who had played baseball at XU for Wulk.

"He went to his first spring training that year (1954)," Boothe said. "He had to leave before the season was over to get to spring training. He was young and fiery. If you're around him now, he hasn't changed a whole lot. He was pretty demanding, pretty intense."

Booth was talking about Bunning there. But he says the same about Wulk.

"(Ned) was a great guy, a great coach," Boothe said. "He was young and fiery and energetic, like the coaches today, really. Very ethical and very easy to live with, though he was tough in practice. The players used to call him 'The Wasp' because he stung in practice.

PHOTO COURTESY OF XAVIER UNIVERSITY

Hank Stein said of Ned Wulk (pictured, right): "He was a defensive coach, and that was one of my weak areas. He really helped me. I was never a great defensive player, but I improved under his tutorage."

"He was very intense. He was always expecting more, more, more. It was good for me. There was no way I was going to get to play by just doing an average job. I had to be in better shape because of my height (5 feet 8). I liked him."

SILENCE AT WKU

Western Kentucky University, under coach Ed Diddle, was carrying a 67-game home winning streak in January 1955 when the Musketeers came to Bowling Green, Ky. The teams had not played in over three years.

It was a back-and-forth affair that went into double overtime. With the score tied, Dave Piontek launched a shot that was partially blocked by WKU's Ralph Crosthwaite. XU forward Duke Schneider picked up the loose ball and laid it in the basket with five seconds left for an 82-80 XU victory.

"Everybody was just shocked," Boothe said. "Afterward we were all screaming and yelling, and all the people were completely silent in the gym. Their young fans had not seen them lose."

The Hilltoppers had not lost at home in six years.

"At the end of the brilliantly played game, a packed house of 4,500 sat in utter disbelief," *The Cincinnati Enquirer* reported. "So difficult was it for them to comprehend that a near deafening silence filled the Hilltoppers fieldhouse. Only after the vanquished Toppers, many of them weeping, did file from the floor to their locker room did the fans begin to leave the arena."

ANOTHER SHOCKER

On Feb. 13, 1956, Xavier was playing host to fifth-ranked Louisville at Schmidt Fieldhouse. The Cardinals came in 19-1, on an 11-game winning streak and with a National Invitation Tournament berth already secured. A year earlier, they had beaten Xavier by 40 points in Louisville.

The Musketeers started the 1955–56 season with seven straight victories and entered the game 13-6, including an upset of No. 20 Cincinnati five days earlier. XU, too, had received a NIT bid.

What happened next could not have been predicted by anyone.

Xavier blasted Louisville 99-59, the worst loss in Fred Hickman's 12 years as Louisville's coach. It was the most points a Hickman team had ever given up.

Boothe led all scorers with 21 points. XU shot 52 percent from the field.

"Everything went right," Boothe said. "Not just for me. The game just went our way. Every time we were on a break, we converted. It just got away from them. They were a fine team. Sometimes you have those kinds of nights. That's one I remember."

Louisville would go on to win the 1956 NIT.

Boothe scored 1,085 career points and was XU's No. 4 all-time scorer when he graduated.

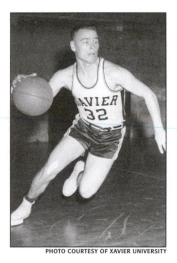

PHOTO COURTESY OF XAVIER UNIVERSITY

Jim Boothe was named XU's Most Valuable Player as a junior, averaging a team-high 16.5 points in 1955–56.

He was selected by the Cincinnati Royals in the 12th round of the 1957 NBA Draft.

He never played professionally but went on to a career in public education. Boothe coached Reading High School for nine years and would later become superintendent of Reading School District. Boothe started working at Xavier in 1987 and has held several positions, including chairman of Xavier's Education Department. He continues in that role at the university.

TAKING A STAND

After Xavier defeated Saint Louis 84-80 in the first round of the 1956 NIT, Piontek celebrated just a little bit too long — and it was costly.

Piontek, the team's star senior forward, averaged 15.7 points and 15.3 rebounds, but he stayed out too late in New York City and missed curfew for the second time. Wulk sent him back to Cincinnati on an airplane the next day. Xavier was to play No. 1 seed Dayton that night without one of its top players.

"We were shocked, devastated," Boothe said. "I think we would've (won the NIT with him). He gave us a little bit of everything. It is what it is. It was part of the whole experience. I was disappointed. I felt I was let down."

Xavier gave up a nine-point second-half lead and lost to the Flyers 72-68. It was the Musketeers first trip to the NIT.

The Enquirer's Bill Ford wrote: "The question naturally arises, would Xavier have won with Piontek, the school's all-time leading scorer? Wulk refused comment. General consensus, an emphatic 'yes.' "

Wulk was praised for holding true to his principles. Jerry Ford, University of Pennsylvania athletic director, called Wulk's decision to suspend Piontek "the greatest thing to happen to college sports in 10 years."

FIRST BLUE CHIP?

Piontek was Xavier's all-time leading scorer *and* rebounder when he left and went on to play pro basketball. When he signed with XU out of Bethel Park, Pa., he may have been one of the best recruits at that point in the program's history.

"He might have been the first blue chip recruit that came," Boothe said. "Dave was a free spirit. He was what I call a happy warrior. He was always one of the guys. He never put on any airs or expected anything different than anybody else. He was a social person. He always pressed the training rules a little bit, pushed the envelope. He was the most likeable guy you'd ever want to meet, but when he got upset ..."

Boothe recalls playing in a tournament in Buffalo in late December 1955. Xavier defeated Niagara 84-63, then St. Bonaventure 95-86 and Georgia Tech 92-67.

"He had a game where he just physically overwhelmed the other team," Boothe said. "The (opposing) coach didn't know what happened to him. He said they must feed Piontek raw meat before the game."

Piontek played on the frontline at only 6 feet 5 and 220 or so pounds.

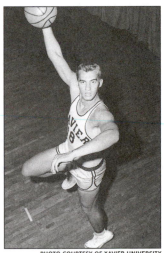

PHOTO COURTESY OF XAVIER UNIVERSITY

Dave Piontek averaged a double-double all three seasons he played and finished with career averages of 15.7 points and 12.1 rebounds.

"He was one of the toughest guys I had ever seen," Tomlin said. "He was going against guys 6-7, 6-8, 6-9. They couldn't handle him. He was that tough."

Piontek was selected in the third round of the 1956 NBA Draft by the Rochester Royals. He also played in Cincinnati, St. Louis and Chicago during a seven-year pro career.

In May 2004, Piontek died at age 69 after suffering a stroke.

Bunning told *The Enquirer* that Piontek was "one of the most talented basketball players I ever recruited."

Piontek's brother, Rich, also played at Xavier. He died at age 69 in September 2007.

MUST WIN

Xavier played at Dayton on Feb. 20, 1957, believing it needed a victory to secure a bid for the NIT. However, only once since 1949 had XU defeated the rival Flyers.

It was Tomlin's only career start (he finished with four points). But the night belonged to sophomore guard Hank Stein.

Stein hit eight free throws down the stretch and scored a game-high 29 points. The Musketeers won 68-65 in a big upset, and teammates carried Stein to the locker room on their shoulders.

"We always had a tough time beating Dayton up there," Stein said.

After the loss, Dayton coach Tom Blackburn had his players change from game uniforms to practice uniforms and took them onto the court for a workout.

A few days later, Xavier received a bid to the NIT.

WILD SWINGS

In 1956–57, Xavier collected the second 20-win season in its history; it also would be Wulk's final year as coach. The Musketeers stormed into the NIT having won six of their last seven games, and they defeated Seton Hall 85-79 in the first round of the postseason tournament.

In the second game, XU was matched against No. 2 seed Bradley.

Xavier led by 21 points in the first half and was in full command of the game. Then Braves coach Chuck Orsborn went to a full-court zone press.

"We had never practiced against it," Tomlin said. "We didn't know anything about it. We frantically tried to get things together during halftime."

The Musketeers still led 52-44 at intermission. But they were unprepared for the defensive pressure and turned the ball over repeatedly.

"The personality of the game changed," said Boothe, who scored all of his 15 points *before* the Braves changed their game plan. "They pressed us, and we just fell apart. "

Bradley won 116-81, setting NIT records for points scored and free throws made. It also set Madison Square Garden records for points and second-half points.

"It was just a collapse," then-assistant coach Don Ruberg said.

"Probably the worst game of our lives," said Joe Viviano, a sophomore that season. "It was really embarrassing."

Bradley went on to win the 1957 NIT title.

Ford wrote in *The Enquirer* that "the incredible turn of events transformed the usually poised Muskies into a disorganized club that appeared as though it never had played the game."

The next day, the newspaper reported that "New Yorkers ... have likened the demise to the 1929 stock market crash."

"Don't blame the kids," Wulk said after the loss. "You've got to credit Bradley. And maybe I made a mistake along the line, too."

COSTLY DEFEAT

There are many who believe it was that loss to Bradley that prompted Wulk's departure from Xavier.

"A Jesuit priest was quoted in the paper saying that the Bradley game wasn't a *loss*, that it was a *disgrace*," Ruberg said. "Ned took that comment very hard; he went over to see Father Paul (O'Connor), the president. I'll never forget it, he came back and looked at me and said, 'The job's yours if you want it, I'm leaving.'"

Wulk, then 37 years old, had taken Xavier to the NIT for the first time in team history in 1956 and '57. He recruited 1,000-point scorers Boothe, Stein, Piontek and Viviano.

"I realize full well what I am leaving," Wulk said in April 1957 when he resigned. "Xavier has a good basketball program. I'd say for the size of the school, its basketball program is the best in the country."

Wulk went on to coach 25 years at Arizona State and become that school's all-time leader in victories. ASU's arena floor was renamed "Ned Wulk Court" in March 1999. Wulk died in November 2003.

"Ned took the Bradley loss very poorly," Ruberg said.

"He took a lot of flak when we lost that game," Stein said.

The trick to replacing Wulk as coach: He was also a physical education professor. Athletic director Al Stephan had to find someone who could perform both roles.

The Enquirer quickly proclaimed that Dudey Moore, who coached Duquesne to the 1955 NIT title, was "rumored to be in line of the job."

As it turned out, he was not the next XU coach.

5

JIM McCAFFERTY
(1957–63)

JIM McCAFFERTY brought his easy-going style to Xavier University in May 1957, after five years as coach at Loyola University in New Orleans. His predecessor, Ned Wulk, liked to yell at players; McCafferty didn't. Wulk liked to run; McCafferty liked to run some offense.

"He wanted to be smarter than everybody else," former Musketeer Joe Viviano said.

Just before his first season, McCafferty told *The Cincinnati Enquirer*: "I make no claim as the world's greatest basketball coach. But we have a few tricks we'll try to work."

Players were cautious at first, as they usually are with a new coach. In part, that was because McCafferty instituted new offensive and defensive sets.

"The guy was a tactician, a great game coach," Viviano said. "He knew the game as well or better than anybody I had run into. But he was not the greatest practice coach."

"Jim was not a motivational speaker," Jack Thobe said. "He basically had a game plan and then he let (assistant coach Don) Ruberg do the rah-rah stuff."

McCafferty, at 6 feet 8, 270 pounds, was the biggest coach

in Division I basketball at the time.

"He was a godfather-type figure," Joe McNeil said. "He was big, but he was the nicest man, a very gentle soul. He was a real Southern gentleman who was physically imposing but carried himself with such dignity. He never cussed and never berated anybody."

MAKING OF A STAR

Paul Arizin, who played for the Philadelphia Warriors in the early 1950s, is credited with perfecting the "jump shot."

When Viviano was at Louisville St. Xavier High School, he was given an 8-millimeter film of Arizin by his coach, Gene Rhodes, who would go on to be an assistant at Western Kentucky and head coach of the Kentucky Colonels of the American Basketball Association. Viviano studied the film all summer before his senior year of high school. He ran it back and forth. It was a slow process that paid off.

"All of us used to shoot that kind of running one-hander, where your leg goes out in front of you," Viviano said. "I thought, now this guy, he stops on two feet, he jumps up and shoots it over his head. God didn't give me speed, and he didn't let me jump very high, so I had to do something. I practiced one whole summer on that stupid jump shot.

"I used it a little in high school. By the time I got to Xavier (in 1955), I could shoot a jump shot off the top of my head from 20, 25 feet. Nobody did that in those days."

Viviano played forward. He was 6-5, about 200 pounds.

"I could go against kids who were much faster and could jump much higher," Viviano said. "I had to get that shot off, so that's what I practiced. If I would've had the 3-pointer in my day, I would've probably averaged another five or six points a game because that's where I was shooting from."

Former teammate Ray Tomlin called Viviano, team MVP in 1958 and '59, "a pure shooter."

"He was a smaller version of (Justin) Doellman," Tomlin said. "He was a perimeter shooter. That's where he spent his time. He'd camp out there. If you turned your back on him, he'd kill you from outside."

Though he finished his career as Xavier's all-time leading scorer, Viviano is quick to point out that he remains seventh on the school's rebounding list, too.

"Don't just tell me I was a shooter," he said, laughing.

A 10th-round pick of the Cincinnati Royals in 1959, Viviano went on to become president of Hershey Foods.

Lou Smith once wrote in *The Enquirer*: "Probably the greatest, well-rounded basketball player ever developed at Xavier is Joe Viviano."

PHOTO COURTESY OF XAVIER UNIVERSITY

In their three seasons together, Hank Stein, left, and Joe Viviano, right, averaged a combined 26.7 points, 33.6 points and 30.7 points.

THE TITLE RUN

Viviano and Hank Stein were Xavier's leading scorers in 1957–58, McCafferty's first year as coach.

The Musketeers were coming off a 20-8 season and returned four of five starters. They started the season with four consecutive victories and were 10-1 in early January. The season held a lot of promise.

But the academic ineligibility of starting forward Cornelius "Corny" Freeman seemed to change all that. Starting with a loss to St. Joseph's, Xavier dropped eight of its next 12 games.

"(Corny) could really jump," said Frank Tartaron, the team's starting center. "He was a good rebounder, and he was a good defensive man. . . . And he could really block shots."

The story is well documented in Chapter 1. Xavier dropped seven of its last eight regular-season games but was still invited to the National Invitation Tournament.

Despite the criticism, the Musketeers were off to New York City that March for a tournament that didn't want them.

"I look back on that year as just an emotional roller coaster and it caused me to really reflect on life," Viviano told Marc Hardin of X-Press magazine in 1998. "I probably experienced every single emotion that year you could experience, and I wasn't even 20 years old."

AN OMINOUS BEGINNING

In its first 1958 NIT game, Xavier trailed Niagara 16-3 early. XU didn't make a basket for the first seven minutes.

Stein remembers thinking he was correct in not packing many clothes. "I was about as negative as I could get," he said.

But the Musketeers rallied in the last four minutes to win 95-86 despite Niagara's Al Ellis scoring 41. Viviano led XU with 26 points. Four other Musketeers scored in double figures. Sophomore guard Bowyer "Ducky" Castelle scored seven points in the final minutes.

The shock waves were just beginning for the Madison Square Garden crowd.

"We were living on borrowed time," Tartaron said. "These were our last games."

SWEET REVENGE

Game 2 in the tournament came three nights later against defending NIT champion Bradley, which had knocked out Xavier in 1957 in an ugly loss that prompted the departure of Wulk (see Chapter 4).

The Musketeers again trailed early but prevailed this time, taking the lead early in the second half and going on to beat the No. 2-seeded Braves 72-62. Stein led Xavier with 23 points.

"Bradley had a number of players returning from the team that had beat us the year before," Stein said. "So when we beat Bradley, I got to thinking, *Heck, we can beat anybody now.*"

RIGHT ON THE MONEY

In the third round of the NIT, Xavier needed to defeat St. Bonaventure to get to the title game. The Bonnies were the No. 3 seed in the tournament and the top team in the East.

McCafferty devised a game plan that had Xavier playing a zone defense, something the Musketeers did not do much.

"Why are you changing the strategy now?" the players asked.

"If you do what I tell you, you're going to win this game," McCafferty answered.

"They can't shoot from beyond here," McCafferty showed his players. "Block them out and you win the game."

Final score: Xavier 72, St. Bonaventure 53.

McCafferty was right on the money.

"He won that game all by himself," Viviano said. "We just shut them down. I was very respectful of him after that. He studied films and he could come up with some very good strategy. We couldn't have won the NIT without him."

CELEBRATE GOOD TIMES

In what remains the only all-Ohio final in NIT history, Xavier shocked Dayton 78-74 in overtime to win the 1958 NIT title. The Musketeers were the first team to bring a national championship to the Buckeye state.

The team was greeted by 10,000 fans when its plane landed at what was then called Greater Cincinnati Airport. That was followed by a ceremony on campus at Schmidt Fieldhouse.

"We couldn't believe it," Tartaron said. "All this fuss, the police (escort) — that was tremendous. Then we went back to the fieldhouse, and they had all the TV cameras there."

The crowd at the airport was so large the plane was stopped short of its gate destination, and the engines were shut off to protect the waiting fans. The plane was towed in from there. Only *two* people were reportedly at the airport to see off the Musketeers when the team left for the tournament.

A side note: In the early morning hours after their victory, the players were still out celebrating in New York City.

The next morning, several Musketeers went to attend Mass at St. Patrick's Cathedral in New York City. Viviano was sitting next to roommate Tartaron. The combination of late-night partying and exhaustion from the tournament caught up to Tartaron.

"I felt terrible," he said. "I felt faint in church. It was kind of like fatigue. I was so skinny then."

"The next thing I know, he gets up and says, 'I've got to go outside,'" Viviano said. "Ten minutes later, what looked like a little old bag lady in tennis shoes comes up to me and pulls my shirt and says, 'You'd better come outside. Your friend's outside.' He walked halfway down the stairs at St. Pat's and apparently must've passed out. He fell right on his chin, so he's now

Jim McCafferty celebrates Xavier's 1958 NIT title. The team's 19 victories in his first season would be the most in his six years as the Musketeers' head coach.

bleeding like crazy.

"Thank goodness one of the coaches was in the church. We took him to the emergency room."

Tartaron was OK and recovered in time to accompany the team back to Cincinnati.

MEANS TO AN END

Stein did not even play organized basketball until he was a freshman at Flaget High School in Louisville. Only Xavier and Centre College recruited him.

"He was tough, determined, gritty, didn't care about anything or anybody," Tomlin said. "He'd go right at you. He was very competitive. Don't block his shot or take the ball away from him or you'll pay for it the rest of the day."

Stein was part of a freshman team at Xavier that went undefeated in 1955–56. He finished with 1,144 career points and was No. 3 on the school scoring chart when he graduated. He was a third-round draft pick of the St. Louis Hawks in '59. Once he got cut from the team, he got married, found a job and never played organized basketball again.

"I think I was tired of it," he said. "Being blessed with natural ability, I didn't have to work too hard at it for whatever reason, and I guess I never really truly loved the game. It was a vehicle for me to go to college."

Stein laughs when he talked about playing No. 6 Cincinnati and Oscar Robertson in January 1959: "He was dribbling and I had to switch off on him. He had to pass the ball; *I made him pass the ball.* I held him scoreless for five seconds!"

UC won 92-66.

NEW YORK CONNECTION

The name Don Fazioli is mentioned by several former players who came to Xavier from New York's Capital Region, the Albany-Troy-Schenectady area.

Fazioli owned D.A. Fazioli and Son Insurance Agency in Troy. More important, though, he attended XU for two years after serving in the U.S. military in World War II. His son, Dave, said Don was called home from Xavier to help care for an ailing parent.

He never returned to school but remained fiercely loyal to Xavier, where he had become attached to the university and the men's basketball program. Among the players he would help steer to Xavier from the Capital Region: Ricky Jannott, Castelle, Leo McDermott, Frank Pinchback, Joe Geiger, Bill Kirvin, Luther Rackley, Perry Ashley and Mark Wilson.

"Don Fazioli was the one who initially made some phone

calls to me, probably in February or March (1958), asking me about XU," Kirvin said. "He went and watched me play a couple of games and he reported back to McCafferty and Ruberg; they never saw me play. They offered me a scholarship based on what he said.

"I went down to Cincinnati for parents' weekend some time in April and the team had a banquet and they introduced me. I came back home and talked to my high school coach who was a big star at Syracuse. From my high school, they only sent kids to Syracuse or Holy Cross. Xavier, Syracuse and Holy Cross were the only schools I visited. I took the trip out to XU and I felt comfortable out there."

Kirvin finished his career in 1962 as XU's No. 7 all-time scorer with 1,088 career points. He scored 27 points and set a then-school record with 13 assists against Loyola of Chicago when he was a senior.

Kirvin was drafted by the Philadelphia Warriors in the eighth round — 74th overall — in 1962, but he chose to enter the U.S. Army after four years of ROTC at Xavier. He played basketball for two years as a second lieutenant in the army, then returned to Albany and played semi-pro ball for five years.

REAPING THE BENEFITS

Xavier's NIT title was impressive to all, but especially to a recruit who was courtside for the Musketeers' championship run.

Jack Thobe, a senior at Cincinnati's St. Xavier High School, was flown to New York to see XU face Bradley in the second game. "It was supposed to be one game and out," said Thobe, who was on an airplane for the first time in his life.

Well, you know the story already: XU won the NIT.

"I was able to stay most of the week," Thobe said. "After the NIT, there was no question I was going to Xavier. I was probably leaning toward Xavier before that. My mom was big on a Jesuit education."

Thobe also was recruited by UC, Kentucky, Notre Dame and Michigan.

SUDDEN IMPACT

At the time, freshmen were ineligible for varsity teams. When Thobe joined the Xavier varsity as a sophomore in 1959–60,

PHOTO COURTESY OF XAVIER UNIVERSITY

When Jack Thobe's Xavier career ended with 1,296 points, only Joe Viviano had more. Thobe was a fourth-round pick of the Cincinnati Royals in 1962.

he went right to work, averaging a team-high 18.4 points and a team-high 10 rebounds. To that point, it was the highest single-season scoring average in Xavier history.

"I think it was basically because I could hook with either hand, like Kareem (Abdul-Jabbar) did when he came up," Thobe said. "That was a big factor."

Thobe was 6-6 as a freshman but grew 2 inches by his sophomore year. That made his sweeping hook more effective.

He developed the shot at a park in Ludlow, Ky., near where he lived along the Ohio River.

"I saw Clyde Lovellette and George Mikan and guys like that on the old black-and-white TV, and it made a lot of sense because a guy can't really block a hook shot," Thobe said. "I taught myself to do it with both hands. I used to believe they couldn't guard you if you shot both ways.

"... I also played with great guards. Jim Enright was the greatest feeder that I've ever had. No matter where the defensive guy was, he'd get it where they weren't."

THE BIRDMAN COMETH

Bob Pelkington came to Xavier from Fort Wayne, Ind., and was known for being a bit of a character and an emotional player.

Pelkington readily said, "I was a hothead when I was a sophomore." This is why he tells this story with such ease.

After fouling out in an 81-69 loss at Illinois early in the 1961–62 season, Pelkington walked off the court and, well ... gestured to the Fighting Illini fans.

"They nicknamed me 'Birdman' down there at Xavier," he said. "I was always giving everybody the bird, flipping them off. I did that at the University of Illinois, and I had people just roaring after me. I was really criticized for it. I played pretty aggressive and got a lot of fouls when I was a sophomore."

HERE COMES THE GROOM

On semester break his sophomore year, Pelkington got married.

McCafferty was not so thrilled with Pelkington's time away from the team. He benched him at the beginning of his first game back after getting married. Roommate Joe Geiger started in his place — against Dave DeBusschere and the University of Detroit.

DeBusschere scored 21 points and grabbed 11 rebounds before fouling out early in the second half. Geiger had 26 points and 11 rebounds and stayed in the starting lineup — alongside Pelkington — the rest of the year.

Bob Pelkington, with the ball, averaged a Xavi-
er-record 16.6 rebounds for his career. He is
No. 2 on the school's all-time rebounding list
behind only Tyrone Hill.

As a sophomore in 1961–62, Joe Geiger led
the nation in free throw shooting (90.2 percent).

Pelkington finished that game with 10 points and 14 boards
off the bench.

DOUBLE-DOUBLE TROUBLE

Pelkington went on to a distinguished Xavier career, *averaging* a
double-double three straight seasons. As a senior, he led the nation in rebounding (21.8 per game).

What made him so good at rebounding?

"Timing, I guess," Pelkington said. "Being aggressive, being
like a bully. I don't know; I kind of knew where the ball was
going. I just wanted to get rebounds."

He also scored 1,075 career points.

"I scored more points when I played for Coach McCafferty than I did when I played for Don Ruberg," Pelkington said.

"With Coach Ruberg, we ran a lot. I used to get the ball and throw it halfway down the floor.

"I always liked playing against better teams than we were. I always seemed to play better."

TO THE GRIDIRON

Pelkington was drafted in the eighth round by the Philadelphia 76ers coming out of Xavier in 1964. But before he went to his NBA tryout, Pelkington got a look from the National Football League's Buffalo Bills, arranged by McCafferty.

"I went to Buffalo first, got cut … then I had like three weeks to get in shape for the NBA tryouts," said Pelkington, who recalls playing just one exhibition game with the Sixers. "I played on the semi-pro football team in Fort Wayne, and I played on three or four other semi-pro teams. Then I got to try out (for the NFL) one year at Dallas, Green Bay and Detroit."

Said Geiger: "He hadn't played football since his freshman year in high school. He played defensive end. If he had any experience, they would've kept him. What an athlete he was. He could run. He was probably the best passing big man until Bill Walton."

ONE-EYED BANDIT

"Timing is kind of an interesting thing," Joe McNeil said.

Sure is.

A 5-8 guard out of St. Henry High School in Erlanger, McNeil had no scholarship offers as a senior. He was a decent scorer but one of the best ball-handlers in Northern Kentucky. There were eight children in the McNeil family, and the only way for Joe to attend college would be with some kind of aid.

Lees Junior College in Breathitt County, Ky., invited Mc-

Neil to an open tryout during spring break of his senior year. After a few days, he was offered a scholarship.

During his first year at Lees, McNeil's father heard that Xavier's freshman guards had become academically ineligible. Maybe it was a good time to contact XU to see if the Musketeers might be interested. Sure enough, Xavier scouted Mc-Neil when Lees played at the University of Kentucky in its last game of the season.

McNeil played well enough that McCafferty offered a partial scholarship.

In fall 1961, McNeil was not eligible to play in games yet. During a New Year's Day practice, he got hit in his right eye and suffered a detached retina. Surgery did not help; Mc-Neil lost the sight in his eye.

"The end of the semester came along and, I don't know if it was a pity move or what, but they put me on full scholarship and the rest is history," he said.

McNeil would go on to play for three years, one under McCafferty and two under Ruberg. He never averaged more than 6.9 points for a season. He moved into the starting lineup in late December of his sophomore year after Enright suffered a season-ending knee injury.

"I'd be a fool to say it didn't affect me as a player, but it didn't affect the way I played the game," McNeil said of his bad eye. "I have no depth perception, but I made up for it other ways. I played defense. I handled the ball. I was very team-oriented. I was one of these guys who just played hard and hustled.

"I wasn't a great scorer but I didn't have to be because I was playing next to a kid who was basically an All-American, Steve Thomas. I was the *other* guard. All I had to do was throw the ball inbounds and turn it over to Steve."

FAST START

The 6-5 Geiger played on the freshman team his first year and said he was the first freshman to average more than 20 points a game (20.7 ppg). He, too, developed the skill of shooting with both hands when he was young. He grew up next to a playground and spent hours shooting with both hands, developing a left-handed hook and his jumpers around the basket.

"It was probably the best thing I ever did," he said.

"He was a fabulous ballplayer," Ruberg said. "I always put him on the other team's best player for defense. Joe was an excellent shooter, excellent defensive player, excellent rebounder … he had it all."

Geiger also played much of his sophomore season on what turned out to be a broken foot (he got X-rays after the season). He suffered an injury early in the season but still averaged 11 points and 7.4 rebounds.

GOING NOWHERE FAST

Xavier played Tennessee in Knoxville the second game of the 1962–63 season. The team flew to the game, but McCafferty had arranged for a train ride home afterward so the Musketeers would not miss any class time the next day. After a good first half, XU struggled and ended up losing 63-48.

"After the game, we went to the railroad station and there was one car waiting for us," Geiger said. "So we all went in the car waiting for the train to pick us up and take us to Cincinnati. Now Jim McCafferty was a pretty big man, and I can remember him at 6-9, maybe 300 pounds, in his jockey shorts.

"What happened that night is we were asleep in the sleep car. We wake up in the morning, and I thought, *Geez, it was a smooth ride.* Well, the train never showed up to pick us up. We slept in the station that night in Knoxville. A car broke down and was on the track. A train hit it. Our train never did show until 8 in the morning. We rode that all the way back to Cincinnati and arrived about suppertime. We missed the entire day of class. It sort of backfired on Coach McCafferty that time."

TRANSITION TIME

In April 1962, McCafferty became the school's athletic director and spent one year as coach *and* A.D. "He feels he can do both jobs," then-university president Rev. Paul L. O'Connor said at the time.

McCafferty already was facing criticism for his coaching, and in 1962–63 the Musketeers were headed for a 12-16 season. In February 1963, *The Enquirer* reported that McCafferty would be asked to step down as coach. The program was hurting financially, and attendance — particularly of students — was down. "Jim's a great guy, but maybe the double role as coach and athletic director is too much," a member of the athletic board was quoted as saying.

McCafferty resigned as coach about a month later.

In six years, he coached seven of Xavier's 1,000-point scorers (Thomas, Viviano, Thobe, Stein, Kirvin, Pelkington and Geiger). His teams had been ranked as high as No. 9 in the Associated Press poll (in December 1958).

McCafferty was athletic director from 1962–79. While he will always be known for coaching Xavier to the 1958 NIT championship, his greatest accomplishment for the advancement of the program may have been his success in getting the Musketeers into a conference in June 1979.

McCafferty, a member of Xavier's Athletic Hall of Fame, died Sept. 18, 2006, in Seattle.

6

DON RUBERG
(1963–67)

YOU NEVER KNOW where life is going to lead you. That was so true for Don Ruberg.

The Elder High School graduate always wanted to coach at his alma mater. It never crossed his mind that someday he might coach at Xavier University, his other alma mater.

"I never dreamed of that," he said. "I always dreamed of coaching at Elder."

He got to do both.

Ruberg attended Xavier from 1947–51, playing basketball and baseball for the Musketeers. An outfielder in high school, Xavier needed Ruberg to pitch — which worked out just fine. After he graduated, the Cleveland Indians signed him as a pitcher and sent him to the minor leagues in Cedar Rapids.

He signed on the Fourth of July. But by the end of August 1951, he was drafted into the U.S. Army, where he spent two years, including one in Korea.

When Ruberg returned to Cincinnati in 1953, Elder hired him as an assistant football coach, head basketball coach and head baseball coach.

In 1956, Xavier coach Ned Wulk — who was Ruberg's baseball coach at XU—called and said: "Xavier has never had a full-time (basketball) assistant coach. I want you to consider that."

Ruberg came to Xavier as the freshman coach/assistant basketball coach, head baseball coach, director of intramurals and a physical education teacher.

"Leaving Elder broke my heart," he said. "But it was a chance to move up, as you can well imagine."

He coached one year at Xavier under Wulk, who left for Arizona State, then six years under Jim McCafferty. When McCafferty resigned to become full-time athletic director in 1963, Ruberg was named head coach.

"We had a great relationship," Ruberg said. "I gave up baseball and intramurals and was strictly a basketball coach."

Even as McCafferty's assistant, Ruberg was the cheerleader, the guy who fired up the players. When he accepted the heading coaching position, he even proclaimed: "I am an optimist."

What players talk about most when it comes to Ruberg is his enthusiasm.

"Maybe the nicest man I've ever met," former Musketeer Joe McNeil said.

PHOTO COURTESY OF XAVIER UNIVERSITY

Don Ruberg is one of four Xavier alums to become the school's head men's basketball coach, joining Harry Gilligan (1919–20), Joe Meyer (1920–33) and Ed Burns (1945–46).

"Probably of all the people I've known in my life, other than my father, Coach Ruberg has had more influence than anybody else — because of his positive attitude," said Joe Geiger, another ex-player. "When I left Xavier and said goodbye to

Ruberg, I was in tears.

"When I attended Xavier, I was very quiet, very shy. I didn't say an awful lot. I just relied upon what I could do on the basketball court. I don't know if I got into sort of a funk or what it was, but with him becoming coach it really lit a fire under my rear end."

The Musketeers averaged 89.7 points a game in Ruberg's first season as head coach — second-highest in school history.

"Ruberg changed the way that we played," Geiger said. "He had us running right from the time we left the locker room."

RENAISSANCE MAN

Ruberg was a man of many talents, but not everyone knew it.

Steve Thomas learned something new about his coach when Xavier played at St. Bonaventure in December 1963.

"We were staying in Buffalo, and we were getting our pregame talk and getting taped at the hotel," Thomas said. "We were in this big ballroom ... and as we're getting ready to go — they had a big baby grand piano on this stage — Ruby jumps up and sits down at the piano and he plays the theme from Clair de Lune — just a little bit. We were flabbergasted. We didn't know he had that talent.

"He finally admitted years ago that all he knew was that one little piece."

QUITE A VISIT

In 1958, Ruberg, then a Xavier assistant, was at Central Catholic High School in Troy, N.Y., to recruit Armand Reo, who would end up going to Notre Dame. While there, Ruberg noticed a 15-year-old sophomore who was shooting free throws. He made about 40 in a row with his right hand, then made about 35 in a row left-handed.

From that moment, Xavier began recruiting Geiger.

Two years later, Geiger was a high school senior choosing among Holy Cross, Villanova and Xavier. In June 1960, he took a recruiting visit to XU. A vast majority of the students were gone for the summer, so Geiger and his dad spent most of their time with McCafferty. Here's what Geiger recalls:

"He took my father and me to a movie in downtown Cincinnati on Saturday night. After about a half hour, I looked to my right and both my father and Coach McCafferty were sound asleep. Even though the weekend wasn't the most rousing, I decided at that time I wanted to come to Xavier."

Geiger may have been the unsung hero of Ruberg's first team in 1963–64 because he played with teammate Thomas, who was one of the top scorers in the country, and senior center Bob Pelkington, who averaged 13.1 points and led the country in rebounding with 21.8 a game.

Geiger, a senior, also averaged a double-double with 19.3 points and 11.2 rebounds.

SCORING MACHINE

No player in Xavier history has ever put together a season like Thomas did in 1963–64.

"He was unstoppable," Ruberg said. "He was totally ambidextrous. They couldn't stop him because he was so quick. He could dribble with either hand, drive either way and put the ball up either way."

"Steve was legendary," McNeil said. "He was just a great shooter and it was fun to play with him."

Thomas, a Roger Bacon High School graduate recruited to Xavier when McCafferty was head coach, *averaged* 30 points a game and had a career-high 50 points against Detroit on Jan. 6, 1964 (see story below). He finished that season second in the country in scoring.

He also led XU in scoring as a sophomore (16.1 ppg).

"I had developed a running one-hander and I don't even know how I developed it," Thomas said. "My (shooting) range was probably all the way back to 18 feet. I could bank it in from the side. I could shoot over the corner of the backboard. I always had confidence in my abilities as a scorer, but in order to score in the 20s or 30s, you have to have good teammates who set picks and things like that."

HISTORIC SCORING NIGHT

Xavier put up a then-school record for points when it beat Detroit 121-113 on Jan. 6, 1964, before 4,789 at Schmidt Fieldhouse. And Thomas did more than his fair share.

The junior guard scored 50 points, which still stands as a Musketeers record.

Bill Ford of *The Cincinnati Enquirer* reported that Detroit alternated four different guards to try to defend Thomas that night. Didn't work.

Thomas was 18-of-34 from the field and added 14 free throws. The 18 field goals were also a school record.

"In the heat of the game, I knew I was having a good game, but I had no idea how many points I had," Thomas said. "I was kind of stunned at the end when I found out. I think in high school the most I ever had was 36. It was nice to break the record and have it be on a winning night, as well. The thing that surprises me, with the 3-point shot, is that (the record) still stands today."

SHOOTOUT (NON CROSSTOWN)

During Ruberg's first season, Xavier scored 100 or more points seven times. "Ruberg didn't refer to it as run and gun, but it was run and score," Geiger said.

Needless to say, the Musketeers won all those games. One was not so easy, though. That was a shootout at Detroit, which XU won 114-112.

Geiger scored 36 points on 15-of-19 shooting. Thomas added 30, and Ryan Williams scored 25.

But the game-winning basket came from McNeil, a 5-foot-8 guard who picked up the ball off the floor after a Thomas miss and scored from close to the foul line as the buzzer sounded. McNeil scored only four points all night.

"Somehow he got the ball, threw the thing up and we got the win," Geiger said. "The only reason we won was because we got the ball last."

The Detroit victory capped a wild three games for Geiger, who scored 29 points against Miami (a loss), tallied 33 points and 20 rebounds against Catholic University (a win), then 36 points against Detroit for a 32.7 average. Geiger was seventh in the country in free throw shooting that season (86.9 percent). When he left Xavier, he was No. 10 on the all-time scoring list.

THOMAS' 45 NOT ENOUGH

Ruberg believed Xavier had a chance to go to the 1964 NCAA Tournament. The Musketeers went into their final two games 16-8 and had UC coming up at Cincinnati Gardens and Marquette at Schmidt Fieldhouse.

The Bearcats went ahead late in the second half, but Xavier came back and pulled within two points late in the game. That, Ruberg recalled, is when UC coach Ed Jucker started complaining about the state of the court, which had an ice rink underneath the floor.

"Ed's all fired up," Ruberg said, remembering the conversation this way:

Jucker: "We've got to call this game; we can't play on this court. They're all slipping and sliding."

Ruberg: "Well, you weren't worried about it about three minutes ago, Ed. Why be worried about it now? What do you suggest — we call it off? There are 13,000 people here. You take the ticket stubs over across the hall over there to that door and I'll take them here and we'll pay us out a rain check. How about that?"

"Well, Ed had no sense of humor whatsoever, so he about died," Ruberg said. "Naturally the game went on."

PHOTO COURTESY OF XAVIER UNIVERSITY

Steve Thomas' school-record single-season scoring average of 30 points in 1963–64 is almost five points better than Byron Larkin's best season (25.3 ppg in 1987–88).

Xavier had cut UC's lead to 94-92 with a tip-in from Jim Bothen. The Musketeers got the ball back and had a chance to tie it, but with 10 seconds to play, Thomas was called for traveling.

He already had scored 45 points that night for XU, 32 in the second half.

"I was convinced that I was going to score," Thomas said. "They kept me off to the right, and coming down the court I was dribbling with my left hand, which I could do. I got bumped out of bounds and instead of the foul, they called walking. That was probably the biggest disappointment of the whole year. They were always at the top and we were always playing second fiddle. I considered myself a good pressure player and I wanted the ball at the end of the game and here was the perfect chance and it didn't happen."

Xavier had not defeated UC since January 1957.

The Musketeers followed the UC defeat with a loss to Marquette and finished the regular season 16-10.

CHANGE OF HEART

Geiger was selected by the Cincinnati Royals in the eighth round of the 1964 NBA Draft. After a successful rookie camp, he was invited to the team's preseason camp in the fall. But Geiger turned down the opportunity and enrolled in graduate school at Xavier, where he also would serve as assistant freshman coach.

"It was with the idea that I'd try out the next year," he said. "But in the year I wasn't playing competitively, I lost the desire and that competitiveness."

TWIST OF FATE

Thomas followed up his junior year with another big season and was leading Xavier in scoring (28.9 ppg) again as a senior.

In the 14th game, however, Thomas — and Xavier — suffered a blow in a matchup against Duquesne and its 5-10 senior star, Willie Somerset.

"We played them in Pittsburgh when I was a junior and they had beaten us, and I didn't have a good game," Thomas said. "So when they came back here, we wanted to beat them."

Ruberg told Thomas: "If (Somerset's) guarding you, go one-on-one the first three times down the floor."

"So I did, and made three baskets, and he hit me three times," Thomas said. "It must have been eight or 10 minutes to go in the first half and we got a rebound and I took off. The pass was behind me, so I had to come back to get it. As it turned out, it was just me and Willy Somerset down at the other end, so I backed him into the basket.

"I'm facing the other way and he's behind me and he's got a hold of my shirt, and he was so strong. When I faked right, his knee hit behind mine and just popped it. I went down."

Before that, Thomas had never suffered anything worse than a sprained ankle. This time, he tore cartilage in his right knee.

"I had major surgery, and that was a nightmare," he said. "Consequently I had four more."

ATTEMPT AT A COMEBACK

Thomas had a half a year of eligibility remaining and came back for the 1965–66 season.

Over the first five games, he averaged 17.4 points and was shooting a career-high 50.8 percent.

But he knew something wasn't right.

"I would play and get 30-some one game and the knee would go out and be dragging around," he said. "Detroit was my last game. I could have played that half a year. But I figured it's not going to get miraculously better, and in my mind, I was jeopardizing my future. I was worrying about being crippled. I wasn't going to have it drained every week. I'm certainly not going to just go out there and make a fool of myself. And if I can't help the team, what's the sense?

"It was a tough decision, obviously. It ended on such a bad note, because I was all fired up to have that extra year."

In mid-December 1965, Thomas had fluid drained from his knee. He did not dress for the next game. The week before Christmas, it was decided that Thomas' career was over.

He was Xavier's all-time scoring leader with 1,722 points, but because of the way his college career ended, he wasn't drafted by any NBA teams. After he left Xavier, Thomas started working out again and his knee was feeling better. He went to South America on a goodwill tour for four or five months.

"I had gotten back into shape and was playing real well and came back and got a call from Pepper Wilson, who was general manager of the (Cincinnati) Royals at the time," Thomas said. "He asked if I wanted to come to rookie camp.

"I was working out with my cousin who was in high school and some of his buddies, playing two against one, just to get me in tip-top shape. I went up to block a shot and I was going to land on my cousin's buddy and I turned sideways and just blew the knee out when I hit. So I had to call Pepper Wilson up and say I couldn't come to the rookie camp and consequently had another surgery, and that was the end of that."

QUICK START

When Bob Quick was a freshman, he looked upon junior center Ben Cooper as a kind of mentor. One day, Cooper was explaining to Quick how a frontline player could get into the action with a sharp-shooter like Thomas in the backcourt. In short: Go to the glass.

"I began to look at: How do I offensive rebound my teammate's shot?" Quick said. "He opened up a whole new arena for me. I became a better offensive rebounder because I began to anticipate. I thought, I can get 20 points even if I'm not in the offense."

Quick averaged 20 points and 11.6 rebounds as a sopho-more and went on to *average* a double-double three consec-utive seasons. He averaged 12 rebounds a game for his career, which ranks fourth in school history.

"He could jump, he could shoot, he could just do it all," Ru-berg said.

When he graduated in 1968, Quick was the No. 2 scorer in school history behind only Thomas.

"Probably the most impres-sive player for me was my best friend, Bob Quick," teammate Joe Pangrazio said. "He was amazing. He was a very hard worker, a dedicated player."

PHOTO COURTESY OF XAVIER UNIVERSITY

Bob Quick holds Xavier records for most free throws made (22) and attempted (24) in a game. He set those against Mar-quette on Feb. 26, 1968.

BIG-TIME RECRUIT

Luther Rackley, a 6-11 senior at Troy (N.Y.) High School in 1965, could have played al-most anywhere in the country. Ruberg heard Rackley had more than 100 scholarship offers. Rackley actually wanted to go to Kentucky or Kansas, two of the nation's most storied and tradition-rich programs.

"But we had some people in town who were pretty friend-ly with Xavier and they thought that I needed some nurtur-ing," Rackley said.

They pointed out some positives about Cincinnati. Oscar Robertson, Rackley's favorite player, was playing there for the Cincinnati Royals, and it was a city with a professional franchise.

"We decided that … if I deserved to play professional basketball, I would get an opportunity because they would see me almost every day," Rackley said.

There were New York businessmen who helped recruit players to Xavier. Chief among them was Don Fazioli (see Chapter 5).

"I thought he was just a good, honest, sincere guy," Rackley said. "He told me if I worked my (butt) off, I would have a chance to do some things."

Rackley said he had never even heard of Xavier.

"I think Don (Ruberg) kind of made up my mind," Rackley said. "Don was like a lamb compared to some of the people I was talking to (in recruiting). That's one of the reasons why I went. He guaranteed (my family), 'Oh, he'll go to class, don't worry about that.' "

"Of course, you see Luther, at 6-11, and, naturally, right away you want him," Ruberg said. "We played Catholic University in Washington, D.C., on a Sunday afternoon (in February 1965) and we had on the hotel marquee: 'Welcome Luther Rackley to Xavier Basketball.' We had Don Fazioli and (Troy coach) Clem Zotto bring him down from Troy to see the game and be our guest."

YOU'RE OUTTA HERE

The first game of Rackley's Xavier career came in a freshman game in the fall of 1965 against the University of Kentucky—and he wasn't even around for all of it.

Keep in mind that UK coach Joe B. Hall and assistant Harry Lancaster had recruited Rackley and wanted him to be a Wildcat. *And* the game was in Lexington. *And* one of Rackley's high school teammates was on Kentucky's roster.

"Now, as you can imagine, they're not going to let Luther beat them," Ruberg said.

"After a bad, bad call, Luther put his hand on the referee's shoulder and said, 'Mr. Referee, I don't think that was a foul.' (The ref) said, 'You're out of here for touching the referee.' He threw him out of the game."

Ruberg said Rackley came over to the bench and was sobbing. "I didn't know I was in the South. I'm going back home," he said to Ruberg. "We had to talk our fool heads off to keep him."

What Rackley remembers is that it was a physical game with some pushing and shoving going on. "So I had to take over," he said.

"One guy … was throwing elbows at me," Rackley said. "I kept telling the referee and he just told me to shut up and play basketball. So I told him: 'Either you get him off me or I will.' I got the ball and I spun right and threw an elbow at him and tried to break his jaw. He went down to the floor. I got sent to the locker room. I heard there was another fight … I took off as fast as I could and I ran back to the floor. I got a couple swings in before they grabbed me again. They took me back to the locker room … and then they put me in the bus."

Ruberg said that when Kentucky's freshmen played at Xavier later that season, Rackley was pretty "pumped up."

"His last three baskets he just stuffed down with two hands, and the UK freshman center was backing off," Ruberg said. "And we beat them. I told the poor (freshman) coach who brought them up: 'I'm sorry we had to do that to you.' I wish Harry would have come up and taken it like a man. But you tell him that I warned him."

THE CRUTCH

They agree on this much: It was one intense game.

We're talking about the March 3, 1967, XU-UC game at the Cincinnati Gardens. Xavier was 13-12, had lost six of seven and was playing its only game of the season at the Gardens. UC was 16-9.

It was the regular-season finale for both teams.

At that point, it was only the second time a UC-XU game had gone into overtime.

"It was a very physical game," Pangrazio said.

To say the least. This is where it enters Crosstown Shoot-out lore.

Raleigh Wynn of UC was dribbling the ball upcourt. Pangrazio was defending.

Wynn's version of what happened: "He was hitting me in the back with his fist," he said in "Tales of Cincinnati Bearcats Basketball." "I said, 'Take it easy.' He hit me in the back again. I dropped the ball and turned around and slugged him. ... He ran up in the stands and got a crutch, and the place just went wild."

Pangrazio's version: "The ball was going out of bounds, right by the side of the court. I screened him off the ball. I thought he was going to throw it off my leg, and as that happened, I stepped in front of him and he pushed me into the stands. ... I landed on these people. I kind of rolled and hit the floor. I just saw the crutch laying there and I picked it up. To say that I picked the crutch up, threw the crutch and hit him, that part's true."

Police quickly got involved. Pangrazio and Wynn were ejected.

"I suppose it was an anger thing more than anything for him

pushing me into the stands like that," Pangrazio said. "It was a spontaneous thing."

UC won 79-69 for its 12th consecutive victory over Xavier.

"I was pretty frustrated," said Pangrazio, a transfer from Tennessee. "We thought we should have won the game."

There were 57 personal fouls, including three technicals, and 79 free throws attempted.

Ruberg's teams went 0-4 against UC.

"It killed me that we lost that game," Ruberg said.

THE END

Ruberg left Xavier with a 52-51 record after four seasons. XU's only winning record under Ruberg came in his first year (16-10). He resigned in March 1967, saying, "I enjoyed the competition, but I'm not having any fun anymore. When it becomes a chore, it's no place for me."

He had failed to get a vote of confidence from the school's Athletic Board of Control in a secret vote by its members. His contract, which was to expire that April, was unlikely to be renewed.

"I look at it as a great time," he said 40 years later. "I had wonderful kids who played for me and I loved every minute of being with them and working with them and coaching them."

7

GEORGE KRAJACK
(1967–71)
DICK CAMPBELL
(1971–73)

THERE WERE CLOSE TO 70 APPLICANTS for the Xavier position after Don Ruberg resigned. Villanova coach Jack Kraft was reportedly the leading candidate until he withdrew his name from consideration.

After almost three weeks, the screening committee and the Athletic Board of Control recommended 30-year-old George Krajack become the school's eighth coach.

For the Clemson graduate and three-year starting forward, this was his first head coaching position.

"I can't promise a certain amount of victories," Krajack said in April 1967 when he was hired. "I can promise dedicated effort to a program that will be a credit to the players, fans and everyone associated with Xavier."

Krajack inherited a team with two senior starters (Bob Quick and Joe Pangrazio) and three juniors.

"If you worked hard, you were fine with him," Jerry Helmers said. "He was just a real straight shooter. I thought he was really fair."

BIG LOSS

Before Krajack coached his first game for Xavier, he suffered a tough loss.

Luther Rackley, his leading rebounder, was declared academically ineligible after the 1967 summer semester.

"We've lost the core of our rebounding," Krajack said in November 1967. "We don't have a man we can stick in the pivot, so we're forced to go to a wide-open offense, which we feel will cause some defensive problems for our opponents."

When asked whether he got along with Krajack, Rackley said:

"Back in those days, it wasn't a choice of getting along or not getting along; it was trying to take advantage of what he had to offer. If he had anything to teach me, I wanted to learn it. I needed to follow instructions to play well."

Rackley did rejoin the team later in that season.

PHOTO COURTESY OF XAVIER UNIVERSITY

George Krajack's teams never won more than 10 games in a season.

SAVING THE BEST FOR LAST

Xavier finished 10-16 in 1967–68, Quick's senior year, but he recalls the final six or seven games as some of his most memorable.

"I really had a chance to express myself on the court more than I had ever been before," he said. "The last few games I had fun on the court because I was in my own world."

His Senior Night, against Marquette, was the first night his mother ever watched him play in college in person. During the pregame ceremony when the seniors were honored, he gave his mother a rose and told her: "Mom, we're gonna win this one for you."

"I think I had more fun that game than I ever had in my life," Quick said. "I was very light that night and 40 points later, we beat Marquette. That was my high game."

Xavier indeed upset NCAA Tournament-bound Marquette in overtime 88-83. *The Enquirer* called it "one of the most incredible victories in many a long season," and XU students rushed onto the court to celebrate when it was over.

No. 10-ranked Marquette, which came in 20-3 and riding an eight-game winning streak, was ahead 77-73 with 45 seconds remaining in regulation. Rackley and Tim O'Connell each scored to send the game into overtime.

"This was a good one for all over the country," Krajack said afterward.

GRAND FINALE

The next game was the regular-season finale against the Bearcats at Cincinnati Gardens.

Xavier had lost 12 in a row over 11 years to UC, and there was no reason to think the results would be any different.

Quick followed his 40-point game with 35 points — including 15 of 16 free throws — and 14 rebounds against Cincinnati in his last college game. But in the end, it was a reserve named John Zeides who cemented his name in Crosstown Shootout history.

The Bearcats were ahead 71-70 after a 30-foot shot by Dean Foster. Xavier called time out with 13 seconds to play.

Zeides, who played just 17 minutes all night, took the inbounds pass, dribbled down the middle of the court and threw up a shot from the foul line that went in.

Final score: Xavier 72, UC 71.

"He knocked it down and we were happy thereafter," Quick said. "That was special. Everybody was all over the court."

After losing five straight, XU closed its season with big consecutive victories.

"We weren't going to the tournament, but to beat those two teams back-to-back like that was pretty impressive," Pangrazio said.

Quick was selected by the Baltimore Bullets in the second round of the 1968 NBA Draft and played four seasons with Baltimore and Detroit in the NBA before finishing his pro career with the Dallas Chaparrels of the ABA.

PLAYING BIG IN BIG GAMES

Rackley averaged 15 points and 12.6 rebounds as a sophomore in 1966–67 but played only seven games as a junior for academic reasons. He came back as a senior in 1968–69 and was team MVP, averaging 17.5 points and 14 rebounds. He finished with a 12.7 career rebounding average, which still ranks second in XU history behind only Bob Pelkington (16.6). Rackley scored 910 points in just a little more than two seasons.

"Luther could have been Bill Russell-plus," Quick said. "He had all of the tools. He had all of the talent. Luther could block shots like Russell but he didn't know what he was doing. If he had a little more push, Luther could have been as good as anybody."

Rackley earned his degree the summer after his senior year. He was selected in the third round of the 1969 NBA Draft by the Cincinnati Royals and played five seasons in the pros with

Luther Rackley was inducted into Xavier's Athletic Hall of Fame in 1982.

the Royals, Cleveland Cavaliers, New York Knicks and Philadelphia 76ers. Rackley spent most of the 1972–73 season with the Memphis Tams of the ABA.

"I think, in the end, Xavier gave me a pretty good education," Rackley said. "One of the ways that I did use it was I taught for 10 years. Of course, it helped me as a business owner. Xavier is not just a basketball, athletic institution. And I think that's what makes it a little bit unique. They keep you on your toes, and that's a good thing."

DID I REALLY MISS THOSE?

During the 1970–71 season, junior Jerry Helmers averaged a team-high 19.4 points and made 81 percent of his free throws.

So when he stepped to the foul line, trailing Cincinnati by one point with nine seconds left at the Cincinnati Gardens on

Feb. 17, 1971, the fans were pretty certain the Musketeers were headed to victory. So was Helmers.

"That crowd thought for sure I was going to make them," Helmers said.

It was a back-and-forth finish that saw the Bearcats go ahead 65-64 on a basket by Steve Wenderfer. But on XU's possession, Wenderfer fouled Helmers. The Musketeers were in a bonus situation. Helmers had to make the first free throw to get another.

Instead, his shot bounced off the front of the rim.

But Xavier's Bob Fullarton rebounded the miss. Then one referee called a foul on UC just before another called for a jump ball.

On the way to the game that night, *The Enquirer* reported, Tom Binegar was telling teammates in the car that he had a feeling one of them would be the one to win the game for the Musketeers. "I hope I'm not the guy to go to the line with four or five seconds left," Fullarton had said.

Well, he was.

And he sank both foul shots with five seconds remaining. They were his only points of the game.

"(Teammate) Conny Warren came up to me at the line and just said: 'Follow through; just follow through, Bob,'" Fullarton related afterward. "I have a tendency to back off on free throws and not follow through, but once I made the first one, the second came a lot easier."

Helmers was still in disbelief.

"We won anyway," he said. "I was so upset about (missing the foul shot), but we had a lot of fun partying after the game."

The Musketeers prevailed 66-65, then lost the final five games of the season.

A LOW POINT

With three games left, Krajack resigned, effective at the end of the 1970–71 season. Xavier would finish 9-17.

Krajack's four-year record was 34-69. He never had a winning season, and neither had the Musketeers in seven years.

That didn't end with the next coach, either.

Dick Campbell became Xavier's coach in 1971 and lasted just two years, the shortest stint for any coach after the 1940s.

Helmers, for one, was upset about the change from Krajack to Campbell. It's no wonder: Helmers' scoring average went from 19.4 points as a junior to 13.9 points his senior year.

"I shot as well but didn't get many shots," Helmers said. "He changed the offense around to get the ball to the big guys. That was disappointing because I thought we could have been a better team. It was 'my way or the highway' (with Campbell). We just kind of kept our mouths shut and did our jobs."

PHOTO COURTESY OF XAVIER UNIVERSITY

In Dick Campbell's second season, Xavier lost 19 of its last 20 games.

After his teams went 12-14 and 3-23 — the worst record in school history — Campbell resigned. The Musketeers had lost their last 13 games in 1973.

It very well may have been the low point in the basketball program's history.

Then the unheard-of happened: Xavier turned to a Bearcat to turn around its fortunes.

8

TAY BAKER
(1973–79)

TAY BAKER HAD RESIGNED as UC's head coach in 1972 and spent the next year as a physical education teacher on campus. The Hamilton native said he had opportunities to coach elsewhere, but he and his wife are from Cincinnati and attended UC — Baker played for the Bearcats from 1947–50 — and they had no desire to leave town.

Baker coached high school ball at Lebanon, Miamisburg and Wyoming before joining the Bearcats staff as an assistant in 1959. He became head coach in '65, and his UC teams went 125-60 in seven years.

In 1973, his name was discussed around Xavier as a coaching candidate. Baker does not know how it started, only that he did not initiate the communication. "One call led to another" is what he remembers, and soon he was invited to a meeting with athletic director Jim McCafferty.

During his year out of coaching, Baker watched Xavier struggle under Dick Campbell, but the notion of taking over the XU program did not cross his mind.

"Never in a hundred years," Baker said. "You're not at UC

and ever thinking about coaching Xavier and vice versa. It just doesn't happen."

He had a good meeting with McCafferty. Baker said he always respected the former Xavier coach and had "high regards" for what the university stood for. But what piqued his interest during their talk was McCafferty's desire to move Xavier from an independent program into a conference.

Schmidt Fieldhouse was XU's primary home court. With no league to lean on, the Musketeers could land games with Michigan, Notre Dame and Marquette, but also ended up with opponents like Indiana-Purdue, Aquinas (Mich.), Thomas More, Delaware and Wheeling College.

PHOTO COURTESY OF XAVIER UNIVERSITY

Tay Baker's teams went 70-89 in six years.

Baker and McCafferty shared the belief that Xavier needed a league affiliation.

"They knew they had to change the direction they were going," Baker said. "He was making a dedicated effort to try to bring that about. That's the thing that got my attention more than anything else.

"He made me feel like they wanted me, and if I were to come over there we could maybe get the thing going and get that league formed and see some brighter days ahead."

So it was done. A Bearcat was about to take over the Musketeers. It was the first and last time that would happen.

And not everyone on Victory Parkway was thrilled.

A member of the athletic board told Baker: "I want you to know that it wasn't a unanimous choice."

"In other words," Baker said, "he's telling me, 'Hey, I don't want you to get the job but I'm not going to stand up against the other people on the committee and the athletic director.' "

What a welcome.

HOW IRONIC

Mike Plunkett always figured he would play for the University of Cincinnati, largely because his father, Dave, played at UC from 1954–56. Xavier didn't even recruit Mike because it was assumed he'd be going to Cincinnati.

But as a senior at Princeton High School in 1971, he was not highly recruited by the Bearcats, whose coach happened to be none other than Baker.

"He recruited me and offered me a scholarship, but I thought his efforts to recruit me were tepid and I didn't feel like he really wanted me," Plunkett said. "So I looked elsewhere."

Plunkett signed with the University of Georgia and played for the freshman team.

"I had a good year, but then I kind of got homesick," he said. "I contacted the University of Cincinnati and I talked with George Smith, who was the athletic director. He was my dad's coach, and they offered me a scholarship again. George Smith told me they would honor the offer of a scholarship even though they didn't even know at the time who the coach was going to be — and eventually it was Gale Catlett.

"Then I called Xavier, and Dick Campbell was their coach and I asked if they would be interested in offering me a scholarship. He said, 'Yes,' and that's how I ended up going to Xavier. I just wanted to come back to Cincinnati."

The irony?

Before Plunkett's sophomore season, Baker became the Musketeers' coach.

"He knew me and knew I was a pretty good player, so I don't think he had anything against me," Plunkett said. "I think he was kind of glad that I was there because at the time Xavier didn't have a lot of basketball players; it was a pretty down period. Coach Baker helped in the first steps to bring the program out of the doldrums they were in."

PHOTO COURTESY OF XAVIER UNIVERSITY

Mike Plunkett was Xavier's leading scorer and rebounder as a sophomore and junior.

THE MAID DID IT

The night after a loss at Loyola of Chicago in January 1975, several Musketeer players were robbed in their Chicago hotel room — by a thief dressed in a hotel maid's uniform, *The Cincinnati Enquirer* reported.

The "maid" stole $50 from Gary Deidrick, $30 from Pete Accetta and $20 from Mark Wilson. Tony Hubbard's empty wallet was stolen, too.

Plunkett and Accetta told *The Enquirer* at the time that they woke up with the thief still in the room but were too "petrified" to prevent the robbery. "I was scared, man," Accetta said. "I figured $30 isn't worth your life."

"We got our rooms broken into," Plunkett said more than 30 years later. "I kind of woke up and saw a shadowy figure in the room. I don't know if I really saw (a man in a maid's uniform) or just made it up to be funny."

After telling *Enquirer* reporter Paul Ritter the story, Plunkett continued to have fun with it.

"I acted like I was investigating the case," he said. "I was always kind of a free spirit. As we were getting more and more into it, I started saying Jim Rippe, a guy on our team, was the main suspect because he was real skinny and could fit into a maid's uniform. Rippe was laughing about it."

EIGHT MEN OUT

In January 1976, when St. Joseph's played XU at Schmidt Fieldhouse, the NCAA prohibited teams from taking more than 10 players on the road.

The game went into double overtime, and by the time it ended, the Hawks had only two players on the floor because *eight* had fouled out of the game.

"It was pretty easy scoring against a one-one zone," Plunkett said laughing. "By the time we got a lead in the second overtime, we just held the ball for the last minute or so because we didn't want to score like crazy on them when they only had two players. That was very strange."

Xavier won 109-96. The Musketeers made 45 of 64 free-throw attempts.

"I'm not embarrassed to win this basketball game," Baker said afterward. "I think the officiating was good, and I don't blame the end result on the two guys in stripes."

Baker instead faulted the NCAA rule, which was opposed by coaches, he said.

St. Joseph's coach Harry Booth also refused to blame the referees, choosing to focus on the fact that his team lost a 90-86 lead early in the first overtime.

He told the *Philadelphia Bulletin*: "The fouls? There were some questionable calls, but I can't blame the officials for the loss. I have to take the blame. Maybe I haven't taught our kids how to play tight team defense or how not to commit silly, senseless fouls."

MOST IMPORTANT RECRUIT

Baker calls Nick Daniels the most important recruit he landed

PHOTO COURTESY OF XAVIER UNIVERSITY

Nick Daniels scored a career-high 32 points against Cleveland State on March 3, 1979, at Schmidt Fieldhouse.

while Xavier's coach. Daniels, a Hughes High School product, was one of the most publicized players in Greater Cincinnati in 1975.

Daniels originally planned to accept a scholarship offer from Georgia Tech. But first, he wanted to come home from his visit there and discuss it with his mother. By the time he called to accept the offer, he said, Georgia Tech offered "his scholarship" to another player. That's when he decided to accept Xavier's offer.

"We worked very hard on recruiting him," Baker said. "We had a lot to sell to him. I think he was convinced the players we were bringing in were going to be good enough for us to make a move.

"He was the best athlete I ever had. He was physical, well-built, had good speed. He's the kind of guy who liked to play. I think he could've been better than he was if he would've really dedicated himself. He could take the ball to the basket. If he could've shot the ball like Gary (Massa), he could've been one of the best players who ever played at Xavier."

'THE OBJECT IS TO WIN'

Daniels was, in fact, pretty good right from the start.

The 6-foot-3 guard was Xavier's No. 2 scorer as a freshman in 1975–76, averaging 15 points and 7.1 rebounds a game. That season, he collected 24 points and seven rebounds in a 90-79 loss to No. 15 Notre Dame, and he had 23 points and 15 rebounds in an 81-74 loss to 13th-ranked Cincinnati.

He continued to climb the school scoring chart during his career, but the teams he played on struggled.

"You lose and what difference does it make? The object is to win," said Daniels, who changed his name to Abdul-Rahim after leaving Xavier.

"My sophomore year was a disappointment (10-17). My junior year we were 13-14, and my senior year we were 14-13. It should have been better both years."

When Daniels left, he was Xavier's No. 2 all-time scorer with 1,690 points, behind only Steve Thomas. But he was bothered by XU's 51-56 record during his career.

"People said I had talent," he said with a laugh. "I just played hard and may the best man win. I played defense and I played offense. I just tried to be the best all around I could be."

LOW MOMENT

Plunkett calls his "most heartbreaking moment" at Xavier a 77-75 loss to Dayton at Schmidt Fieldhouse in February 1976, his third-to-last game.

The Musketeers trailed by one point with 12 seconds left

when Plunkett was fouled. He made both ends of a one-and-one bonus situation.

"It looked like we were finally going to beat one of the Valley teams," Plunkett said.

Xavier's defense blanketed Dayton freshman star Jim Paxson. But Paxson passed to an open Doug Harris, who launched a 15-foot jumper with three seconds to go for the win. It was Harris' only basket of the game. He also made a free throw with one second remaining.

"That was really tough," Plunkett said.

Baker's Xavier teams would go 2-20 against so-called Miami Valley teams (0-6 against UC, 1-3 against Miami, 1-11 against Dayton).

IT'S ABOUT TIME

After 12 consecutive seasons without a winning record, Xavier finished 14-12 in 1975–76. The last time the Musketeers had finished over .500 was in 1963–64, Don Ruberg's first season as coach, when they went 16-10.

Xavier came into its second-last game, against Duquesne at Schmidt Fieldhouse, with a 13-11 record, one victory from clinching a winning season. The Dukes had Norm Nixon, who later played 10 years in the NBA, mostly with the Los Angeles Lakers.

The Musketeers shot 66 percent from the field in the 98-86 victory over Duquesne. XU center Joe Sunderman scored a career-high 24 points and had 15 rebounds.

"I don't know why I played so well," he said after the game. "Things just fell together. I was loose and relaxed and things happened."

Sunderman had been responsible for another key victory a

few weeks earlier. He scored on a layup with five seconds left to give XU an 82-80 overtime victory against Detroit. The Musketeers had trailed by 13 in the second half of that game.

On the final play, Xavier guard Garry Whitfield passed it to the 6-foot-10 Sunderman, who called the game-winning shot "just a reflex action." Meanwhile, Baker had been trying to call a timeout to set up a shot.

"Luckily they didn't hear us," he said afterward.

A SEASON OF DISCONTENT

The 1976-77 season was Baker's worst as Xavier's coach. The team went 10-17.

Sunderman was lost for the season in December because of knee surgery. A 3-0 start was followed by nine losses in the next 12 games.

By mid-January, Baker was holding a team meeting to try to placate unhappy players, who wanted a faster-paced offense than what Baker was running. It came after a disturbing 63-62 loss at home to Ashland, and just before a 42-point loss at No. 8 Marquette.

"Things like this always crop up when you're not winning," Baker told *The Enquirer*.

Before the season ended, players were ignoring their coach, looking disinterested in huddles and talking about quitting the program. Cleveland State coach Ray Dierenger observed after beating Xavier in March that players were "defying" Baker.

The season closed with four consecutive losses.

SHHH, IT'S A SECRET

Massa remembers playing a lot with the first team in preseason practice, but even as Xavier rode by bus to West Lafayette, Ind., to open the 1977–78 season at 12th-ranked Purdue, the fresh-man had no idea he'd be in the starting lineup.

"I think he was trying to protect me from my own nerves," he said of Baker.

After the team warmed up on the court, Baker announced his lineup.

"That was a welcome to the big time," Massa said. "It was great that he had that kind of confidence (in me). It was fun to be at that level, to play all of a sudden."

Massa struggled with foul trouble in a 90-82 loss to the Boilermakers.

But the start affirmed one of the reasons Massa chose Xavier coming out of St. Xavier High School: Baker told him he'd be able to play right away.

"I didn't really recruit him," Baker said. "I got a lot of help. He was very close to the Deters family. He was younger than Joe. The Deters (family) lived on the same street I did. That was more of a factor in his recruitment than anything. He was close with the Deters boys, and they talked to him all the time about going to Xavier."

Massa's final choices for schools included Miami, Richmond and North Carolina-Charlotte.

"It made a lot of sense for me to stay in town," Massa said. "We've got a big family locally, a fun family, and I feel blessed to be a part of it. The basketball program was not in great shape then, so beyond the opportunity to get a great education ... the fact that they weren't very good played to my advantage because I knew I could play."

Xavier needed some perimeter scoring and Massa was a good outside shooter. He played small forward and began scoring in double figures right away.

"He fit in with the other guys perfectly," Baker said. "He wasn't a speed merchant, but he had the ability to come off screens and get open. He was a marvelous 15-foot jump shooter."

MARVELOUS INDEED

Twelve games into his college career, Massa rewarded Baker for the confidence the coach showed in his young forward.

Entering a Jan. 7, 1978, game against Dayton, the Flyers had won 10 in a row over Xavier, whose last victory in the series had come six years earlier.

It looked like more of the same with Dayton leading by 12 at Schmidt Fieldhouse.

Then Daniels brought Xavier back. The score was tied with 14 seconds left, and during a timeout Baker called a play for Daniels to win it.

"I, as a stumbling freshman, went to the wrong corner," Massa said. "I was running to my corner and our point guard, Keith Walker, handed me the ball because he thought I was coming to get it.

PHOTO COURTESY OF XAVIER UNIVERSITY

After scoring in double figures three consecutive seasons, Gary Massa averaged only 4.7 points as a senior and played sparingly because of injuries.

"So I get the ball at the top of the key and make a dribble literally off my foot to the right, and I take about a 20-foot jumper to win the game. All of a sudden, after kind of a crummy game and being in the wrong place and dribbling off my foot … that was a last-second shot that certainly was not scheduled for me."

It was Massa's only shot of the second half; he was 2-of-7 from the field in the first half. "Give the real credit to (Daniels)," Massa said afterward. "He's great."

That would turn out to be Baker's only victory against UD in 12 tries.

SPEAKING OF DAYTON...

The next time Xavier and Dayton were scheduled to meet was Jan. 28, 1978, at Dayton. But the game ended up being postponed until Feb. 28 because neither team could make the first date.

You see, both were caught on the road in a good ol' Midwest blizzard.

Baker and Xavier assistant coach Tim Meyer had gone recruiting and scouting in Chicago after a Jan. 24 loss at Marquette in Milwaukee. With all flights into Greater Cincinnati canceled, they tried to drive, but they ended up in a ditch off the highway.

A trucker passing by picked them up and took them to a truck stop, and the two ended up at a National Guard armory in Remington, Ind., 30 miles north of Lafayette.

Meanwhile, the entire Dayton team was stuck in a hotel in Bowling Green, Ky., unable to travel by plane or bus back to Ohio.

Baker and Meyer spent three nights sleeping on a concrete floor at the armory. They eventually made their way back to Cincinnati on Jan. 29.

Meyer told *The Enquirer* there were about 100 people at the armory "and all the cots were gone. They gave us one blanket, and we ate soup and chili for three days."

GLORY DAYS

The highlight of the Baker era came in December 1978 during the four-team Volunteer Basketball Classic in Knoxville, Tenn.

The top team in the field was 12th-ranked Southern Cal. Clearly, what organizers were hoping for was a final game between USC and Tennessee, the host school.

The Musketeers came in 4-2 and had to face the Trojans in the first game. XU had lost 20 of 20 games against ranked teams under Baker.

"I knew the cards were stacked because of the pairings," Baker said. "We were a pretty daggone good team. I felt we could've played with anybody. And the kids kind of felt that way, too."

Xavier upset Southern Cal 75-68, earning a meeting with the host Volunteers in the final. Tennessee had trounced Niagara in its first game.

The XU-UT game went down to the wire. The Musketeers, trailing by one point, had the ball out of bounds under their basket with two seconds remaining. Walker passed to Massa in the corner, and his high-arching jumper went in as the buzzer sounded.

Xavier 51, Tennessee 50. It was the second big-time upset in two nights.

"We just ran a simple play," Massa said. "Nick (Daniels) went one way and everybody went with him and nobody went with me. I happened to be open and was fortunate enough to make a shot to win the tournament. It was pretty neat. I remember the quotes in the paper talking about the fact that Tennessee didn't even scout us.

"(Daniels) was the most talented guy that I played with. Whenever we played some of these prime-time teams, he always came to play."

Daniels led all scorers that night with 22 points. Massa finished with 12.

"People gave us no chance of winning that game," Daniels said. "So the guys banded together. We played hard and we believed in ourselves, and I knew I had to be on the top of my game."

"Sure, that was the highlight of my career there," Baker said. "I was really hepped up. The media and the people down there couldn't believe it happened."

THE DOWN SIDE

The bad news? Massa was out for several weeks after that tournament. He had developed an Achilles-related injury that required much rest.

"It was a critical time when we had some momentum," he said.

Losing their second-leading scorer and the only other player averaging in double figures certainly hurt the Musketeers. They went 4-9 over the next six weeks. It was not a team with depth.

"He never did come back until the end of the season, and he was very important to us because he could score," Baker said. "Massa could shoot that ball. He was a threat from all over. We had pretty good chemistry. The guys liked each other. They got along real well. That was kind of broken up when Massa missed all those games. It could've been a heckuva good season for us."

THOSE DARNED BEARCATS

Naturally, being a former UC coach, Baker really wanted to beat the Bearcats during his tenure at Xavier. But Cincinnati went 6-0 against his Musketeer teams. The closest XU came was in Baker's last season when UC won 60-58 at Riverfront Coliseum on Feb. 12, 1979.

Xavier actually was ahead by five points with 4½ minutes to play. But the Musketeers did not score again. UC's David Kennedy scored the final basket — the game-winner — with 1:40 remaining.

Shoving matches broke out at the end of the game. UC assistant coaches exchanged words with Baker. Players had to be restrained.

"I think we gave them all they could handle 'til the very end," Massa said.

CAREER CUT SHORT

Sunderman started his first two seasons at Xavier, but he injured his knee playing pick-up ball with high school players at Colerain High School and — after surgery — had to sit out the 1976–77 season.

He still had two years of eligibility remaining and returned to the starting lineup in 1977–78 and 1978–79.

Sunderman, who would go on to greater notoriety as a Xavier radio announcer, picked XU over Miami coming out of La Salle High School.

"Why I chose Xavier, to this day I am not really sure other than I loved the city and respected the Jesuits and liked the coaching staff," Sunderman said. "I had always thought from Day 1 that Xavier had a lot of potential. I really did."

Baker called Sunderman one of the program's great role players.

"He was a banger around the boards, he screened very well and played good, hard defense," Baker said. "Joe and Gary

Joe Sunderman was the Musketeers' top rebounder in 1978-79, averaging 8.6 a game.

(Massa) weren't guys that mouthed off much; they just worked hard and brought their lunch pail every day and did what they were asked to do and did it very well."

Said Massa: "There's not a better human on the face of the earth than Joe. First-class guy, genuinely nice person. Pure character and integrity. Joe was certainly a nice guy to have around. He was like a big brother."

Sunderman's best statistics came during his senior season when he averaged 9.6 points and 8.6 rebounds, both career highs. But his career ended when he suffered a thumb injury late in the season.

In February 1979, Sunderman was driving his car back to his dorm room when it slid down a hill and bumped into a slow-moving train at a railroad crossing. His thumb was broken in two places and required surgery "to put it together again."

"I was coming down Herald Avenue where there are two sets of train tracks," he said. "And in between there's an area to stop. I'm coming down the sloping hill, and I hear a train. I am going 5 miles an hour, and I hit my brakes. I hit the front of the train, but I was able to turn the car parallel. I was very, very lucky.

"Did it shake me up? Sure. It was not something you were happy about."

ON THE AIR

When Sunderman was sitting out the 1976–77 season, he spent some time on the radio with Bill Meridith, broadcasting a couple of La Salle and Elder high school games.

"He would tap on the table when he wanted me to talk, and when he had heard enough, he would tap again," Sunderman said.

In 1980, a year after Sunderman graduated from Xavier, Musketeers coach Bob Staak wanted a former player on the radio broadcast team. XU booster Paul Olding, who had heard Sunderman on the high school broadcasts, suggested to Xavier officials giving Sunderman a chance.

"It wasn't an automatic 'yes.' I had to think about it," Sunderman said. "I thought, 'Well, why not? It could be a good opportunity not so much to establish a radio career but just good experience, speaking and that kind of thing.' "

Sunderman has been on the broadcast team ever since, over the years serving as an analyst, then a play-by-play man. He was inducted into Xavier's Athletic Hall of Fame in 2007.

"I like staying connected to the program," he said. "I enjoy doing the games. I enjoy the Xavier community. I've really enjoyed watching the university grow in terms of the success on the basketball court and outside of that.

"It's been fun to be part of. I really enjoy the players, I enjoy the coaches and I've had really great broadcast partners."

MIXED EMOTIONS

Baker was considered an "old-school" coach by many of the players. "A straight shooter," Daniels calls him. "Well-prepared and well-organized," Plunkett said.

"He was not real dynamic, joking," Plunkett said. "He was not going to motivate you a whole lot and pat you on the back and that kind of thing. When we would go on the road, Tay would sit in the lobby and work crossword puzzles. He wasn't the type of coach where you developed a close, personal relationship with him.

"Despite the fact that I didn't always get along with Coach Baker, I always admired him for his work ethic and really felt bad that we didn't do better for him. He was very stoic. He would take (a loss) hard, but you couldn't tell through his outward emotions. He was pretty even-keel through a lot of tough times. I've always said that the hardest thing in sports, the toughest thing to do, is to turn around a losing program; that's so difficult."

Massa grew up in Baker's neighborhood and was a bit shaken when Baker resigned.

"I trusted him," Massa said. "So when he left, for me, it was a little bit disappointing and a little bit of a fear of the unknown. You know, here's a guy that looks out for you, plays you a lot, and all of a sudden, what's the future going to hold? And I just didn't know what to expect."

BIG CHANGES AHEAD

Baker announced his resignation as Xavier's coach, effective the end of the season, in late January 1979. He said at the time that he knew it was going to be his final year, "it was just a question of when I decided to announce it."

It probably didn't help that there was growing dissatisfaction on campus. About 250 students wrote negative comments about Baker in response to a random poll during student government elections. Some Xavier officials were openly critical of Baker's recruiting and his ability to relate to student-athletes.

Baker's last team finished 14–13, his second winning season with the Musketeers.

Baker remained on XU's faculty in the Department of Physical Education.

"I had my shot at it," he said. "The only regret I had is I never did get to coach in that conference, and that's the thing that took me over there to begin with.

"Yeah, there's a piece of me over there (at Xavier). Maybe not as big a piece as at UC, but I was always treated very fairly over there and was given an opportunity. It was an honor for me to be selected to coach there. It fulfilled my desire to coach a couple more years, and it's a great school. I didn't get as much done as I wanted to get done. It's just kind of unfortunate the conference affiliation didn't materialize any quicker than it did."

Baker did leave the job feeling that he had something to do with Xavier getting into a league, something he pushed for with McCafferty, who resigned as athletic director in February 1979, effective the end of May that year.

"I've said this to a lot of people: Xavier should be thankful they had Coach McCafferty. Not only did he win an NIT championship for them, but he wanted to get that conference started and he really worked hard and spent a lot of time on it," Baker said. "That was really the salvation of that program."

THE DEED IS DONE

In June 1979, the Musketeers' long-awaited goal of being in a conference was realized.

The Midwestern City Conference was born with six teams: Butler, Evansville, Loyola of Chicago, Oklahoma City, Oral Roberts and Xavier.

McCafferty, a driving force in the formation of the league, was named its first commissioner.

Make no mistake: This was a pivotal moment for Xavier basketball. It helped the program attract its next coach, it helped make the NCAA Tournament a consistently attainable goal and it would set the stage for decades of success at the conference level.

9

BOB STAAK
(1979–85)

AT THE SAME TIME TAY BAKER was resigning as Xavier's coach, an assistant for the University of Pennsylvania was in Cincinnati recruiting. Bob Staak read all about it in a local newspaper and found himself thinking about the Xavier job on the flight back to Philadelphia.

Great city. Good area for recruiting — surrounded by Kentucky and Indiana. Some history of success.

"I just thought there was some potential for it to be a very good situation," Staak said.

As he looked into the job, he found out Xavier was planning to join a conference and there was a renewed commitment to winning and doing it "the right way."

All that appealed to him.

He quickly became one of the top candidates, along with Pat Haley, an assistant coach at Dayton, Roger Blalock from Purdue's staff and Indiana assistant Tom Miller.

Bill Daily, head of Xavier's Athletic Board at the time, was close to a one-man search committee (See Chapter 2).

"I watched Staak on three or four games and I saw that he could really coach," Daily said. "Some assistants, you know, just sit there ... I was impressed by his coaching, and I knew he could recruit."

Staak came to Cincinnati to interview on a cold, icy day.

"I really wanted the job when I went through the interview process," Staak said. "I was extremely impressed with the people that I met, what I thought to be their sincere commitment to building a winning program there. The fieldhouse was an old, old building. It wasn't really something you could sell (recruits), but they said that we could do something to spruce it up, which is what we did."

In fact, Staak said laughing, the first time he got on campus and saw the facilities, "I was ready to quit."

"I had never seen a basketball coach's office like that," he said. "It was like in the extreme corner of the basement of Schmidt Fieldhouse. The tile was broken, there was a broken wooden desk, there was a chair and it was dilapidated. It was like a glorified phone booth. I said: 'If you want to do what you say you want to do, and the reason I took the job is because you said that, this doesn't match, so I've got to have something different.'

PHOTO COURTESY OF XAVIER UNIVERSITY

Bob Staak coached Xavier for six seasons. His first three years, the Musketeers went a combined 28-54. His last three years, XU was 60-32.

"They moved me into the O'Connor Sports Center. They converted a conference room into my office. Within a couple, three years, they renovated that O'Connor Sports Center. They built an office for me that was adjacent to the conference room, so it worked well."

A native of Darien, Conn., and a University of Connecticut graduate, Staak came highly recommended. "I would hire him in a minute," Villanova coach Rollie Massimino told *The Cincinnati Post*. "My son plays for him at Penn, and he thinks Bob is the backbone of the Penn staff."

In the first six months or so after Staak's arrival, the Schmidt Fieldhouse floor was repainted, "All for one and one for all" was painted onto the sideline, the locker rooms were refurbished, new uniforms were ordered and the coaches were moved to their new location.

It was time for some changes.

GETTING GROUNDED AGAIN

When Steve Wolf played basketball at St. Xavier High School, he loved high-flying North Carolina State star David Thompson. He vowed to himself that if he got a chance to play for the Wolfpack, that would be his first choice.

Sure enough, N.C. State offered him a scholarship, and off he went to Raleigh, N.C.

Wolf's father, legendary Cincinnati coach Charlie Wolf, wanted his son to go to Richmond. But he told Steve: "I'll give you an opportunity to make your decision. You're 18 years old."

Wolf played as a freshman at N.C. State through 14 games until a lower back injury ended his season. But it was his off-the-court attitude that bothered his father most.

"What happened was in the summer (of 1979), I got a little bit big for my britches and my dad said: 'Listen, here's the deal: You can do family or N.C. State.' So he made me make a decision," Wolf said. "One night we sat there together and he said:

'I think you need to come home because you're losing your values and everything else. You're starting to think you're something special.'

"So I decided to come back."

Staak recently had been hired. He met with Wolf that summer. In August, the transfer was announced.

"Staak really took me under his wing," Wolf said. "He was so passionate. He helped me grow into being a leader."

MOREHEAD MONDAY

If the players didn't know what Staak was about already, nine games into his tenure as Xavier's coach they found out exactly what they were in for.

On Jan. 5, 1980, the Musketeers lost at Morehead State 99-84 on a Saturday night, and the new coach was none too pleased. But he didn't say much after the game.

"We played terrible," Wolf said.

Staak already had invited all the players to his home for dinner for that Sunday. They were a little nervous about going because they knew Staak was upset about their play.

"I talked to them and joked a little bit," he said. "They were a little bit on edge. But we had a good time and then I said, 'I'll see you at practice tomorrow.' "

The next day forever will be known as "Morehead Monday."

"I ran their asses off," Staak said. "It was the worst practice they ever went through."

Wolf recalled it that way, too.

"He was pissed because we didn't hustle, we didn't play hard," Wolf said. "So we get there at 9 o'clock. It was cold. We go to the film room after we've all been stretched out and we watched the first 10 minutes of the game and he yelled the whole time.

"Then he turned off the projector and said, 'Friends, I want to let you know something. This day will live in infamy in your minds.' We go out, we stretch and we were out there for four or five hours. We had guys throwing up. He would do full-court lay-up drills. People passed out or threw up. I'm exhausted. That was a helluva practice."

HERE COME THE BEARCATS

In early February 1980, Xavier was preparing for Staak's first matchup with rival Cincinnati.

XU was practicing the day before at Riverfront Coliseum, where the game was going to be played.

Staak remembers getting pretty upset — again.

"I took a ball and kicked it," he said. "I kicked it from about the foul line at one end all the way down to the other end, and it went over the backboard. John Shimko put his hands up like I'd just kicked a field goal. The guys didn't want to laugh. But I started laughing, and it just improved the whole practice."

The next night ushered in a new era of Musketeer basketball with a bold statement.

UC, coached by Ed Badger, brought an eight-game winning streak in the Crosstown Shootout. The Bearcats had beaten Xavier 22 of their last 24 meetings.

"They really looked down their nose at us, and there was not a whole lot of respect for the (XU) program because I don't think, prior to that, we were taken seriously," Staak said.

"That was the first time Skyline got involved and *The Cincinnati Enquirer* got involved. It was more than just a game; it was more like an event that year."

Xavier came out red hot and built a 17-point lead by halftime. The Musketeers ended up winning 77-69.

With just more than a minute left, Staak called time out and gathered his team close together. "Sixty-seven seconds and we own this (bleeping) city," he said.

"That's the first time we ever thought every year we ought to beat UC," Wolf said. "That's what you want and that's really what turned around the program to where people actually thought, *Man, this is a rivalry.*"

Over the next 28 meetings, the Musketeers would win 15 times.

Staak said, "I think that was the thing that gave us the first bit of credibility, at least locally."

FIRST LEAGUE TITLE

Xavier spent its first 58 years as an independent program with no conference affiliation. The 1979–80 season was the first in the new Midwestern City Conference. Xavier went 0-5 in the MCC and lost its first game in the postseason tournament.

But the next season, Staak's second, would be different.

The Musketeers won six straight conference games and took a 7-3 league record into their regular-season finale against Evansville at Schmidt Fieldhouse on Feb. 28, 1981. The winner would be the league's regular-season champion.

"That place was electric that day," Staak said. "You couldn't get a seat."

Xavier won 59-57. The Musketeers were ahead by 14 points with 14½ minutes left, then held off a late Aces rally. Evansville missed three opportunities to tie or take the lead.

When the game ended, music played in the arena. Dwight Hollins stood on top of one of the baskets. Fans were celebrating like crazy. Gary Massa, who missed the game with a dislocated finger, cried.

"It was the loudest crowd I ever heard in Cincinnati," Wolf said. "It was loud and it was hot."

The Musketeers lost to Oklahoma City in the second game of the league tournament and finished 12-16. But that first conference title proved the program was headed in the right direction.

WILLING TO WORK

Despite XU's loss in the 1981 MCC Tournament, the most valuable player was Xavier sophomore Anthony Hicks, who averaged 16.7 points during the season, the only Musketeer to average in double figures. Hicks averaged 26.3 points over the final four games of the season.

Hicks was known for his pre-practice routine of stretching, jogging, ball-handling, free throws and shooting jumpers from all over the court. He would regularly show up 75 minutes before practice started. "I thought *I* went to practice early," Wolf once told *The Enquirer.* "Tony sweats more before practice than most of the guys sweat during practice."

"The way I look at it," Hicks told the newspaper, "you can be as good as you want to be. I look at the Olympic athletes. They work four years, all the time, to participate in one event.

"You have to sacrifice. It hurts to be good. But I want to be one of the best, period."

He was.

Hicks averaged 16.3 points for his career, finished with 1,805 points and was Xavier's all-time leading scorer until Byron Larkin came along. His 466 career assists are the most among the school's top 14 scorers. Hicks is the only 1,000-point scorer to have at least 100 assists four consecutive years.

INJURY PROBLEMS

Massa's senior year 1980–81 did not go as he had hoped. A three-year starter, he suddenly found himself battling one injury after another.

He turned an ankle during preseason practices. He then favored his other ankle so much he developed an Achilles tendon problem. During the season he was elbowed in the mouth during a practice and got eight stitches. In mid-February—just before his final crack at UC—he suffered a compound dislocation in his baby finger that required surgery, and he sat out another three weeks.

"I ended up getting hurt a lot my senior year, but (Staak) always included me," Massa said. "He took me on the road. Even though I didn't contribute a whole lot to the team, he never discarded me."

Massa later worked in the Xavier athletic department, then was part of the school's radio and broadcast teams for about 12 years.

"When Mike Bobinski became the athletic director, they hired some real talent," Massa said, laughing. "Actually, we've got four kids and I didn't have an interest in going to New York on the weekends anymore. That's when I stopped."

In 1999, Massa returned to Xavier to work full-time in the development office.

PERSONAL HIGHLIGHT

One of Massa's favorite memories as a Musketeer came Jan. 10, 1981, the night he scored his 1,000[th] career point—against Dayton at Riverfront Coliseum.

It came on a free throw, and officials stopped the game to give Massa the ball.

"I ran over to Coach Staak and said, 'Can I give this to my dad?' And he said, 'Nobody's going to stop you.' I was able to walk into the stands and give the ball to him," Massa said. "That was a really cool thing because my dad had been to so many games."

Later, somebody gave Massa a photo of the foul shot that gave him the milestone. In the background of the picture is a Dayton cheerleader named Mary.

She would become Massa's wife.

HARRIS GETS MOTIVATED

Richie Harris, a recruit out of New York, arrived at XU in the summer of 1982 with a lot of hoopla about his abilities. But any notion that he would come in and take over was quickly eliminated after Staak caught a glimpse of him during an open gym.

PHOTO COURTESY OF XAVIER UNIVERSITY

Richie Harris averaged 15.4 points during his last two seasons at Xavier; he had averaged just 4.7 points during his first two years combined. He finished his career with 1,109 points.

"You have a tremendous reputation," Staak told Harris. "But I'm not sure we did a good job recruiting you and assessing your capability. I watched you play, and I don't think you can get your shot off on this level."

Harris was stunned.

"Rather than telling the coach he's crazy, I thought, *Well, he's the coach; he probably knows what he's talking about.* So rather than allow him to be right, I ended up perfecting my shot enough that I could get it off," Harris said.

"He might not have even believed that, but ... he motivated me subtly. It was his psychology on how to get the most out of his players."

MORE STAAK TACTICS

Walt McBride actually made a verbal commitment to Arizona State and former XU coach Ned Wulk when he was a senior at Summit Country Day. Western Kentucky, DePaul and Xavier were his other final choices.

People at Summit wanted him to go to Xavier and stay home. His brothers wanted him to go to DePaul and play for legendary coach Ray Meyer, who wanted McBride to play guard.

But McBride and Staak were a good fit: A tough player and a tough coach.

Right at the beginning of McBride's freshman year, Staak put Shimko, Wolf and McBride together at the same basket. They would toss the ball off the backboard, then battle for it and try to score. Anything goes.

"It was just pushing and shoving," McBride said. "We all played the same position. Coach Staak was just sitting back there at halfcourt with the other coaches laughing. I didn't understand what was going on. I played for a hard-nosed, tough man, very competitive."

McBride admits to being a bit of a "dual personality."

"I'd be low key, just playing the game," he said, "and then something would trigger me and I would just fly off the handle."

He was a gifted athlete who sometimes thought his teammates were not "giving it their all." He would get in teammates' faces and yell. He knows some thought he was a jerk.

"At that time, we were 21 years old," McBride said. "You haven't really matured yet."

NOT GOOD ENOUGH

If you want to trace the exact year Xavier turned around for good, it has to be the 1982–83 season.

The Musketeers were coming off what would be their final single-digit-win season (8-20). Staak was done rebuilding now. His starting lineup consisted of senior Hicks, juniors Dexter Bailey, Shimko and Victor Fleming, sophomore Eddie Johnson and a freshman point guard coming off the bench named Ralph Lee.

Lee had verbally committed to XU before Staak ever saw him play. Xavier assistant Wayne Morgan loved Lee's skills, but Lee broke his thumb at the beginning of his high school senior season. Staak still offered him a scholarship. Connecticut would get Lee to visit in the spring but already had signed players of similar size and position.

"Wayne Morgan is probably the best recruiter you'd ever want to meet," Lee said. "He made you feel like you were a part of the family before you even got here."

Lee's friends back in Baltimore were critical of his decision to join a program coming off such a lousy year. Johnson, also from Baltimore, told Lee the team needed someone who could distribute the ball.

A few months later, Lee was wondering, too, if he had made the right call.

XU opened the season with a 75-62 victory over Union (Ky.) College, but Staak did not like the way his team played. Xavier led most of the game but didn't put away the Bulldogs the way Staak wanted.

"There was no intensity, no emotion, no mental sharpness," the coach huffed after the game. When a fan handed him a cigar to light up, Staak snapped: "This is not a victory cigar. It's just something to take the edge away from my anger."

He did not let the media talk to players afterward.

Meanwhile, the Musketeers were in the locker room waiting an unusually long time for Staak.

"He finally comes in," Lee said. "He looks at all of us and says: 'You guys think you're going home tonight? I'll be damned if you guys are going home tonight. You guys are going to be running. That was absolutely unacceptable.'

"And he takes his hand and puts it through the chalkboard. *Puts it straight through the chalkboard.* He said, 'You son of a guns are going to be running till your tongues drop.'"

PHOTO BY GREG RUST/XAVIER UNIVERSITY

Ralph Lee, Xavier's career assist leader, also holds the two best single-season assist totals in school history.

He instructed Terry Kofler, team athletic trainer, to clear out Schmidt Fieldhouse.

The players then returned to the court and started running. And running. And running.

"I can remember guys screaming," Lee said. "I can remember guys pissed off. Then he stops us and says, 'OK, shoot free throws.' We shoot free throws. You miss a free throw and you had to run up and down the side. I'm sitting there thinking: *This is a nightmare. I can't believe this guy. We won by 13! This is not good."*

After it was over and everyone showered, Lee returned to his room and sat down on his bed with suitemate Harris. Lee then called his mother.

"Ma, I don't know what I've done," he said. "I think I've gone to school with Bobby Knight."

"What happened?" she asked.

Lee told her how much they had to run despite winning by 13. "Who did you play?" his mom wanted to know. Union College, he told her.

"Who is Union College?" she said.

"A small Division III school in Kentucky," Lee told her.

"Well, I see why y'all ran if you only beat them by 13," she said.

No sympathy there.

"Coach Staak thought we were supposed to beat them by 50," Harris said. "He set a bar that said with all this ability that we have on the team, you cannot play down to your competition. (At the time) I thought he was nuts. But I respected him because he held you accountable."

THE HANLEY SAGA

Staak recruited Jon Hanley out of a junior college in California. Hanley had been one of the top high school players in Pennsylvania as a senior. As a sophomore at Xavier in 1979–80, Staak's first season, Hanley led the Musketeers with an 18.4-point scoring average. Pro scouts were already high on him.

Still, he and Staak had issues. Staak disciplined Hanley during that season for violating team rules. The next season, Staak openly criticized Hanley in January 1981, saying, "I think Jon should be doing other things besides scoring points."

In October 1981, Hanley was kicked off the team for "disciplinary reasons" and missed what would have been his senior season. In August 1982, Hanley was reinstated. "I feel he has paid his dues," Staak said at the time. "I am different, but I can only be myself," Hanley said four months later.

On Jan. 29, 1983, Xavier won 76-58 at Oklahoma City to improve to 12-3. Staak put Hanley into the game. Wolf said that during a missed Oklahoma City free throw, Hanley tipped in a shot for XU's opponent. Staak grew upset on the bench and started yelling at Wolf, "You better get his (butt) together."

That night at the hotel, Wolf set the menu for the players but later noticed that Hanley exceeded the spending limit, including an order of two alcoholic beverages, Wolf said.

"That was a no-no," Wolf said. "I went over to talk to John Shimko and Jeff Jenkins and I said, 'Guys, I'm going to tell Coach Staak we need to get rid of this guy.' I was in Staak's room for about four hours that night, talking about how we are going to get rid of him."

Xavier lost at Oral Roberts 87-71 two nights later, then flew back to Cincinnati. On Feb. 1, Staak dismissed Hanley from the team — again.

Nobody was talking much about what had happened on the road. Staak would only tell *The Enquirer*: "...I have to make decisions as a coach on what is best for the team."

And then the real craziness began.

The day after he was dismissed, Hanley said Staak had a personal grudge against him, accused the coach of once punching him in the mouth and made other charges of NCAA violations. Staak denied all of the above.

Xavier conducted an internal investigation and cleared Staak of all charges. Hanley consulted with an attorney but eventually decided not to pursue any course of action.

"I have decided what good would this do Jon Hanley to destroy a man's career and a team I cared for," Hanley said in a statement released Feb. 15. "I felt I would come out looking like sour grapes."

Thus ended the incident.

"He could have been the best player to play at Xavier *ever*," Wolf said. "He was that good. But he never would abide by the rules.

"We ended up really growing as a team when Hanley was gone. What Staak did really fostered a team effort."

The Musketeers won 10 of their next 13 games.

IN HONOR OF DAD

Staak is quick to recall the exact date: Feb. 21, 1983.

One of his most memorable games at Xavier was an 86-85 *loss* at Loyola of Chicago late in his fourth season.

"That was the day my father died," Staak said.

The Musketeers were holding a team meeting in Staak's hotel room in Chicago when his mother called from Stamford, Conn.

"She said that my father had taken a turn for the worse and she wasn't sure what was going to happen," Staak said. "The suite wasn't a separate bedroom, it was just like a partition, so the players could hear what I was talking to my mother about."

The meeting ended. Players walked up and told their coach, "Hope everything works out." At 4 p.m. the call came. His father, Ernest, died at age 72. He told his mother he was going to leave right away.

"No," she said. "Your father wants you to coach the game."

"So I went to the game and it was tough," Staak said. "I didn't tell the players that he passed. I said, 'Just go out and play hard.' And they played their asses off."

Xavier trailed by nine points in the second half but rallied to an 80-77 lead with 4:20 remaining. Alfrederick Hughes, who finished with 27 points, took over and helped Loyola win it.

Said Staak: "I'll never forget coming out of the locker room at the end of the game and I said to the kids: 'You know, I told you that my father never got the opportunity to see you play a lot. Well, he saw you play today.' And I told them what happened. They all rushed up and hugged me. It was a great experience. That meant a lot to me."

Staak left the next day to go back to Connecticut for the funeral. He missed two days of practice and didn't return to the team until just before the start of XU's home game against Oral Roberts at Schmidt Fieldhouse.

"I got there maybe 10 or 15 minutes before the start of the game," Staak said. "I wasn't even in the locker room before the game, and then I walked up on the court just before the game started, and the crowd gave me a standing ovation. And we won (87-79 in overtime). That week really … just kind of solidified what the whole team meant to me."

RECORD-SETTER

When Xavier faced Oklahoma City on Feb. 26, 1983, it wasn't expected to be much of a game. Oklahoma City had lost 15 in a row and was down to seven players after academic ineligibility claimed several guys.

But the story of the night was Hicks, who came in needing 10 points to become Xavier's all-time leading scorer.

With a jump shot from the corner with 9:21 left in the game, Hicks surpassed Steve Thomas on the career points list. The game was stopped, and teammates rushed to his side. Hicks received the game ball and a personal congratulations

Coach Bob Staak is surrounded by, from left, John Shimko, Dexter Bailey, Jeff Jenkins and Victor Fleming after Xavier defeated Dayton 72-61 at Cincinnati Gardens in February 1984. The players are holding the original Blackburn-McCafferty Trophy, which has gone to the winner of the XU-UD game since 1981. Fleming was named MVP of the game.

from Thomas, who was in attendance. Hicks presented the ball to his mother, Betty Hicks, who was in the stands after making the trip from Birmingham, Ala.

"When I took the pass from Ralph (Lee) and let it go, I felt relieved," Hicks said that night. "I knew it was in. Still, it was a very emotional moment. Tears ... I tried to hold them back. I still had the rest of the game to play."

Not to worry. The Musketeers won 79-53 and got a career-high 22 points from Wolf, who started in place of an injured Victor Fleming.

FIRST TOURNEY TITLE

In 1981, Xavier won its first regular-season league title.

In March 1983, it won its first conference tournament championship, defeating Loyola of Chicago 82-76 in Evansville in the final of the MCC tourney.

The Musketeers rallied from an 11-point second-half deficit with an injured Fleming, who was still suffering from bruised ribs. "He's playing, but he can hardly breathe," Lee said. Fleming scored only two points, but Hicks had 23. Xavier earned the second NCAA Tournament berth in school history and its first in 22 years. "Only three of the current Musketeers were alive ... when the Musketeers last breathed NCAA air," wrote *The Enquirer's* Tim Sullivan.

Alcorn State knocked out XU 81-75 in the first round of the NCAA, but the Musketeers finished 22-8 and would not have a losing season until 14 years later.

BIG (MAN) LOSS

Eddie Johnson was Xavier's starting center for two seasons, but in 1983–84, he missed the entire season after being diagnosed with acute viral pancreatitis in September 1983.

Johnson had been hospitalized for two weeks while undergoing tests.

"I lost probably 40 or 50 pounds," Johnson said.

"I was in the dorm room talking with Victor Fleming and I just passed out. I woke up in the hospital. I didn't feel sick or anything. I couldn't come back (that season). I missed probably two months of school, so I had to make up a lot. The home games I sat on the bench when I could. It was hard.

"When the summer started and school was over, I stayed and went to summer school. Most everybody stayed so we had pretty good pickup games, and I just kept playing every day and I started lifting and I got back to almost where I was."

BROTHERLY LOVE

On Dec. 28, 1983, Fleming squared off against his twin brother Vern, an All-American guard at the University of Georgia.

Victor also was offered a scholarship to Georgia, but both played guard and they didn't want to compete for playing time. So Fleming, an inch taller than his brother at 6 feet 6, chose Xavier.

"I have no regrets," the quiet Victor said in March 1983. "I like it here."

When they met in college, it was the first time they went head-to-head since they were high school juniors. Both insisted it was "just another game."

No. 11 Georgia won 73-70. Victor finished with 21 points, Vern with 20 and the victory. "We lost the game and that's what is important," Victor said.

"Vic was a real quiet leader," Lee said. "You did not want to let him down."

WELCOME, MR. LARKIN

On Valentine's Day 1984, Xavier got a sweet gift: An announcement from Byron Larkin, a Moeller High School standout, that he would attend Xavier to play basketball.

Larkin averaged 28.1 points at Moeller and was the top scorer in the city. He also owned Moeller records for single-season and career scoring.

Purdue was Larkin's second choice. He also took visits to Minnesota and Vanderbilt. Unofficially he visited Michigan and Notre Dame, where he had brothers (Michael and Barry) in school.

Larkin did not get a good vibe from Purdue coach Gene Keady during his visit. "He didn't strike me as somebody I'd like to play for," Larkin said.

Notre Dame football coach Gerry Faust, a former Moeller coach, also spoke with Larkin about playing football for the Fighting Irish. Larkin was a high school All-America football player and he briefly considered playing football in college.

"At Xavier, I was their No. 1 recruit," Larkin said. "X wanted me from the very beginning."

NIT RUN

The Musketeers could have used Johnson in 1983–84. They lost in the final of the MCC Tournament and had to settle for an NIT bid — their first since they won the event in 1958.

Xavier's first game was against Ohio State at Cincinnati Gardens. It was the first game between the schools since 1934 and only their third meeting ever.

This was a great battle, too. The game was tied 15 times and no team ever led by more than six points. OSU's Ron Stokes hit a short jump shot at the end of regulation to send the game into overtime.

Fleming scored six points in the final 1:35 and helped the Musketeers win 60-57. Senior center Jeff Jenkins scored a career-high 30 points and added 11 rebounds.

"I'm just not ready to quit yet," he said that night.

Xavier held Ohio State star Tony Campbell to just 11 points and three rebounds.

"It's my biggest victory here," Staak said afterward.

Xavier defeated Nebraska in the second round and then played Michigan in Ann Arbor. The Wolverines nipped XU 63-62. "A very heart-breaking loss," Lee called it.

It would be another 10 years before Xavier would be back in the NIT.

PRO-X AND PROUD OF IT

He never played for the Musketeers nor was he an alum, but it's hard to talk about Xavier basketball without including Andy MacWilliams, who was renowned for his unabashedly pro-Xavier radio broadcasts for more than 13 years.

MacWilliams was working TV and radio broadcasts for the University of Cincinnati for Channel 19 for about three years and had grown close to Bearcats coach Ed Badger. Badger was fired after the 1982–83 season, UC decided to change radio stations and MacWilliams was finished with the Bearcats.

In March 1983, MacWilliams went to see Xavier play Alcorn State in the NCAA Tournament in Dayton. The Musketeers lost 81-75, but Andy Mac came away impressed with XU.

He came back to Cincinnati and talked with Dave Ashbrock, Channel 19's producer.

"I think these guys are going to be good if they stay healthy and Staak has a few more recruits," MacWilliams told Ashbrock. "I think it's a viable product and I think we ought to go try and sell it to the Channel 19 management."

"They went for it," MacWilliams said. "We put on 11 or 12 games the next year. This was really the first viable TV package that Xavier ever had."

MacWilliams selected Joe Sunderman as his TV partner.

"We hit it off personally," MacWilliams said.

Ratings were good. When the Musketeers went to the 1984 NIT, WLW-AM (700) broadcast two games on radio when WHKK, the team's regular station, had scheduling conflicts.

MacWilliams said that after that season he convinced WLW general manager Dave Martin to carry Xavier games regularly. In July 1984, Xavier announced a two-year deal with the "Big

One" to carry all Musketeer games.

XU went from 3,000-watt WHKK to 50,000-watt WLW.

"This is another step that enhances our program," Staak said at the time.

MacWilliams, a Syracuse graduate who is originally from Albany, N.Y., worked XU games until 1997. He stakes claim to being the person who dubbed the UC-XU annual game as the "Crosstown Shootout" in January 1985.

He is loved by Xavier fans for his hatred of the Bearcats. He became close with former Xavier athletic director Jeff Fogelson and coaches Staak and Pete Gillen. He definitely was not a fan of former UC coach Bob Huggins.

Radio listeners enjoyed MacWilliams' blatant "homer" attitude on the air; he was clearly in Xavier's corner at all times, even chastising officials when he deemed necessary.

"My attitude was, *if I can't get excited, who the heck else is?*" he said. "I always had a point of view and it favored Xavier because I figured 90 percent of the audience was pro-Xavier. I legitimately felt an allegiance to Xavier, and the other 10 percent were UC fans, and why not piss them off?"

He laughs.

"There was a game against Detroit at the Gardens, and Detroit was pretty good back then," MacWilliams said. "A Xavier guy had a breakaway — I mean a *clear* breakaway at center court — and a Detroit guy grabbed him by the jersey; it was just a flat-out, intentional foul all the way. I got up and did the old ax for the intentional foul and got really upset on the air, and Sunderman pulled me down in my seat and calmed me down. The next home game Fogelson did a presentation before the tipoff; he had a chair modified with a seatbelt for me."

BYRON ARRIVES

Larkin actually grew up a UC fan. When he was a sophomore at Moeller, Badger frequently left tickets for Larkin and his mother to attend Bearcat games and sit behind the Cincinnati bench. Larkin thought (no gasping, please) that one day he might like to play for the 'Cats.

Xavier? He hated Xavier.

As a junior at Moeller, Larkin started to experience the recruiting process. And it was Morgan, a Xavier assistant, who "really put the full-court press on me" and started to change his mind. Larkin decided he would pick the school that wanted him most.

PHOTO COURTESY OF XAVIER UNIVERSITY

"And no question, Xavier came after me with both guns blazing," he said. "They were there at every open gym. Every time I looked up, they were there. They were calling, and Wayne Morgan just kind of overwhelmed me."

Larkin remembers sitting in the Schmidt Fieldhouse stands watching a practice one day

Byron Larkin set a Xavier freshman record with 492 points during the 1984-85 season, bettering the old mark of 391 set by Gary Massa in 1977-78. To no surprise, Larkin also holds XU scoring records for sophomores, juniors and seniors.

when, at the end, he was called down into the team huddle.

"I was like a little kid," Larkin said. "They brought me in the middle and were like: '*All right, 1-2-3 — Go Xavier!*' They had me after that."

Staak knew for a long time that Larkin was an important recruit.

"I think we saw every game he played for like three years," Staak said. "He was a great kid, good student, great reputation, great athlete. From a basketball standpoint, he really could score. ...You could just see his ability.

"We knew he was going to have a steep impact. Byron was game-ready. He was a very confident kid, like nothing ever really fazed him."

DOES MAMA KNOW BEST?

Staak was almost a reason Xavier *did not* get Larkin.

"My mom did not like him," Larkin said. "During the home visits, Bob Staak came with Wayne Morgan. The whole staff comes into your living room and they've got this flip chart. *Hey this is what it's like, here's a picture of the campus* ... Coach came in with a cigar, just really cocky, and my mom, she told him, 'I really don't care for you because you're a little cocky.'

"What was even worse is when Villanova came in. Rollie Massimino walks into my house with his assistant coach, hair slicked back, and you hear the violin straight out of 'The Sopranos.' While they're talking, I just see my mom's head churning and I'm thinking, 'Uh oh, here it comes.' "

"Massimino, can I ask you a question?" Shirley Larkin said.

"Yes, ma'am."

"You're not involved with the Mafia are you?"

Larkin's first thought: "OK, let me just cross them off the list really quick."

IN OVER HIS HEAD?

Staak may have thought Larkin showed up supremely confident, but there was a moment the summer before his freshman year in 1984 that Larkin had his doubts.

Leroy Greenidge was a year ahead of Larkin, who said Greenidge encouraged him during the recruiting process to come to Xavier. "And after I signed, he was like, 'You're going to sit the bench for three years.' "

We'll see, Larkin thought.

Then came pick-up games in Schmidt over the summer.

"He was bigger and stronger than me," Larkin said. "The first time I played him, he just mesmerized me with his handle. He was flashy, flashy. I was used to playing in the GCL (Greater Catholic League). I wasn't used to all that fancy ball-handling."

After the games ended, Larkin went to the office of assistant coach Harry Krohn.

"I was crying. I said, 'Coach, I'm sorry, I made a mistake. I cannot play at this level.' I told the coaches I was just going to go play football," Larkin said. "I was recruited hard for football. I told them I didn't think I could be successful (in basketball) at this level."

Krohn told Larkin to calm down.

"Stay with it," he said. "You'll be OK. You just have to adjust."

Adjust he did.

ONLY THE BEGINNING

Larkin was a freshman in 1984–85, a first-year player vying for the ball alongside four juniors: Harris, McBride, Johnson and Lee. He started the season as a reserve before moving into the starting lineup for good.

"He brought leadership, he brought commitment, he brought passion, and he was really efficient with his abilities," Harris said of Larkin.

"Staak was tough on him," Wolf said. "Byron was scared of Staak. His mom and dad didn't like the way Staak cussed; Byron didn't like the way Staak cussed. But Byron was a winner and Staak saw that."

Larkin does not deny that he was afraid of Staak. Coaches had screamed at him before, but not like his new coach.

"That was a little different for me," Larkin said. "My freshman year, I was just trying not to get yelled at and to just fit in.

"He was always on me about my shot selection and playing defense. When we would lose, he'd start picking apart my game. I was fine with that. It just made me become a better player. I was OK with him screaming and yelling, and I got used to the cursing. I'm grateful that he was hard on me."

Lee said veteran players had a hard time accepting that their best player was a freshman. Larkin led Xavier in scoring (17 ppg), and it was clear he was a special player.

"I was in so many huddles where Walt is yelling at Byron to pass the ball, Eddie's yelling at me to tell Byron to pass the ball, and Richie's being the gentleman saying, 'Hey we got to share the ball.' We didn't let him lead as a freshman," Lee said of Larkin. "We just couldn't accept it.

"It's not like we froze him out or did anything like that; we just didn't play as a unit and play together as we could have."

Larkin laughs.

"I was just a scared little kid playing with all these older dudes who were screaming at me," Larkin said. "Walt wanted to fight me. And I was like, man, I don't want any part of that. It took some time for us to kind of jell and everybody to settle in on their roles."

It was clear what his role was. Before the season, Staak would sit down with each player individually and tell him what was needed that season.

"We need you to score," he told Larkin.

"I had a job to do and I was going to do it," Larkin said. "As long as the coach was telling me I was doing what I was supposed to do, I was OK despite what some of the older guys were saying to me.

"I had a lot of expectations of myself. When I was in high school, I put so much pressure on myself to be consistent. I never wanted to see someone in the street after I played them and have them say, 'Oh, we stopped you.' That was my worst nightmare."

It didn't take long for Larkin to win over his teammates.

In the second game of his college career, Larkin scored eight straight points in the final minutes of a 61-58 victory at the University of Pittsburgh. In his fourth game, he came off the bench and scored a team-high 19 points on 7-of-10 shooting in an 87-79 victory over George Washington in the Kactus Klassic in Tempe, Ariz. He played only 23 minutes that night.

"I started feeling comfortable in that (Pitt) game," Larkin said.

"That first year, you have a lot of questions in your mind. I know I did. *Did I pick the right sport? Can I play at this level?* The coaches told me: Do what you did in high school, and that was score. So that's what I did. After I had a couple big games offensively early in my career, I guess that answered some questions. I just kind of expected that of myself from then on."

WHO'S IN THAT ROOM?

There was more to the Pittsburgh victory than Larkin's heroics.

The night before that game, the team was staying in the Hyatt Regency hotel across the street from Mellon Arena (AKA The Igloo), which was playing host to the Fresh Tour, which included Run-DMC, Houdini, Curtis Blow and other popular rappers at the time.

Curfew was midnight. Lee, Harris and McBride heard the rappers were staying in the same hotel. So around 12:30 a.m., they decided to sneak out of their rooms in search of the stars.

"I know several members of Run-DMC because we used to get our hair cut at the same barbershop in New York," Harris said. "I was looking for them because I know them."

They went from room to room listening at doors to see if they could hear the artists. Finally, they heard voices and thought: *Maybe this is it.*

"Hey, they're in this room," Harris said.

They knocked.

And who should answer the door?

"It's Coach Staak," Lee said. "We just look at each other and look at him. He says, 'What do you guys want? Why'd you knock on my door? It's past curfew.'

"That's the last we heard because we all three turned and ran up the steps. And as we were running up the steps, we could hear him downstairs saying, 'I'm going to get you ...' And we just kept right on running right to our rooms."

One of the assistant coaches showed up. The guys didn't even want to answer the door. They explained the situation. They were told they violated curfew and to get to bed.

"We all are scared to death," Lee said.

The next morning at the team shootaround, Staak said

nothing about the incident.

The Musketeers returned to the hotel. Nothing.

Pregame meal. Still nothing.

Before the game that night, Harris told his partners in crime: "We've got to win this game. That's the only way to fix this."

Xavier did win and went back to its locker room celebrating. Harris remembers this part:

"Staak comes in and says: 'Great win! Big win! This is exciting for Xavier basketball.' Blah, blah, blah. 'But you know what? I'm not freakin' happy. Let me tell you a story. Last night …' and he's looking at me, Ralph and Walt and he's telling the story and he starts cussing us out."

"He's yelling at the top of his lungs, 'I'm going to get you when we get back,' " Lee said. "Needless to say, we got back (to Cincinnati) and we ran so hard, it was unbelievable."

CROSSTOWN SMACKDOWN

The Crosstown Shootout on Jan. 30, 1985, at Riverfront Coliseum was billed as the first showdown between the city's sensational freshmen — Larkin and Cincinnati's Roger McClendon.

Even though Larkin grew up in Cincinnati, the event surpassed his expectations. "I had never played in any game that intense before," he said.

In the end, that meeting would be remembered for this: It was the night UC's Myron Hughes decked Xavier center Eddie Johnson.

"It was a very physical game," Lee said. "People were talking trash back and forth."

"They were kind of dirty players," Johnson said. "It all started from the introductions."

Xavier had just scored, and as the teams ran down the court,

Hughes punched Johnson and knocked him down.

The officials did not see it. No foul was called, and no players were ejected. The media missed it, too. There was no mention of it in the morning newspaper.

"Myron was a pretty quiet guy, but he was very physical," Lee said. "I remember Eddie and Myron going at it. We're running up the floor and then Eddie turns and Myron takes a forearm and goes right across his face and knocks Eddie down."

While video of the incident often makes its rounds just before each Shootout, Johnson said he doesn't recall getting clocked.

"He swung his elbow in my face and I fell backward," Johnson said. "Did he hit me enough to knock me out? I remember it happening, but I don't remember him hitting me. If he hit me, it was like a glancing blow."

Hughes said Johnson elbowed him first.

"I just reacted," he said in the book "Tales from Cincinnati Bearcats Basketball." "I turned around and slugged him and knocked him down. He wasn't knocked out, but he was stunned. ...The referee came up to me and said, 'I don't know what happened, but I know something happened. You guys need to clean it up.'"

A crowd of 16,342 watched the game — a record for a UC-Xavier game. McClendon outscored Larkin 20-12, but the Musketeers won 55-52.

FIGHT'S ALL RIGHT

Harris scored only 10 points in an easy Xavier victory over Evansville 83-63 on Feb. 11, 1985, at the Cincinnati Gardens.

But for him, the real action that night came afterward.

"I had a girlfriend who would wait for me after the game,"

Harris said. "So I go out and I can see from the corner of my eye like five guys standing around and I'm thinking: *Who are those dudes?* As I got closer, I could see that she was very uncomfortable, like they were invading her space. So I went in between her and one of the dudes and I said, 'Excuse me.' And when I did that, I threw my elbow at him and hit him in the face.

"Well, I don't know how many guys he had with him and he started going crazy and starts swinging at me. I said: 'You want to fight? Then take your coat off.' And this dude actually went to take his coat off, and when he went to take his coat off suddenly I attacked him and started beating the dude up. This was inside the gym.

"I'm fighting six people by myself and out of the corner of my eye I see Leroy Greenidge, and he starts running over. He didn't ask questions, he just started swinging. The police came and broke it up. Staak goes bananas.

"We were thinking he was going to suspend us. Staak pulls everybody back in the locker room and he says: 'This is what I'm trying to instill in you as Xavier basketball players — to be tough, courteous and respectful. But let me tell you, Richard was being attacked and here's Leroy coming to his aid. That's what we're about. We don't let anybody (mess) with us.' He's just going at it, and the team's like, 'Whoa, what just happened?' He didn't punish us; he gave us compliments for fighting."

'A BAD CHOICE'

After six seasons at XU, another job caught Staak's attention: Wake Forest.

Friends in the business encouraged him to look into it. It was more money. It was the prestigious Atlantic Coast Conference.

"I guess it was the competitive juices in me," Staak said.

The night before his interview, he said, he almost backed out. Then he figured he should at least go through the process and "see how it goes."

Staak was offered the job. And he accepted. It was a decision he would grow to regret.

"I think I made a bad choice," he said. "I went to a place where I didn't really know the people, I didn't know the culture. ... I just think that I was different from what they were used to and what the culture was.

"I never would have done it if I had to do it over again. I never would have left (Xavier), never should have left."

Staak might very well be the unsung hero of the Xavier program.

His teams were the first to win a league regular-season title and the first to win a conference tournament championship. They were the second to earn an NCAA Tournament berth and the first to win 20 games in back-to-back seasons. Also, the players were devoted to him.

Harris recalls Staak's departure being "traumatic."

"I can remember feeling like we lost a family member," Lee said. "Everyone loved Staak. He yelled at you a lot but then he hugged you and he gave you positive reinforcement."

"I think out of all Xavier's successful coaches, Bob Staak has gotten the least amount of credit," said Mike Plunkett, a Musketeer from 1973–76. "And he's the person who really turned that program around."

"I saw the apathy (with Xavier basketball) for so many years before Staak got there," Wolf said. "Staak was something special."

10

PETE GILLEN
(1985–94)

THIS WAS JEFF FOGELSON'S first big hire as Xavier's athletic director. He had to find a men's basketball coach to replace Bob Staak in August 1984, not an ideal time to find a coach.

His leading candidates were all top assistant coaches: Tim Grgurich from UNLV; Wayne Morgan, a former XU assistant then at Syracuse; and Pete Gillen from Notre Dame.

"I think the problem I had was, the guys who were being pushed were perceived as — if not actually were — the other schools' chief recruiters," Fogelson said. "I found myself asking, 'OK, I understand he can recruit, but can he coach?'"

Grgurich was recommended by then-Georgetown coach John Thompson, a former colleague of Fogelson's. Then-Fighting Irish coach Digger Phelps had called Fogelson on Gillen's behalf.

What Gillen really wanted was a program that had a plan. He was looking for a school that already had some talent, was in a good recruiting area and was competitive.

"I didn't want to go to a place that needed three years before you had a winning season," Gillen said.

"Pete came in (to interview) and did a great job," Fogelson said. "He was very high-energy about everything. The clincher was, one night at home, I get a call from Hubie Brown. At that time, Hubie was the coach of the New York Knicks, and I had heard that Hubie was trying to hire Pete to become an assistant coach for the Knicks. I didn't know if it was true.

"Hubie just called me out of the blue. I maybe had met him at some point, I don't know, but it's not like we knew each other that well. He was wonderful, and I remember he said to me: 'Jeff, I wouldn't try to hire Pete because I needed him to recruit for the Knicks. My interest in hiring him is because he can coach.' That's how it came about."

HANGING ON TO 'B'

Perhaps Gillen's most important "recruit" was Byron Larkin, who was about to begin his sophomore year at Xavier.

"He wasn't going anywhere unless I screwed it up, because he loved Cincinnati," Gillen said.

When Staak left, Larkin was on his way to Syracuse to work a basketball camp. Morgan, who helped recruit Larkin to XU, had left for Syracuse in 1984. He made it known that there was a place for Larkin at Syracuse should he want to transfer.

"While I was up there, it kind of turned into a visit," Larkin said. "They were showing me around the dorms, and I was talking to the athletic people. I considered (transferring) for a second, but after I came home from that trip, Coach Gillen had been hired. He had already been out to my house and had dinner with my mom and my dad."

Larkin first met Gillen in the Schmidt Fieldhouse parking lot. Gillen introduced himself and quickly asked Larkin to sit down and talk.

Gillen told him: "We're going to play up-tempo, we're going to press a lot, you're going to have free reign to shoot it. I think you're going to enjoy playing. We'll have fun. We're going to work hard, and you're going to be a catalyst. We want you to be the leader. Your role is not going to change at all."

Larkin had been nervous. He worried that Gillen would not like him or would want to bring in his own guy to build the team around.

"It was a really scary time for me," Larkin said, "but after I met Coach Gillen I knew it was going to work out fine. I liked the role he had planned for me."

BRINGING IN SKIP

Gillen and Skip Prosser got to know each other when both worked at the Five-Star Basketball Camp, which was held at the time in Wheeling, W.Va., where Prosser was a high school coach.

"It was unbelievably impressive how hard Pete worked," Prosser said.

The two kept in touch. Prosser went to Villanova when Gillen was an assistant there to visit and watch practices. He did the same after Gillen went to Notre Dame as an assistant.

"Pete Gillen treated me like a king," Prosser said. "I started working Notre Dame's camp, and we became friends."

After Gillen got the Xavier job, he hired Jeff Nix as a full-time assistant. Prosser called to let Gillen know he was interested in a spot on the staff, too.

"I just knew him a little bit," Gillen said. "I was kind of leery. Skip was maybe the third or fourth guy I asked. I was impressed with his love of the game, his passion. He was aggressive, but not too aggressive. He was loyal; he'd work hard. I thought, *Hey, I don't know him that well, but I like what I see.*"

It was 6 p.m. on a Friday in September. Prosser was on his way to scout a high school football game, helping out his school's coach. His interview with Gillen was from a phone booth in West Virginia.

"I know he offered the job to three other guys, and all three said no," Prosser said. He didn't much care.

Gillen offered, and Prosser accepted. Who knew he would spend 15 of the next 16 years in Cincinnati?

PHOTO COURTESY OF XAVIER UNIVERSITY

During Pete Gillen's nine years as Xavier's coach, the Musketeers never had a losing season and won 20 or more games seven times.

SENIORITIS

Gillen walked into a situation that had its pluses and minuses.

He inherited a team with four seniors — almost all with strong personalities — and a sophomore (Larkin) who was his best player.

The seniors were Walt McBride, Richie Harris, Eddie Johnson and Ralph Lee. They all felt comfortable talking back to Gillen. They also wondered amongst themselves what Prosser, a high school coach from West Virginia, could teach them.

"Coach Gillen was the boss," Larkin said. "Everybody knew that. But we would have some disagreements with him."

Gillen would want to play zone defense. The players would break the huddle, gather on the court and decide to go man-to-man.

"Pete would call time out and Ralph would yell at him

for calling a timeout," Larkin said. "It was a struggle between Ralph and Pete on when to call timeouts, what plays would be called. Ralph was such a leader. If Coach Gillen did something Ralph didn't like, he would let him know."

Lee said he and Gillen did not have a great relationship early in the 1985–86 season.

"I had to figure out what he was trying to accomplish," Lee said. "I figured it out later on. And I *really, really* figured it out after I stopped playing for him.

"He did a wonderful job of coaching; he didn't come in to change much. He kind of rolled with everything we did, but he made sure in the last two minutes we took care of the little things. That was a big issue. He really concentrated on that, got us in shape to be able to win those games down the stretch."

On Dec. 21, 1985, Lee collected 10 assists in a victory over Wayne State University and became Xavier's all-time assist leader. "That was my goal when I first arrived here," he said that night. Lee finished with 699 career assists.

TECHNICALLY SPEAKING...

Xavier was in control of its game at Evansville on Jan. 20, 1986, leading by 12 points with 4½ minutes left. Then McBride lost control.

After getting called for a charge on a play when he clearly thought he was fouled, McBride snapped, yelling expletives at the officials. He received three technical fouls and was ejected.

"I went to the basket and the guy called a charge," McBride said. "I said, 'No!' and that was a technical. I started going off, and that was a technical. Then I said, 'You can kiss my ...' and that was a technical. That was pretty much my character ... but that was one of the extremes."

Evansville went on a 9-0 run and pulled within three points, but the Musketeers prevailed 78-69.

"Walt was kind of his own man," Lee said, then started laughing. "He had a couple issues that we had to address, and I talked very sternly with him in the office a few times. I think he was a little bit afraid of me, and Walter wasn't afraid too much. He was like the hard-rock guy — he was tough; he'd fight you in a second. But he was a great kid, still is.

"The good thing about Walt — and I always said this — was no matter what, you know Walt had your back."

ENCOURAGING WORDS

Xavier finished the regular season 23-4 and was heading into the 1986 MCC Tournament in Indianapolis. After a practice, Larkin recalls an unusual conversation on the telephone with his father.

"Byron, do you want to be the tournament MVP?" Bob Larkin asked his son. "Well, go out and do it. You know you can do it."

"That was kind of significant," Larkin said. "He would always support me. He would go to games and say, 'I love you,' but we wouldn't have any long talks. He had never said anything like that to me before. Those words maybe galvanized my focus a little bit."

Indeed, Larkin put on a show in a 99-91 victory over Loyola of Chicago. Then a sophomore, he scored a career-high 45 points, hitting 17 of 20 shots from the field and 11 of 12 free-throw attempts.

According to the next day's *Cincinnati Enquirer*, Larkin "hit hanging jump shots. He hit fast-break layups. He hit shots with hands in the face and slaps on the arms."

His previous high was 32 points.

"We were playing against a team that was going to play us man-to-man," Larkin said. "They weren't going to play any tri-angle-and-two or box-and-one (defenses). I was kind of insult-ed ... I was like, *You have the nerve to play me one-on-one, especial-ly with a freshman? OK.* That was my attitude."

Perhaps not coincidentally, Lee dished out a career-high 15 assists that night.

"I would score eight points a game just on layups because Ralph would keep his head up and throw it to me," Larkin said.

Larkin followed that with 19 points in a victory over Saint Louis in the MCC final and was named tournament MVP. Xavier earned its third NCAA Tournament berth but lost in the first round to Alabama 97-80.

"I think that year we were just happy to be there," Larkin said. "The next year our mentality was totally different."

HILL PICKS XAVIER

During the summer before his senior year at Withrow High School, Tyrone Hill was playing pick-up basketball at Stewart Park in Madisonville. Larkin was there with some friends, too.

"I didn't even know who he was yet," Hill said. "Our team played against his team. He was making jump shots, driving. I was like, *Who is this cat?* Later he told me."

They built a friendship. One day, Larkin invited Hill to play with some of the Musketeers at Schmidt Fieldhouse.

"From that point on, everything kind of took its course, and I decided to go to Xavier," Hill said.

Other schools that were interested in Hill — UNLV, DePaul, Loyola of Chicago, to name a few — backed off because there was a chance he was not going to be academically eligible as a college freshman. When Hill achieved the necessary test score, schools renewed their interest, but it was too late.

"Xavier was there from Day 1," Hill said. "They just kept the heat on; even if I had to sit out, they still wanted me. That meant a lot to me."

He signed in April 1986.

REBOUNDING MACHINE

PHOTO BY GREG RUST/XAVIER UNIVERSITY

Tyrone Hill led Xavier in scoring and rebounding as a junior and senior. During the 1988–89 season, he grabbed 23 rebounds against Loyola of Chicago.

Hill didn't set out to be Xavier's all-time leading rebounder. But here's how he found his way there:

He remembers a game early in his career when guards Larkin and Stan Kimbrough would not pass him the ball. He was getting upset about it, and the two players knew it. The next day at practice, Hill said, both passed to him all the time. "Oh, you guys will give me the ball in practice, but I can't get it in a game?" Hill asked.

"They were just trying to bust my chops a little bit, (telling me) to quit being all about me," Hill said. "I think from that point on I kind of came into my own as far as what I was really good at: being a rebounder and good defensive guy, playing my role. I wanted to play, so I did whatever it would take to play. My career just kind of blossomed. I loved to rebound."

Hill became the first player to lead Xavier in rebounding

four consecutive years.

"I think you've got to have it in you," he said. "You've got to have a passion for it, you've got to have desire. Like every great shooter, they know their shot's going in; every great rebounder knows every shot that goes up is a missed shot, and is already getting into position to rebound.

"I was not a raw-talent guy at all. I wasn't a big weight-room guy until my junior year. What I realized was a lot of guys didn't want to play hard the whole game."

SPEAKING OF ROLES...

Kimbrough had to adjust his role when he arrived at Xavier.

Coming out of St. Joseph Academy in Cleveland, the 5-foot-11 guard started his college career at Central Florida, recruited there by Bob Huggins and Chuck Machock, who later would coach together at Cincinnati.

In 1984–85, Kimbrough led Central Florida in scoring at 18.1 points a game and was one of the top-scoring freshmen in the country. But after his first year, Machock was out as coach, Huggins was head coach at Akron and Kimbrough wanted to transfer.

"(Xavier) talked to me and I came and visited," Kimbrough said. "Byron and I talked because we knew there was going to be a ball that had to be shared. We thought we could make it work."

When Kimbrough became eligible in 1986–87, Lee would have graduated, leaving the point guard position open.

"I thought it would be a good fit," Kimbrough said.

It also was going to take some adjusting. Larkin was a junior, and it was, after all, *his* team.

TOUGH AS NAILS

As soon as Kimbrough arrived, the competition in practice between him and Larkin was intense. Especially because Kimbrough liked to use a secret weapon: his nails.

"Me and Byron went at it a lot," Kimbrough said. "I would take my fingernails and run them up the back of his leg just to let him know, *You better relax, man.* I liked playing against him; he was bigger and stronger, so that meant I had to compete every single day."

Larkin remembers all that too well.

"Stan had these long fingernails," Larkin said. "He would stay in his room and put hardening solution on his nails, and he would slay you like Wolverine. He would scratch you to pieces. Stan's mentality is he's going to pick you up 94 feet in practice; he's just hard-nosed. He would scratch you on purpose most of the time. Sometimes when he wasn't trying he'd get you, too, because his nails were so long. I've still got marks on my body from him. One time he reached for the ball and scratched me on my face. I had two lines going down my face like tear tracks."

PROGRAM MILESTONE

Xavier won the MCC Tournament for the second straight time in 1987 and got into its fourth NCAA Tournament. The Musketeers' first-round matchup was against 14th-ranked Missouri in Indianapolis.

The Musketeers, eight-point underdogs, came out early before the game, took the balls from the ball rack and started shooting at one of the baskets. A little while later, the Missouri players came out. Larkin said that instead of just asking for some balls, one of the Missouri assistant coaches started yelling and cursing at the Xavier players. Larkin punted one toward the Tigers.

Kimbrough said the Missouri players came to the basket where Xavier was shooting and insisted the Musketeers walk to the other end of the court.

"I ain't going nowhere," Kimbrough said. "So we get into a little skirmish. ... No matter what, I was not going to let you get a mental edge on me; it just wasn't going to happen."

Turns out, that was the Missouri basket and Xavier had to switch sides. But the banter was under way.

"Their players started talking," Larkin said. "Then our guys were like, *We don't care where you're from.* So when the game started, we were in the huddle saying, 'Hey, let's get 'em.' We were kind of chirping the whole game. They came out and were really combative."

Xavier led most of the way and held off a Missouri rally to win 70-69.

"It was a fun game," Kimbrough said. "It was one of those things that no one expected us to do."

It was the first NCAA Tournament victory in Xavier history. Larkin, who finished with 29 points and 10 rebounds, calls it the most satisfying game of his career.

"No question about that," he said. "It's special. We had done something no other Xavier team had ever done.

"And after the game, we're walking down the tunnel together with Missouri. We're all hyped up and they're down. Dexter Campbell — he was our enforcer — runs up behind (Missouri coach) Norm Stewart and slaps him on the butt and says, 'Have a good trip home, Coach.' Dexter was crazy. I couldn't believe he did that."

BRINGING IN SOME 'TUDE

Jamal Walker, out of Cardinal Hayes High School in New York, started his Xavier career in the fall of 1987. Gillen calls Walker one of the key guys he brought into the program, along with keeping Larkin and signing Hill.

"He brought a little New York cockiness," Gillen said. "Jamal was cocky and confident and I think his confidence rubbed off on our guys. He was a freshman and he wasn't afraid of anybody. He gave us a toughness that we needed."

PHOTO BY GREG RUST/XAVIER UNIVERSITY

Jamal Walker is the only Xavier player to record at least 1,000 career points and 500 assists.

"We call it a swagger in the streets," Walker said.

Gillen first saw Walker with the New York Gauchos Amateur Athletic Union program. That's when Xavier started recruiting him. Walker, like many top players out of that area, grew up playing against pros and former pros from New York City.

"I showed up to Xavier ready to play," Walker said.

"I was going to do what I had to do to be successful. I wanted to win. I knew if we weren't going to win, nobody would come see us play, nobody would put us on TV."

GILLEN'S PREGAME TALKS

Larkin said one consistent trait of the Staak and Gillen coaching staffs was their interest in getting the Xavier players angry at the other team.

Jerry Wainwright, a Xavier assistant under Gillen, would talk about each opposing player, not only describing strengths and weaknesses, but also calling them thugs and low-lifes and worse.

"It was so funny," Larkin said. "He'd talk like he knew these guys personally and they were terrible people, according to him."

Gillen took a similar approach. When the Musketeers would come into the locker room after warming up, Gillen — face getting redder and redder — would have them sit down. Then begin:

"Those guys out there, they think they're better than you. I want you to go out there and act like they're trying to come in your house and kill your family. That's what they want to do to you! What are you going to do about it? Now LET'S GET 'EM!"

"We were ready to run through a brick wall," Larkin said. "He would always give us that kill–your–family speech. We went for it every time. I would hop 5 feet off the chair."

JUST ANOTHER UC GAME

Xavier clobbered UC 98-80 on Jan. 12, 1988, but that game will be remembered mostly for the fight between Campbell and Cincinnati's Keith Starks.

The Musketeers were ahead 79-74 when the two got into it near UC's bench. Bearcat players rushed onto the court. UC was called for two technical fouls — one on Starks and one on the bench. A technical also was called on Campbell. There were 45 fouls called in the game.

Roger McClendon, UC's star, missed both foul shots. Larkin made 3 of 4 for XU. The game wasn't close after that.

Starks would say later that he thought he was retaliating for a blow to his face by Campbell. But Starks found out it was UC teammate Levertis Robinson who hit him. "It was just a big mistake," Starks said.

FINALLY: THE TOP 20

The Associated Press national college basketball rankings started in 1948–49. Xavier first entered the poll 10 years later, rising to No. 9 in the country. That was the season after the Musketeers won the NIT championship.

It took another 29 years before Xavier joined the AP rankings again. The Musketeers came in at No. 20 in late February 1988 after winning their 11th straight game.

"It was kind of uncharted waters," Gillen said. "We wanted to be ranked, of course. Our kids were excited about it. It was just a little bit of a distraction."

Xavier's next game was at Niagara. The Purple Eagles led by as many as 14 points before the Musketeers rallied for a 93-80 victory. Walker came off the bench for a season-high 12 points.

"We were getting our tail kicked," Gillen said. "We came back and played great the second half."

PASS HAPPY?

Xavier would finish 26-4 in 1987–88, with the MCC regular-season title, a third consecutive conference tournament championship and a third straight NCAA appearance.

The Musketeers lost to Kansas in the first round 85-72. Larkin hurt his right leg in the first half, fouled out with 1:23 left and scored a season-low 16 points.

Larkin finished his career with 2,696 points and is No. 1 on Xavier's all-time scoring list by more than 500 points over second-place David West. At the time, he ranked 13th in career scoring in the NCAA.

Perhaps his favorite stat, though, is his career assist total. That's because former teammates *still* give him a hard time about never passing the ball.

"I just pull out the book all the time on those guys," he said, laughing. "That shuts them up real quick. Just look at the data." Larkin's 370 career assists are ninth-most among the school's 1,000-point scorers (Lenny Brown, Anthony Hicks, Lionel Chalmers, Gary Lumpkin, Jamal Walker, Maurice McAfee, Michael Hawkins and Stanley Burrell have more). Larkin actually led Xavier in assists as a junior and senior.

His No. 23 jersey was retired in 1990.

WHAT A START

Xavier opened the 1988–89 season against No. 4-ranked Louisville, led by Pervis Ellison, at Riverfront Coliseum in the Preseason NIT.

Larkin had graduated. Hill and Derek Strong were juniors. Kimbrough was the lone senior in the lineup.

"We came out to warm up," Michael Davenport said. "Louisville was out there, and there were no Xavier people. It was like, *Wow, we're not going to have any fans here.* We go back in (to the locker room) for the pregame meeting and when we came out, it was full, whatever it seated (16,574), and it was pretty much red on one side and blue on the other."

This was a night Kimbrough won't ever forget. He calls it his "signature game."

The Cardinals jumped in front 12-0.

"I don't think I even touched the basketball," Kimbrough said. "At that point, we took a timeout, and it was the first and only time I ever used choice words with coaches. I was saying,

'Get me the ball.' They immediately drew something up for me. I touched the ball next time down and hit a shot."

It was the first of many. Kimbrough, a fifth-year senior, would score a career-high 35 points. He finished 14-of-20 from the field and 5-of-6 from the foul line and also had a career-high eight steals.

"Up until that year, I had sacrificed so much," Kimbrough said. "I took a backseat to Byron. I got Byron the ball. I got Tyrone the ball. That's just the way the system went. But this is *my* team now. I was the only senior that played. I was a verbal leader. I wanted the players to know that I was the guy that would do anything and say anything in order to get a win. That meant *'you are all going to follow me'* because I'm not afraid."

Xavier won 85-83 when Walker drove the length of the floor and passed to Hill, who scored with two seconds left.

"They pressed and I went through the whole press," Walker said. "Everybody thought I was going to shoot it, so I passed it to Tyrone."

PHOTO COURTESY OF XAVIER UNIVERSITY

Stan Kimbrough scored 2,103 points in his college career – 1,596 in three years at Xavier and 507 at Central Florida.

NOT EXACTLY A BURGLAR

While at Xavier, one of Strong's close friends was Brent Kohlhepp, whose father, Bob, is a former member of the Xavier Board of Trustees who helped spearhead efforts to build Cintas

Center (see Chapter 2).

The Kohlhepps owned a house near the Xavier campus where their children lived when they were in school. Strong spent a lot of time over there.

During a holiday break in 1988, when Strong was a junior, he went over to the house while Brent was gone. Brent had given him a key and told him to come by whenever he wanted. Strong didn't have cable TV in his apartment, so he went over to Brent's house to watch television and play video games.

"On this particular night, I was watching TV and out the window I saw this flashlight going on in the backyard, shining into the house," Strong said. "The first thing I thought was someone was trying to break into the house. I'm kind of ducking and dodging through the house, trying to figure out where I can hide out in case this person breaks in, so I can get the jump on them. Then I realized there were a whole bunch of flashlights going on. I went to a window and saw a Cincinnati officer. It was the police. I went outside."

Kohlhepp had received a phone call from a family friend who said someone was in the house near campus. The friend's son was about to go in, saw the person and didn't know who it was. Kohlhepp called the house, and nobody answered. Then he called 911.

When Strong left the house, the police told him they received a call about a break-in.

Strong tried to explain that he was a friend of the homeowners. But until they could reach someone in the Kohlhepp family, they had to handcuff Strong.

The Kohlhepp children and parents arrived at the house around the same time. There they saw Derek in handcuffs. "It's OK," Bob Kohlhepp quickly told police. "He's a friend."

"Derek, thank God, has a good sense of humor," Bob Kohlhepp said.

"I was laughing," Strong said. "I thought it was funny. I thought somebody was breaking in, and somebody called the police on me thinking *I* was the criminal."

HUMBLE BEGINNINGS

Hill and Strong were seniors, and Xavier went into the 1989–90 season having lost only Kimbrough. There was plenty of optimism about the new year.

Until the opener at home against Southern Utah State, which shocked the Musketeers 97-90 at Cincinnati Gardens.

"We were really cocky going into our first game because we knew we had a good team," Hill said. "We didn't expect to lose to anybody. When those little guys came in and upset us, we felt small the whole week until we played again. Pete Gillen was mad at us. We were mad at ourselves. We had a good week of practice and from that point on we said we've got to stay humble and stay grounded."

Xavier rattled off 12 consecutive victories after that.

RUN AND GUN INDEED

Xavier agreed to a two-game series with Loyola Marymount, in part, as a response to criticism over weak nonconference scheduling. And it turned into one of the more fun series ever for the Musketeers.

This was during the time when Loyola Marymount featured star players Bo Kimble and Hank Gathers and a run-and-gun mentality unmatched by any program in the country. LMU set an NCAA scoring record by averaging 122.4 points per game in 1989–90.

In January 1989, Xavier won 118-113 in California. In January 1990, the Musketeers prevailed 115-113 at Cincinnati Gardens.

In the second meeting, Hill scored a career-high 38 points, and XU won on a 10-foot jumper by Walker with one second left.

"I remember going back and forth," Hill said. "That was the most fun I had playing college basketball. Nobody was playing defense. It was just an exciting game. I'm a defensive specialist, so it was a lot of fun for me because I didn't play any 'D' that game."

BEHIND THE SCENES

Xavier lost at Evansville 59-51 on Jan. 18, 1990, ending a 12-game winning streak. And there was some drama in the locker room at halftime with the Musketeers ahead by two points.

Davenport had a decent game with 17 points. But Hill was complaining that he wasn't getting the ball enough.

"We hardly ever beat Evansville at Evansville," Walker said. "We were playing well, Mike Davenport is killing, but Tyrone didn't get the ball a whole lot so he comes in the locker room and he's yelling, 'Give me that damn ball!' So I just walked over and said, 'Shut the hell up!' I think I had his jersey or something like that. I don't know what I did."

"Jamal had his hands around Tyrone's neck and he's telling him, 'If you don't throw the ball back out, I will kill you,' " said Jay Ross, the team's athletic trainer at the time. "Now, you've got the biggest guy and the littlest guy on the team. Tyrone's sitting there not saying anything, and Jamal's in his face."

Gillen walked in and yelled, "What's going on here?" That was that, Walker said.

"That was the extent of it," he said. "It was still a family. Stuff like that was rare in our situation because we were always together."

GETTING AN EDUCATION

Aaron Williams arrived at Xavier in 1989 a quiet, humble, down-to-earth guy just trying to battle homesickness and make the transition to college life like all other freshmen.

He was not that highly recruited out of Evanston, Ill., and had scholarship offers mostly from schools such as Eastern Illinois, Western Illinois and Loyola of Chicago.

"I guess Coach Prosser would be the one responsible for (Xavier recruiting me)," Williams said. "I guess he saw something in me that he liked."

Xavier was Williams' only official recruiting visit.

The visit was anything but memorable. Gillen said it rained the entire weekend. When they took Williams to see Cincinnati Gardens, it was a mess from a tractor event there. "It smelled like manure," Gillen recalled.

The players who hosted Williams told Gillen he barely spoke. When Gillen went to dinner with Williams and his mother, Williams didn't say much.

"He might have been the shyest guy," Ross said. "His mother ordered everything off the menu for him. You would have thought, *Does this kid talk?* But when Sunday rolled around, he said, 'I'm coming to Xavier. I'd like to play here.' "

As a freshman, Williams had an almost ideal situation: the chance to learn on the court from two future NBA players (Hill and Strong).

"It was kind of the best of both worlds," Williams said. "You come there and you want to play, but on the other hand you have two great, great basketball players to learn from. They pounded against me. *I* didn't do too much pounding when I was a freshman.

"Those two guys didn't back down to anyone. ... After my freshman year, I went straight to the weight room. I credit those two for getting me in shape, getting me ready and really giving me the motivation to go work out even harder."

At 6 feet 9, Williams was tall and skinny. But not for long.

After totaling 62 points and 76 rebounds as a freshman, Williams went on to average 11.4 points and 7.2 rebounds over the next three seasons.

Williams became dedicated and proficient in the weight room.

"We had to lift weights at like 7 in the morning," Steve Gentry said. "And you got to do the bench press one time with as much weight as possible. And these guys, Erik Edwards, Dwayne Wilson and Brian Grant, they'd all be putting it on 325 (pounds), 350 and doing it one time and pumping their chests. And Aaron would come in there and put on 400 and get down there and do it with no help. He was just a strong guy."

PHOTO COURTESY OF XAVIER UNIVERSITY

Aaron Williams is second in career blocks with 197 and has Xavier's third-, fourth- and fifth-best single-season block totals.

AARON'S BLOCK PARTY

When Xavier played at Loyola of Chicago on Feb. 6, 1990, Williams was making a homecoming of sorts, returning to the state in which he played high school ball.

With his parents in the stands at the Rosemont Horizon, Williams blocked seven shots which, at the time, tied the school record (David West would get eight in November 2001). Remember, Williams was only a freshman. It was his first start, and it came because Hill was suffering from lung inflammation and was taken to a nearby hospital before the game.

Williams played 39 minutes — he came in averaging just 6.4 — and he added eight points and 10 rebounds.

"My father was able to come to the game and he passed away shortly after that," Williams said. "But he got to see me play. It just happened to be Chicago where I'm from and I had a lot of people there, friends and family, so that's one of the memories as far as basketball that I remember the most."

TEAM FIRST

Though he grew bigger and stronger, Williams was not someone who was going to take over games. He was still quiet. He excelled on the defensive end. And, in general, he felt as though there were enough "scorers."

"He blocked a lot of shots, he dunked on a lot of guys, but he really didn't care about that," Gentry said. "All he wanted to do was win. One night he'd have 20 (points) and 10 (rebounds) and the next night he'd come back with eight and six.

"We always said, 'Man, you can be a lottery pick, Aaron.' But I don't think he thought that; he was a down-to-earth guy. I knew he was all about winning, but sometimes it would get frustrating because we knew he could do a lot more than what he was doing. ... When you made him mad and he turned red, you best believe he was coming at you. Once he got upset, he wanted to play, and nobody could touch him."

When Williams was a freshman, teammate Maurice Brantley told him he had "NBA talent." Williams thought he was crazy.

"We had some pretty good teams, we were winning games," he said. "I guess I didn't even try to score more. It probably hurt me to some extent as far as getting drafted to the NBA. But I was just there to help the team win any way I could — playing defense, getting rebounds, blocking shots."

Williams' high game was 25 points against Loyola of Chicago in February 1991. He never led Xavier in rebounding for a season.

"I thought he was very, very talented," Grant said. "Some of the things that I would see him do in practice, I would be like, *Wow, I wish I could do some of those things.*"

Williams was in his 14th NBA season in 2007–08. Not bad for a guy who wasn't even drafted and spent time in Europe, the USBL and the CBA.

"No way," Williams said, when asked if he could have predicted such a long pro career. "I talk to my wife about it all the time. In high school, I would go to the career development room and look at all the different jobs they had and I was trying to pick a career, trying to find something that made pretty good money that I'd be interested in.

"Never in my wildest dreams did I think I'd be in my 14th year in the NBA. I'm proud of it. When I'm done, I'll probably look back and reflect properly. Right now, I'm just going to enjoy the ride."

WHAT *REALLY* HAPPENED?

When it was over, Xavier had another victory over UC in thrilling fashion. And like so many others, this Crosstown Shootout on Jan. 31, 1990, won't be forgotten.

Walker's 3-pointer from the corner with seven seconds left gave the Musketeers a dramatic 90-88 victory in overtime at Cincinnati Gardens.

Huggins was in his first year as coach at UC. And he left the court furious.

After a 3-pointer from Davenport cut the Bearcats' lead to 88-87 with 20 seconds remaining, UC had the ball. On the in-bounds pass, Davenport tied up Lou Banks of UC with the ball, which then went out of bounds with 17 seconds on the clock.

Rather than calling a jump ball, an official ruled the ball went out of bounds off Banks, giving Xavier a chance to win it.

The thoughts that night?

Gillen: "It was a bizarre ending."

Banks: "It was a bad call, but that's the breaks."

Davenport: "I slapped the ball, and I don't know if it went off him or not."

Huggins: "I thought we deserved to win, and that's all I'm gonna say."

Walker finished with 21 points. Hill had 20 points and 11 rebounds before fouling out.

"It didn't go off his leg," Walker said almost 18 years later. "It looked like it, but it didn't. It was a bad call. Michael's a good actor; he should have gotten an Emmy on that one."

XU WON MORE THAN THE GAME

One person keeping a close eye on that Crosstown Shootout was Gentry, a Withrow High School graduate who was attending Maine Central Institute.

Gentry called his mother back in Cincinnati during the game and had her giving him a play-by-play. UC and Xavier both were recruiting Gentry, and he told his mom: "Whoever wins that game, that's what school I'm going to."

"Jamal hit the long shot from the corner, and I called Xavier the next day and told them I wanted to come," Gentry said. "If Jamal would have missed that shot, I probably would have been a Bearcat."

IN THE BOOKS

Xavier went to a fifth straight NCAA Tournament in 1990 and advanced further than any other team in school history, getting to the Sweet 16 before losing to Texas 102-89.

It was the end of the Tyrone Hill era. Hill finished as Xavier's all-time leading rebounder with 1,380 and No. 2 scorer behind only Larkin with 2,003 career points.

Hill set a school record with 24 doubles-doubles in 1989–90.

"Xavier was just a great school," he said. "If I had to do it all over again, I would still make Xavier my first choice."

Hill was picked in the first round, 11th overall, in the 1990 NBA Draft by the Golden State Warriors. He played 14 years in the NBA for five different teams before retiring in 2004.

In February 1996, he became the second XU player to have his jersey (No. 42) retired by Xavier.

"I was very surprised," he said. "It wasn't about the records or the rebounding titles. It was about winning. And they appreciated everything I had done for them. That meant a lot."

CALIFORNIA KID

Strong was a rare Xavier recruit out of California, discovered by assistant coaches Mike Sussli and Nix. Strong grew up in Los Angeles and attended Pacific Palisades High School. He knew little of Xavier until he received recruiting letters. Turns out, it was just the kind of place he was looking for.

"I wanted to go to a smaller school where classrooms weren't auditoriums," Strong said. "I wanted the same kind of atmosphere I had in my high school. I had a good time on my visit. They showed me around the city, the people at the university. It was a good experience."

He was fairly quiet when at Xavier, saying he didn't do much beyond school and basketball.

"My best times were hanging out with the friends I made on campus," he said. "I didn't really get out a lot. If I had free time, I went to the gym and worked out, worked on my game. I basically just stayed in my room and went to class."

The 6-9 Strong played center at Xavier and started three years. He probably was underpublicized because he played alongside Hill.

Still, Strong ranks among XU's top 10 career rebounders, scored 1,291 career points in three seasons and was a second-round pick in the 1990 NBA Draft by the Philadelphia 76ers. He played in Spain, the USBL and the CBA before beginning a 10-year career in the NBA with six different teams.

Strong graduated in 1990 and gave way to another quiet, 6-9 center who would develop into an NBA Draft pick. A guy named Brian Grant.

WHAT A FIND

Naturally Gillen would be skeptical.

Grant was a fine player for tiny Georgetown, a Division IV high school in Brown County, Ohio, east of Cincinnati. But really, how good could he be? The village of Georgetown had around 3,500 people with fewer than 1,000 families. President

Ulysses S. Grant grew up there.

During Xavier's summer basketball camp in 1989, Cincinnati high school basketball coach Bob Callahan told the Musketeer coaches about Grant (Brian, not Ulysses). Assistant Dino Gaudio called Georgetown coach Tim Chadwell, a former XU player. Gaudio said Chadwell did not think Grant could play at Xavier's level.

In December, Chadwell called Gaudio back. "Remember you called me about one of my kids back in the summer? I don't want to sell this kid short. Maybe you should come and see him."

Gaudio went to see a Georgetown practice. "I'm in the gym 15 minutes and I'm like, *Wow*," Gaudio said. "He plays hard, runs the floor. I really liked him."

He watched Grant play a game. In February 1990, Gaudio and Prosser went to see Grant, driving from Indianapolis in a snowstorm after a Xavier victory at Butler.

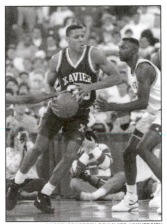

PHOTO COURTESY OF XAVIER UNIVERSITY

Brian Grant was the second player to lead Xavier in rebounding four years in a row. He is ninth on Xavier's all-time scoring list (1,719 points) and fourth on the career rebounding list (1,080).

Gillen still had not seen Grant.

When in Dayton practicing for the 1990 MCC Tournament, Gaudio and Gillen went to see Grant, who was also playing in Dayton during the Ohio high school state tournament.

"We jump in the car, and we fly over," Gaudio said. "We get there and it's halftime. They come out, and Pete says, 'Where is he?' Brian's on the bench. He's got three fouls. Chadwell doesn't start him in the second half. When the kid comes in, he plays his brains off.

"Pete sees him play 12 minutes and offers him a scholarship."

"He only had one scholarship offer at the time, which was Youngstown State," Gillen said. "He was 6-7½, almost 6-8, quick, athletic. I loved him."

Grant averaged 19.3 points, 13.5 rebounds and eight blocks as a high school senior. He signed with Xavier in April 1990, despite some bigger schools trying to get him late in the recruiting process after his performance at a postseason all-star game.

"Xavier was the biggest team recruiting me and it was in Cincinnati and they just had a great year prior to that with them beating Georgetown," Grant said. "Coming from a town with 3,000 people, I was the first person to ever get a Division I scholarship. I was the first person in my family to really go to college. That was a big deal."

CHAOS ON THE ROAD

Several former teammates refer to Colin Parker as the best prankster of his era and one of the funniest guys on the team. Tyrice Walker tells a mean story:

"We were on the road my freshman year. We were in the hotel in Evansville and it was the night before the game. Coach would always pair up an upperclassman with a lowerclassman, and we would always fight.

"I was in a room with Colin. We were right next to Moe Brantley — and I can't remember who was rooming with him. You know how they have the door in between the two rooms?

We're sitting there playing around, talking, whatever, and next thing you know, Moe's kind of sliding stuff under the door. Well, Colin, who was the prankster, he lights matches and he slides these matches under the door. Then the fire alarm goes off. The fire department was coming.

"Coach Gillen didn't hear about it that night. Well, we didn't *think* he heard about it. The next morning, we're sitting there eating breakfast and he's acting like everything is peachy and then all of a sudden, we get done eating, and he said he wants to have a meeting. You could tell he had a chip on his shoulder. He was mad about something.

"He's calling us in one by one, and I don't know what's going on. I get in this meeting with him and he said, 'You could have had a true fire. There are old women in this hotel.' He was just flipping out. He blew everything out of proportion. I'm like, 'Coach, I had nothing to do with it.' I think Colin may have talked to him after me, and Colin told him I had nothing to do with it.

"Well, he ended up making two or three guys go to Shriner's to the burn unit here in Cincinnati when we got back for like a week straight."

A DIFFERENT APPROACH

Larry Sykes attended St. Francis, an all-boys high school in Toledo, and was recruited by Indiana, Dayton, Miami, Florida and Wisconsin. His visit to Xavier, he said, was unique.

"It was the only school that recruited me where, when I came on the recruiting visit, I didn't stay in a penthouse, I didn't stay in a suite, I was with the players," he said. "I stayed in the Manor House. I went to class my first day there to see what the experience of class was like. I went to practice my first day there. It was like I was already a student there."

But on the visit, the Xavier coaches were anything but impressed with Sykes.

"For like a day and a half, he kept talking about Dayton," Gillen said. "So finally, we brought him into a room and we say, 'Hey, what are you doing talking about Dayton? That's a fine school, but you're here at Xavier. Your attitude's not real good; what's going on?' "

The coaches told Sykes they were going to leave him alone with his parents so he could decide whether he wanted to stay or go.

"They met for about 15 minutes," Gillen said. "He had (an attitude) change and we wind up getting him."

CHECK'S IN THE MAIL

When Xavier traveled, the mini-bars in the hotel rooms were locked and players were not to purchase any amenities. When Xavier played two games in Tokyo in December 1992, Ross remembers looking over the final bill from a hotel and noticing a $200 charge for kimono robes from one room.

The team's trainer didn't have his rooming list with him, so he climbed on the bus and started yelling.

"I'm flipping out," Ross said. "I'm looking at everybody on the bus and suddenly I hear a voice. 'Jay, it was me.' I'm looking around, *Who the heck?* 'I bought the robes for my wife and my daughter.' "

It was Gillen.

"I just shook my head," Ross said. "I went back inside, paid the bill and I got on the bus and left. He paid for them when we got back to the United States."

UM, THAT'S NOT MY CAR

Several players and staff members remember one afternoon when Gillen went to leave practice at Schmidt Fieldhouse. He walked out to the parking lot and got frustrated because his keys weren't working. Ross calls it "the missing car incident."

"We all were at the window looking out and he's trying to get in somebody else's car," Gentry said. "He's got his keys out, and he's trying to jam the key in there and we all just sat back cracking up. He's going around to every door. He goes to the trunk. We laugh for about 10, 15 minutes and we went out and told him: 'Coach, that's not your car, your car is over here.' I thought that he was colorblind. I don't know what was wrong with him that day."

IN THE 'HOOD

How could Sherwin Anderson say no to Xavier after this? When he was being recruited, most coaches wanted to meet him at his high school. Gillen was the only one, Anderson said, who insisted on coming to his home.

"I lived in a very bad neighborhood in Brooklyn," Anderson said. "It's all private buildings and a lot of guys on the streets selling drugs and a lot of gangs. Just a negative situation. I remember about 15 to 20 guys standing in front of the building and Coach Gillen walked in and walked past some of my homeboys. One of them even asked him if they had a scholarship for him. It was something out of the movies.

"I was nervous. He walked through and they said something to him and he said something back, and they all laughed. There was nothing to it."

Gillen concedes that he was nervous, too.

"That was a real tough area," he said. "I think Skip was with me. Great parents. Lovely people. But it was a little scary for a couple of white coaches to go in there. I probably tried to have a little fun with those guys. That's what you do as a coach."

WHO'S WATCHING?

Gillen's paranoia was legendary. One of Sykes' favorite examples comes from a practice at Duke's Cameron Indoor Stadium the day before Xavier's game against the Blue Devils on Dec. 4, 1993.

"He had people up in the scaffolding looking for people," Sykes said, laughing. "He sent the managers up there; we checked the garbage cans; he had people going up in the rafters looking for scouts. He was just freaking out.

"They were top 10 in the country and they really didn't need to do that."

No. 6 Duke defeated Xavier the next day 82-60 for its 83rd consecutive nonconference victory at home.

WHO CAN FORGET THE NON-HANDSHAKE?

Going into the Crosstown Shootout on Jan. 19, 1994, Xavier had lost three in a row to UC. None of Xavier's starters, including seniors Grant, Gentry and Tyrice Walker, had ever defeated the Bearcats.

"They were just too tough," Grant said. "Yeah, all of us were frustrated."

The Musketeers came in ranked No. 22, and UC was 19th. The game was billed as a showdown between Grant and Cincinnati's heralded freshman, Dontonio Wingfield. But Wingfield played just 15 minutes and finished 0-of-7 from the field.

UC led by two points at the end of regulation when Walker threw up an air ball and Grant rebounded and scored for Xavier with one second on the clock. That tied it at 71 and sent the game into overtime. "Maybe it wasn't an air ball; it was a pass," Grant said, laughing.

Jeff Massey, who finished with a team-high 20 points, and Gentry each hit 3-pointers at the beginning of overtime. UC would get within 77-76, but Damon Flint missed a short jumper. Massey nailed another 3 with 24.7 seconds to play.

"After regulation, I felt like it was life or death," Grant said afterward.

Xavier fans rushed the court following the final buzzer.

Meanwhile, Huggins refused to shake hands with Gillen after the game. Gillen didn't take the snub well. He tried to make his way back to Huggins but was held back.

"It's a bitter, bitter game," Gillen said later. "If we would have lost, I would have shook his hand."

"Their guys were yelling things at my players and coaches," Huggins countered in the postgame press conference. "I'm not going to act like everything's all right and shake hands after the game. I'm not going to be phony about it."

Gillen and Huggins did not exactly get along. But this took their relationship — and the Shootout — to a new level.

"I was surprised," Gillen said 13½ years later. "That had never happened before. I think he regretted it; he called me a day or two later and apologized. I have no animosity. Both sides were cursing at each other, the benches and stuff. That happens. In the heat of the game, things are going to be said and you forget it. I don't hold a grudge. We see each other, we're cordial; we say hello."

The day after the game, Gillen suggested the series between the schools take a year off. "Something's got to be done," he said. "It's not healthy."

The wear and tear of the rivalry with Cincinnati — and Huggins — wore on Gillen. One of the reasons he was ready to leave Xavier at the end of the season had to do with the stress of the Crosstown Shootout.

Gillen finished 4-5 against UC. He never liked when the game came in the middle of the conference season, which it usually did during his era.

In his final season, after beating the Bearcats, Xavier went 5-5 over its next 10 games. Gillen thought that sometimes the players let up after the UC game, thinking it was the biggest game of the season.

"That game against UC took a lot out of me," he said. "I'm sure I was wacky other times, but I'm sure I was more wacky then. I used to get uptight because it was a big game. Like a week before, they're writing stories on the stars, the team, blue and white cookies, red and white cookies, chili three-ways. I got a little paranoid, I guess. It was fun for the players, fun for the alumni, fun for the administration, but it wasn't fun for me. Those are tough games because if you lose, you're a bum."

GRANT DOMINATES DARE

Grant was ready for this matchup. Xavier played George Washington on Feb. 12, 1994, at the Gardens. The Colonials were led by 7-foot-1 Yinka Dare.

"He had a lot of publicity because of how big he was," Tyrice Walker said.

Grant stole the attention of NBA scouts sitting in the stands that night. He finished with 28 and 16 rebounds. Dare fouled out with just nine points.

"Brian truly dominated him," Walker said. "And I mean dominated him in every facet of the game."

The tough part about that night is that GW came away with a 93-92 victory in double overtime, ending Xavier's 23-game winning streak at the Gardens when reserve guard Vaughn Jones hit a running bank shot at the end to win it.

NO NCAA

Xavier went 20-7 in the regular season but did not get in the 1994 NCAA Tournament. That was a big disappointment for a team that started three seniors and two juniors.

The Musketeers were invited to the NIT and advanced to the quarterfinals before losing at Villanova 76-74.

After the season, Grant heard a wide array of opinions from various agents about his NBA potential. One agent thought he might not even get drafted. Others thought he was a solid second-round pick. Most thought Grant should not play in pre-draft camps.

Mark Bartelstein, out of Chicago, had a different take. "I've been watching you for the past week and I think it would be a travesty if you do not go to the combines," Grant remembers Bartelstein saying. "You need to go to Phoenix because I think you're going to show everybody who Brian Grant really is. I believe in you and I think you can be a first-round draft pick."

"He was the first person to tell me that," Grant said. "I'm like, 'Shoot, I'm going with this guy.'"

Grant played well. He performed well in workouts with teams. He was rising on teams' draft boards. He ended up as a lottery pick, selected eighth overall by the Sacramento Kings. It remains the earliest any Xavier player has ever been drafted.

"It was surreal," Grant said. "I couldn't believe it. It was very gratifying and very terrifying, too."

NEVER SAY NEVER

It seemed like an annual event at Xavier. The season would end. Gillen's name would get mentioned in connection with job openings. Gillen would proclaim his love for his job at Xavier but was known for adding, "Never say never."

"I think the way I used to refer to that was it was an aggravating form of flattery because we had a coach that other people wanted," Fogelson said.

The spring of 1994 was no exception. But this time, it was for real. Providence College came calling. It was in the Big East Conference. But mostly, Gillen felt it was time to leave.

"It had been nine years and I was a little frustrated," Gillen said. "I love Xavier, but little things kind of bothered me. I thought, *What would it be like to coach at a higher level?* I don't want to be 75 years old and sitting on a porch and not knowing what it's like to coach in the Big Ten or the ACC or the Big East.

"Providence was certainly not a super, super high-tier job. I loved New York, but I didn't want to live there at the time. Providence is outside of New York, and I like New England. My wife's family had a place in Massachusetts. I said, 'Well, let's see what it's like.' "

Gillen's Xavier teams went 202-75 in nine seasons. He took the Musketeers to seven NCAA Tournaments and coached them in more NCAA games than any coach in school history.

"I was most proud of the fact that we had a very competitive team and we had all our kids graduate," Gillen said. "We tried to do it the right way. We didn't take advantage of players. We tried to make them go to class. We had some bumps in the road, but they received their education and we were a Top 25 team a bunch of years."

11

SKIP PROSSER
(1994–2001)

SKIP PROSSER, then an assistant, first left Xavier in 1993 to become head coach at Loyola College, a small Jesuit university in Baltimore. It was a program that was coming off six straight losing seasons, including 2-25 in 1992–93.

In one year, Prosser's team went 17-12 and accomplished the unimaginable, going to the NCAA Tournament for what remains the only time in school history. Following that magical 1993–94 season, Loyola would endure 11 losing seasons in a row.

Once Pete Gillen made his decision to leave Xavier, then-athletic director Jeff Fogelson had only one candidate in mind to replace Gillen: Prosser.

"When Pete left, my bosses where adamant that we had to conduct a national search," Fogelson said. "I said, 'Look, if you want to conduct a national search, fine, but at least talk to him and then I'll do whatever you want. But I'm telling you this guy is everything that Xavier could want in a coach.' They agreed."

Prosser flew in from Baltimore on a Wednesday night and met with Fogelson. The next day, he met with the Rev. James

E. Hoff, Xavier's president, and Board of Trustees chairman Mike Conaton.

"Skip came out and my immediate boss pulled me aside and said, 'That's the guy.' They never interviewed anyone else after Skip," Fogelson said. "This is someone who philosophically understands who we are. This is someone who will push for more. There was no question that he was going to be successful."

Prosser was offered the job that Thursday, March 31. But he refused to give an answer before going back and talking with Loyola officials that night.

PHOTO COURTESY OF XAVIER UNIVERSITY

Among Xavier's top 20 career scoring leaders, Gary Lumpkin has the most assists (470). He finished with 1,507 points. Among all 1,000-point scorers, only Jamal Walker has more assists (639).

"Everyone thought it was a no-brainer, but it really wasn't," Prosser said. "Loyola had given me the opportunity as head coach and I thought we had some good young guys coming.

"I went back to Loyola, met with the president and the AD. I'll never forget it: They were almost in tears. They said, 'As your bosses, we really want you to stay, but as your friends, we think it's a job you have to take.'

"So I came back to Xavier. I felt like I was coming home. Xavier wasn't just a job for me. It was my first opportunity to coach at a collegiate level. I loved the city. Bellarmine was my parish. It was my church, my school. It was a town I considered my home. The minute I left Loyola, I felt great about being back at X."

He was introduced as Xavier's coach on Saturday, April 2.

CHANGE GOOD FOR HAWKINS

One of Prosser's first orders of business was to help senior point guard Michael Hawkins regain his confidence.

Hawkins started as a freshman and sophomore but struggled as a junior and came off the bench, playing behind Steve Gentry and Jeff Massey.

"He was ready to transfer," Prosser said of Hawkins. "He and Massey were not getting along. I brought them both in my office and said, 'Listen, Hawk, you need him because you're not going to get any assists if he doesn't finish. Mass, you need him because you're not getting any baskets if he doesn't throw the ball to you. So you guys better get along.' "

Prosser was right on the money. Massey led Xavier in scoring (19.9 ppg), and Hawkins was second (14.1) while averaging 5.8 assists.

"He shined," fellow guard Sherwin Anderson said of Hawkins. "He was amazing in certain games."

Hawkins actually got off to a slow start, averaging just 6.5 points over the first four games. Fans wanted Anderson in the lineup. But Hawkins turned it around and had his finest season as a Musketeer.

During one five-game stretch at midseason, he scored in double figures every time and connected on 20 of 32 shots from 3-point range.

"I never felt like people didn't have confidence in me," Hawkins told Rory Glynn of *The Cincinnati Enquirer*. "Most of it was me not having confidence in me."

"With Mike, you've got to let him go," teammate Larry Sykes said. "You can't pull him out every time he makes a mistake. Coach Prosser just said, 'Mike, you're the point guard, take it and run with it.' Coach said we were going to play up-tempo, and that played to Mike's strength because he's fast, he can shoot and he likes to get out and run. He was very glad to run the system."

Hawkins averaged 7.5 points a game during his first three seasons, then averaged 14.1 points as a senior. He finished with 1,029 career points.

FEELING BETTER NOW

On Feb. 12, 1994, Sykes thought he cost Xavier a game. George Washington, ranked No. 25 at the time, escaped from Cincinnati Gardens with a 93-92 double-overtime victory when Vaughn Jones went coast to coast and scored the game-winning basket.

"I lost that game because I let him go," Sykes said. "I was sick. I just sat in the locker room and cried."

A year later, the teams met in Washington, D.C. Sykes had not shaken the memory of that defeat. He went out and collected 19 points and 18 rebounds and got Alexander Koul, GW's 7-foot-1 center, in foul trouble early in the game.

"He was a man out there today," Prosser said of Sykes afterward.

Xavier won 88-75. Sykes felt vindicated.

"I needed that game because I had lost it for the whole university the year before and I wanted it back," Sykes said.

A TOUGH CALL

Xavier completed an undefeated regular season in the Midwestern Collegiate Conference, finishing 14-0 after defeating Butler 81-66 on Feb. 25, 1995. It was the Musketeers' final go-around in the league.

They were upset by Wright State in their first MCC Tournament game and were given an 11th seed in the NCAA Tournament. Their first-round opponent: good ol' Georgetown, the team XU knocked out of the NCAA in 1990, which was led in '95 by All-America guard Allen Iverson.

But before Xavier left for Tallahassee, Fla., two key players were arrested following an incident at a bar in Corryville. Pete Sears, a senior starting forward who averaged 12.9 points and 5.1 rebounds, was charged with assault after allegedly punching a bouncer. Forward DeWaun Rose, one of the first players off the bench, was charged with resisting arrest and disorderly conduct. Both pleaded not guilty.

"It was a gut-wrenching, tough week," Prosser said. "I think Xavier really tried hard to do the right thing."

Both players made the trip to the NCAA game. Xavier did not make an announcement about their status until game day.

"I remember talking to Tim Floyd who was coaching Iowa State and we're flying to Tallahassee where the game is going to be played and I told him what happened," Prosser said. "I said, 'We haven't announced it yet, but those two guys aren't going to play.' It was a hard decision because the legal process hadn't played out. There were a lot of meetings."

Georgetown won 68–63.

"Whether it was the right decision or not, who knows?" Prosser said. "But I think that Xavier took a stand that we're going to err on the side of trying to do the honorable thing."

Charges later were dropped, but both players had violated team policies.

MOVIN' ON UP

The 1995–96 season was the start of a new era in Xavier basketball. After 16 years in the MCC — during which XU went to the NCAA Tournament nine times — the Musketeers were headed to the Atlantic 10 Conference. This was a step up to a league that, in theory, could get more than one or two teams in the NCAA on a regular basis.

From 1980–95, the MCC never had more than two teams in the NCAA, and only four times did it have more than one.

"I think we reached a point … (where) we were dominating the league," Fogelson said. "The A-10 had been talking to me for a long time and they kept up the possibility of coming in. I felt like we had kind of reached a point where not all the schools in the MCC were making a commitment that was necessary.

"We were just waiting and waiting and waiting to get an opportunity to present ourselves to the A-10. It was very important for Xavier. We, the staff at Xavier, covered every base. I think it put Xavier on a national scale. It generated more income and consequently was a big contributing factor that an on-campus arena got built. It was a move that benefited the university as a whole."

WELCOME TO THE TEAM

Pat Kelsey, Elder High School Class of 1993, started his college basketball career at the University of Wyoming, coached by former Miami University coach Joby Wright. Kelsey started 22 of 28 games and averaged 24.3 minutes a game. But he was not happy being so far from home.

His father, Mike, played at Xavier for two years and graduated in 1971, and Pat grew up a Xavier fan who attended Gillen's camp as a kid. "I kind of always dreamed of wearing blue and having the X on my chest," Pat said.

When he decided to transfer, Pat's first call was to Prosser. Prosser said there could be a spot on the team for him, but

Kelsey would not start on scholarship and nothing could be promised.

"That's all I wanted to hear," Kelsey said. He paid his own way and would be put on scholarship during his junior season.

The first time Prosser told Kelsey to drop by practice, before he was even enrolled at XU, he did.

"I came into Schmidt Fieldhouse and I sat way at the top in the very corner," Kelsey said. "It was about 15 minutes into practice and he looked up and kind of blocked the lights out of his eyes and he saw somebody sitting up there and he pointed to the manager. So a manager came up and I said who I was. Skip told the kid to have me come down and sit right by the court.

"Some of his legendary practices were the first ones after Christmas break because he wanted to run off all the cake and ice cream and Christmas dinners. It was three hours of just up-and-down the floor, bodies flying around; it was almost like you needed helmets and shoulder pads. As I'm sitting there, I'm salivating watching this practice. I could not wait to lace them up and get out there; it was such a high-energy practice. There was no down time, just what I wanted to be a part of.

"So the practice is over ... nobody knows who I am except for Coach Prosser. They get done stretching and they all huddle up in the middle of the court. At the very end, everybody always puts their hands in and says, '1 ... 2 ... 3 ... Xavier,' so everybody puts their hands in. And Coach goes, 'Whoa, hold on a second.' Everybody puts their arms down. He kind of moves the huddle out of the way and looks at me and he says, 'Kelse, come here.' So I run to the middle of the huddle and he says, 'OK, now we're ready. Everybody put your hands in here.' *1 ... 2 ... 3 ... Xavier!*

"From that moment on, I was his. He could have told me to run through 60 brick walls and I would have done it 61 times."

ALL-OUT ALL THE TIME

As soon as Kelsey joined Xavier's practices, he quickly made an impact.

He was relentless. He was physical. He was a kamikaze.

"I always thought how you worked and how you played and how you performed in everything you did, even in practice, says a lot about you as a person," Kelsey said. "I took pride in making those starters better and getting them ready for that next game.

"If I was running the scout team, those four other guys that were with me — sometimes they were scholarship guys that didn't play as much or sometimes they were other walk-ons — they better lock in when we were prepping for that scout. If Coach (Jeff) Battle was giving us six sets that La Salle runs and Kenny Harvey forgets two of them, I'm going to be in his rear end because it makes me look bad and it's letting the guys down that have to play on Saturday afternoon."

A PAIN IN THE…

If anyone took issue with Kelsey's day-in-and-day-out intensity, it was fellow guards Gary Lumpkin and Anderson, who constantly had to square off against Kelsey.

They could not take a second off or he'd steal the ball from them, knock them around, outhustle them or outwork them.

"From 3 to 6, from the time practice started till the time it ended, they must have thought I was the biggest pain in the ass in the world," Kelsey said. "I think, typically, 99 percent of the coaches in the country want their walk-ons to take it easy on the scholarship guys.

"Coach Prosser was totally different. He let me be me. He didn't want me to hold back. He wanted me to get in fights with Gary and Sherwin — scratch and claw them and dive at their knees for loose balls and take charges on them. Never once did he call me over and say, 'Hey, scale it back a little bit.' I think he thought that helped develop the toughness identity of Xavier basketball and our team."

Were there fights? You betcha.

Lumpkin (repeatedly). Anderson. Nate Turner. Torraye Braggs.

"Looking back on it, I didn't have much to do on the court with a lot of victories, even though there were a couple games I had a little bit of an impact in," Kelsey said. "But I think the mark I wanted to leave on Xavier basketball was: I wanted to be a tone-setter in practice that would then bleed over into games. I think at the end of the day, Sherwin and Gary realized that it made them better and they respected me for it."

The relationship among the three point guards was strained at times.

Anderson was recruited by Gillen. He was an enthusiastic leader, but not the best shooter. Kelsey was the transfer and crazy practice player. Lumpkin was recruited by Prosser to lead the program into the Atlantic 10.

"It was awkward," Anderson said.

And they were all from different backgrounds.

"I remember Pat's family coming to the games and cheering for him *and* for me," Anderson said. "It was tough not to like Pat. We were both fighting for the same position, but he was great; he was the guy I wanted to be. We respected each other's work ethic. We both ran hard, we both played hard, we both loved the craft that we did."

Anderson waited for Gentry and Hawkins to leave, then thought he'd be the starter. Then Lumpkin arrived. Prosser had to sell Anderson on taking a reserve role despite being more experienced.

"For me, it was a tough situation," Anderson said. "Gary was the one who took my position. I thought I lost my position because I didn't have the seriousness they expected of me.

"I accepted the role because of the team. I love Xavier. I love everything about it. I loved being on that team and I think I couldn't, for whatever reason, be mad at the decisions the coaches made."

GARY & LENNY

Their names were connected long before they arrived at Xavier. Gary Lumpkin and Lenny Brown were teammates in middle school and again in high school. As juniors, they led William Penn High School in Wilmington, Del., to the 1994 state championship. Brown was Delaware's Player of the Year.

Lumpkin grew up playing organ at his church and spending time with his family. Brown, raised by a single mother, grew up five miles away in the Riverside federal housing project and has said he was selling drugs at age 15 to help pay family expenses.

Brown didn't play at William Penn as a senior. His high school eligibility had expired, and he ended up at Maine Central Institute, a prep school.

That's where Prosser found him.

"Coach Prosser was actually coming to see someone else on the team," Brown said. "We had open gym. I think I won the first two games and lost the third one. I walked out of the gym and the next thing you heard was a big boom. I had kicked the trash can."

MCI coach Max Good yelled at him. He didn't care how many games Brown's team lost — that was unacceptable behavior.

That did not deter Prosser, who loved Brown's competitiveness and toughness.

"Off the court, Lenny was totally misunderstood," Lumpkin said. "I know that Lenny's not a mean person. He might come off like it, but Lenny's one of the biggest-hearted guys I know. He won't ever admit that, but he is."

"I appreciate him more now than I did when I was in school," Brown said of Lumpkin. "He does everything a coach could ask. He's great in the locker room. He's one of the guys I could call Monday through Sunday. I love him as a friend, but I didn't appreciate his friendship until we got older."

ROCKY ROAD

Brown rode from Wilmington to Xavier with Lumpkin's family in the summer of 1995 and met some of the guys from the team. Campus life seemed OK to him when just the athletes were around. Then the rest of the student body showed up.

"When school started, I felt like an outsider," Brown said. "It was a culture shock. I didn't think I was going to fit in. I didn't think anyone would like me. I was thinking all negative."

He wasn't sure whether he liked all the guys on the team. He didn't know if he even wanted to play basketball. He knew he had a stubborn attitude and he wondered whether Xavier was a good match for him.

"For the first month or month and a half, it was terrible,"

Brown said. "I pretty much walked around with my hood up and my headphones. I didn't want to speak to anybody, and I didn't want anybody speaking to me either. I just wanted to go to class and go back to my room."

After a couple of weeks, he told Prosser: "Coach, I don't like it here."

"Why?" Prosser asked.

"No one likes me, no one talks to me," Brown replied.

"Lenny," Prosser said, "no one can see you because you've got that hood on."

GO GREYHOUND

The second game of the 1995–96 season, Xavier played at Virginia Commonwealth. Brown calls it "probably the worst game I ever played in college basketball."

"I stunk the gym up," he said.

Some friends and family members had traveled from Wilmington to see him play. Prosser was trying to work with Brown, but that wasn't easy. Prosser took him out of the game, and Brown was on the bench steaming. He finished 0-of-3 shooting with one point.

"I'm upset at Coach, not thinking I'm playing terrible," Brown said. "I thought Coach was giving me the short end of the stick."

He decided right then and there that he was finished.

"It wasn't really just about the game," Brown said. "It was everything."

When the team got back to Cincinnati, Brown packed his things and prepared to leave town. Teammate James Posey was there.

"I did *not* help him pack," Posey said. "I just took him to the bus station. I remember he was crying. He just wanted to go home to his family. He asked me not to tell anybody."

Brown went to the bus station and got a ticket.

"I made it from Cincinnati to Columbus," he said. "I thought that was it. I never thought I was going to play for Xavier again."

Back at Schmidt Fieldhouse, practice was about to start and Prosser noticed Brown was missing. He asked assistant coach Jeff Battle to find out where he was.

"Obviously I went to Gary Lumpkin and said, 'G, where's Lenny?' I could tell he didn't want to say anything," Battle said. "He was mumbling stuff under his breath. Then he said, 'Coach, Lenny's gone. He's going back to Delaware.' "

Battle jumped in his car with trainer Jay Ross, and drove, uh, fast, up I-71 toward Columbus.

Brown was in the Columbus bus terminal playing a video game and waiting for his transfer bus. Then he heard a voice yell: "LB!"

Brown was about to board his next bus. Battle told him he wasn't getting on it. "I'm out, I'm out," Brown kept saying. "No, you're *not* out," Battle replied. "I told the bus driver to get his bags off the bus."

Battle "poured his heart out" to Brown, trying to convince him that he needed to come back to Cincinnati and stay in school. "What are you going to do — go home and hang out with your boys on the corner?" Battle asked.

"I just broke down and cried," Brown said. "Tears were going everywhere. I didn't know what I was going to do. I was just reacting on anger and being young and not knowing what was going on."

Battle talked about all the people Brown would be letting

down if he quit. He told him to get in the car. Together they drove back to Cincinnati.

"I was pretty adamant about not letting him get on that bus," Battle said. "He bought what I was trying to sell, I guess you could say."

"That's a big moment in my life," Brown said. "I can't imagine if JB didn't come and get me. I can't guarantee that I would've went to another college and graduated. I think about that moment a lot."

In fact, Brown told that story the night he was inducted into Xavier's Athletic Hall of Fame in 2006. Prosser and Battle were able to attend because Wake Forest, where they coached at the time, was in town to play Cincinnati.

"I broke down again just to hear him relive that story," Battle said. "Every time I hear it I get emotional just because of the kid and what he went through."

MAKE IT SNAPPY

Before the 1996–97 season, Prosser changed the Musketeers' style of play. He always favored playing faster, but he was turning it up a notch.

"It all started with preseason conditioning," Lumpkin said. "He brought us all in and told us that he wanted to press up and down. He brought in Torraye (Braggs) and said, 'We're going to go 40 minutes all out. We want to play ugly, we want to make teams turn the ball over and we want to score and put pressure right back on the defense. And if they score, we want to get out, push it back down their throats, score and get right back on it again. We want teams to hate playing against us.'"

Prosser had a reason for the change.

"What made me go to the press was UC," Prosser said. "I

thought the perception was that they were tougher than we were. They would press. That was their persona at the time. One of the reasons we went to the pressure was to sort of fight fire with fire. We were going to come after them harder than they came after us. And Lenny personified that. He had great courage and I think that rubbed off on the other guys."

Oh, and Prosser also had Posey to play at the top of the press.

SITTING OUT

Posey had to sit out the 1994–95 season. He was academically ineligible to play or practice with the team, nor could he be on scholarship.

He committed to Xavier out of R.B. Chamberlin High School in Twinsburg, Ohio, because the coaches told him they wanted him whether or not he was eligible to play as a freshman. Only Dayton and Indiana gave him the same assurance. Prosser and Battle made numerous visits to Twinsburg.

"It wasn't even about basketball then; it was about being able to graduate from college," Posey said. "That really won me over."

His first year on campus, Posey would play intramurals and see his Musketeer teammates at study table. He attended only a few games at Cincinnati Gardens.

"It was tough," he said. "For the first time, I went to school without playing a sport. It was just class and study hall and that was it.

"I couldn't take going to the games and just sitting in the stands. I couldn't sit on the bench or anything. I was sitting up there with the families. It was killing me."

He called home often to talk to his parents and his high school coach, Bob Pasci. He talked about leaving Xavier and going to a prep school or junior college. Meanwhile, his father, James Sr., was working two jobs to pay for his son's first year of college.

"I just wanted to play basketball," Posey said.

He would get his chance as a sophomore, and he couldn't wait.

But first, Prosser had a pitch to make: He wanted Posey to come off the bench as the team's sixth man.

"I think the key component there is trust," Prosser said. "I brought him in and I said, 'I think you're one of our best five players, without a doubt in my mind. I think it's better for this team if we bring you off the bench.' I think he trusted me that that's what was best for the team. I think he's a unique kid."

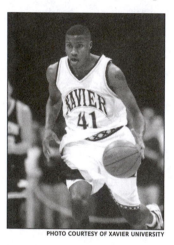

PHOTO COURTESY OF XAVIER UNIVERSITY

James Posey was 12th on Xavier's all-time scoring list when he graduated, scoring 1,455 career points despite playing only three years. He has won NBA titles with Miami and Boston.

Posey accepted his role. And later embraced it. Even off the bench, he was the Musketeers' leading rebounder and he was a disruptive force at the top off the press with his long arms, getting steals and easy transition baskets. He averaged 13.3 points a game.

"I guess it was just about growing up, accepting my role on the team at the time," Posey said. "Everybody wants to start. Coach just sat me down and said, 'It's not about starting, it's about playing.' It took a little to settle me down and realize you just have to take advantage of those opportunities when you're out there playing. After that, it was easy to accept. I had fun. I started to get recognition for being the top sixth man."

Posey, who won the Atlantic 10's Sixth Man Award in 1997 and '98, became known quickly for how hard he practiced. He knew only one way: all out.

"That was just how I approached it," he said, "but it also came from Coach Prosser. Those are the types of practices that we had — very hard and very intense. Whether it was diving into the ball rack to save the ball or whatever, it was about whatever it was going to take for us to win games."

STEELERS RULE

On Dec. 29, 1996, the Indianapolis Colts and Pittsburgh Steelers had an NFL playoff game in Pittsburgh. On that day, Xavier played host to Kansas State at Cincinnati Gardens.

On Xavier's roster was Matt Terpening, a walk-on whose father, Bob, just happened to be an executive with the Colts. Prosser, as is widely known, was fanatical about *his* Steelers.

During practices leading to the K-State game, Prosser would bring his Steelers "Terrible Towel" to practice to taunt Terpening.

Well, the Musketeers drilled Kansas State 95-54, and Terpening thought he might have a chance to get in the game since it was lopsided.

"The game was getting to the point where Coach Prosser was ready to let the bench out," Terpening said. "There was like five minutes left, and he comes walking up and down the bench and he says, 'Hey, I just wanted to say the Steelers are up by 30.' *It was in the middle of our game.* So that kind of caught me off guard. I think he had maybe (sports information director) Tom Eiser giving him updates during timeouts. That was probably the most memorable moment for me because I was focused on our basketball game and Coach Prosser was in there saying, 'Hey, my Steelers are beating you!' "

The Steelers won that day 42-14.

Terpening, who never did get in that game, is now a scout for the Colts.

'WE'RE THE INTIMIDATORS'

Since we're talking about the Steelers, one of Prosser's more memorable pregame talks came just before Temple's visit to Cincinnati Gardens on Jan. 19, 1997.

Temple was led by veteran coach John Chaney and was perennially one of the Atlantic 10's top teams. The Owls had clobbered Xavier 73-56 the previous season at Temple and again 67-50 in the A-10 tourney in Philadelphia.

Prosser played for his team a highlight video of Steelers great Jack Lambert. Hit after hit after hit.

"You can't push us around, you can't intimidate us," Terpening remembers of Prosser's message.

"*We're* the intimidators," Prosser said, firing up his team. "You've got to hit them first; don't give up a step. I want people to feel when they come inside the Gardens, you are not giving up a floorboard."

It was a classic game: 10 ties and 18 lead changes. It went into overtime, and Lumpkin made some big plays. He nailed a 3-pointer with 2:41 left in overtime for a 60-56 XU lead and got a steal and layup with 36.1 seconds to play that made it 66-61.

The Musketeers won 68-64.

"That was a big win, not only for our team but for our school also," Lumpkin said afterward. "We're the new kids on the block (in the A-10). In order for us to make our name known, we have to beat tough teams in the league. I think we're making our way toward doing that."

SOMEONE CATCH ME

Darnell Williams already had endured some setbacks during the 1996–97 season. He missed most of preseason conditioning with bone spurs in his knee, then he got a virus.

Xavier didn't just lose a game to Duquesne (78-70) on Jan. 25, 1997; it lost the *real* Williams. The sophomore forward injured his knee jumping over the Cincinnati Gardens courtside press table. He continued to play the rest of the season but endured endless treatments and his knee never felt the same.

"It was really bad because I just had to slow down a little bit," Williams said. "I wouldn't be able to practice for three hours or two hours. I would have to sit out a couple plays (in games) because it would swell up. It was a mental hurdle."

He had surgery April 2 and was back on the court close to three weeks later.

BEST FRIENDS FOREVER

They met on their first day on Xavier's campus.

The coaches had given Maurice McAfee and Alvin Brown each other's phone numbers during the summer of 1997 and encouraged the two to call and get acquainted. Neither picked up the phone.

When McAfee unloaded his belongings in his room, he locked the door when he left because he didn't trust Brown. Brown had locked his room, as well.

The Xavier team was in Ireland on a tour when the two arrived on campus. McAfee and Brown were the only scholarship freshmen that season.

After their parents left, the new suitemates talked. They were skeptical hearing about each other's basketball accomplishments, but as they started discussing more personal issues, they discovered they had much in common.

"I guess the rest is history," McAfee said. "He is one of my best friends. He was one of the best men in my wedding. It's in God's plan, that's all I can really say about that situation. He places people in your life for a reason. And for some reason, He placed Al in my life ... to help me develop as a person, and also I believe He placed me in his life to help him develop as a person."

McAfee had a bad temper when he was in high school. Brown was pretty mellow.

Neither played a lot as freshmen. Brown broke a bone in his left wrist during practice and did not play again after Dec. 13. McAfee averaged less than nine minutes a game.

They were both frustrated and wondered whether they made the right college choice. They consoled and encouraged one another.

"We built a trust," McAfee said.

"We kind of had two completely different personalities, and we just balanced each other out," Brown said.

McAfee graduated in 2001; Brown a year later, staying on for a medical redshirt year due to his wrist injury.

They both interned at Chrysler and ended up in the company's managerial program. They both moved to Philadelphia in 2002 and worked for Chrysler. They lived in the same apartment complex.

In 2008, McAfee lived in Cincinnati and Brown in Pittsburgh. Both still worked for Chrysler.

"When we first got there (to Xavier)," Brown said, "Skip Prosser was telling us … when you leave Xavier, you're probably not going to remember every game that you played in or all the practices and things like that, but you'll have those relationships with the players on the team. Moe and I are best friends. We talk pretty much every day."

How fitting.

ONE STEAL AFTER ANOTHER

In January 1998, Williams was in his Ford Escort waiting to make a left turn when he was hit from behind by a pick-up truck. The back of his car caved in. His stomach hit the steering wheel hard, and his head hit the roof of the car. He was taken by ambulance to University Hospital, where he was treated and released.

He missed some practice time and was stiff, had a headache and couldn't turn his whole body at the same time as his head. Williams sat out the next game against Fordham.

That set the stage for Posey's fourth career start. In a 77-43 victory over the Rams, Posey set an XU record with nine steals. Xavier tied an Atlantic 10 record and set a school record with 24 steals.

"They were sort of scared," Posey said after the game. "They didn't want to face the press. After awhile it seemed like they were just throwing the ball away to get rid of it. They probably thought there were 20 of us out there."

Posey also had 21 points, eight rebounds and four assists in 35 minutes that night.

"Our style of play was to cause havoc," he said. "I would get my hands on a lot of balls. I guess I was in the right place at the right time; I don't even know, it was crazy. I guess our overall style of play helped."

Williams returned the next game to face George Washington on the road. The Musketeers lost a heart-breaker 78-73 in overtime, but Williams was back with 20 points and 12 rebounds.

ALL-STAR BLOWOUT

Williams led XU in scoring (17.3 ppg) and added 3.9 rebounds as a junior in 1997–98. He quietly mulled declaring for the NBA Draft that April but decided to return to school.

PHOTO BY BOB ROSATO

One of Darnell Williams' favorite shots was what he called the "tear drop," when he jumped into the lane, leaned toward the basket and lofted the ball in the air. Williams went on to score 1,572 career points and finished as XU's No. 11 all-time scorer.

"I was even on the Internet researching agents," he said.

Williams was selected for an NIT All-Star team that would play in Italy that June. Prosser thought it would be good exposure for Williams and Xavier. Williams says he wasn't really keen on going.

"I was so close to graduating," he said. "I had to drop my summer school class and leave."

In the NIT team's third game, Williams got "a little nudge" while driving to the basket. He came down wrong and "heard it all snap."

It was his knee.

Williams had surgery to repair a torn anterior cruciate ligament. He didn't even start jogging until seven months later. He had to sit out the 1998–99 season. "By the time I took that cast off, my muscle was gone," Williams said.

He was never the same.

TIME TO GROW UP

As for many freshmen, Kevin Frey's first year at Xavier in 1998–99 was an eye-opener. In addition to the typical adjustments to college and Division I basketball, Frey struggled at times to deal with Prosser, who was hard on him from the start.

Prosser wanted Frey to be tougher inside, show more consistency and eliminate bad fouls.

"He beat on me," Frey said. "I was, I don't want to say a troubled kid, but I battled a little bit with discipline from male figures. I think he taught me a lot. He wanted the best out of me and he wanted me to be responsible for my actions on and off the court."

One of the reasons Frey chose Xavier over Cincinnati (and Notre Dame) out of Maine West High School in Des Plaines, Ill., was that Frey's mother was impressed with Prosser.

Though he found himself starting as a freshman alongside seniors Lumpkin, Brown and Posey, Frey had a hard time and even considered transferring after his first season.

"I was thinking about going to UNLV," Frey said. "To be honest with you … I didn't want to take the risk of leaving. I liked the family environment at Xavier. I liked the fact they were going to get a new arena. I liked my teammates. I'm glad I never left. Who knows if I would have graduated? I don't think I would have become the man I am today."

SENIOR SLUMPING

"G," Prosser would say to Lumpkin throughout his career, "You can only be one of two things: You're going to be a basketball or you're going to be a football. When you drop a football, you don't know where it's going to go. It's very unpredictable. I want basketballs. I want to know when I bounce it on the ground it's going to come right back to my hands."

For Prosser, Lumpkin was a basketball. Until his senior season.

In his fourth year as a starter, Lumpkin averaged a career-low 11.1 points and shot just .394 from the field.

"I did see a different confidence level," Brown said.

After scoring a season-high 25 points in a loss to Cincinnati, Lumpkin averaged only 9.4 points during the team's final 16 games.

"I lost all that confidence," he said. "I tried to work at it; I tried to keep my same regimen, but for whatever reason it didn't come as easily as it came earlier in my career.

"I stayed out there and practiced and shot and I wouldn't leave until I made 10 3s in a row. I would come in on off days and try to make 100 3s. I was always doing things to help make me better, but when game time came, for whatever reason…

"Every time I look back over my career, that was one of the toughest points of my life. I don't blame that on anybody. I don't know what anyone thought about me at that point. One of my main hang-ups was that I was always worried about what people thought of me and what I did on and off the court. That had the biggest effect on me."

What he never talked about during that season was this: His girlfriend, Caley, whom he married in July 2001, had given birth to his son, Jalen.

"It had an effect on me because there were times where I tried to be there to help Caley out and maybe there were a lot of times where I stayed up a little later than usual," Lumpkin said. "I wasn't over there a whole lot, but I tried to be there. I was feeling I wanted to be responsible."

He couldn't help but be distracted from basketball at times.

"Subconsciously I played with a little heavier spirit than I did my first couple years," Lumpkin said. "I had that responsibility that I never had before. I had to own up to it and be a man to the best of my ability. I didn't know anything about being a father and taking care of a child. I was learning on the move.

"I didn't broadcast it. I wanted to keep it in-house as much as possible. My teammates respected me on that, and I appreciated it. They just kept it quiet and never really brought it up."

VERY UNSATISFYING

Posey, Lumpkin and Brown won 83 games over four years — but none at UD Arena.

The last chance for a victory on Dayton's home court came Jan. 30, 1999. Xavier led by three at halftime but ended up losing 91-86. Flyers fans chanted "You — can't — win — here" in the final seconds and stormed the court after the final buzzer.

Posey scored a career-high 32 points on 9-of-17 shooting. He made all 14 of his free-throw attempts and added nine rebounds. Still, he was distraught in the locker room afterward.

Mention that game, and he is quick to remind you that it was a loss.

"Stats have never really been a big thing for me," he said. "It was all about winning."

GARDENS PARTY

Xavier did not make the NCAA Tournament in 1999 but was invited to the NIT. After a victory at Toledo, the Musketeers came home to play Wake Forest, then Princeton.

That meant one more victory and XU would head to New York for the semifinals.

Only 7,815 fans showed up, but they were loud. "You didn't even think you were in an NIT game," Posey said.

Princeton led by as many as 16 points and was ahead 35-23 at halftime. Prosser was none too pleased.

"Where are my seniors? Is this how you all want your careers to end?" he shouted at halftime.

"We came out there and started pressing and turned it on," Brown said.

With 13:03 left, Posey went up for a rebound and came down hard on his back. A few minutes later, he called time out and fell to the floor. He stayed there close to a minute, then left the game. Despite pain in his lower back, he re-entered the game limping with 9:38 to play. "I was hurting bad," he said.

No matter. Posey totaled 19 points and 11 rebounds and led Xavier to a 65-58 victory. He ended up with the final rebound and dribbled out the final six seconds with his left hand in the air signaling "No. 1."

"Everybody was excited at the Gardens," Posey said. "The students rushed out there and picked me up."

They had Posey on their shoulders and were giving him high-fives. "New York, New York" played in the arena.

"It was a good feeling, the way we were able to come back," Posey said. "That was another big game for us."

TILL THE END . . .

Xavier lost to Clemson 79-76 in the NIT semifinals, then defeated Oregon 106-75 in the consolation game at Madison Square Garden.

In an odd way, Brown's final college game summed up what he was all about. He scored a career-high 34 points.

"That was one of those games where you kind of get him the ball, get out of the way, let him do what he does and jump on his back and go for the ride," Lumpkin said.

"I remember pulling up on the foul line in transition," Brown said. "One of their guards literally smacked me on the arm, and I went up and still made the shot. I was on fire."

With his mother, Jerina, in the crowd, Brown also nailed a career-high six 3-pointers.

"Pack it in? I think that's what Oregon did, and I think that's what they were expecting us to do," Brown said. "My family came up. I'm going to play. The game still counted. I wasn't taking a night off."

PROUD DAY

Brown walked in graduation ceremonies in May 1999. He was joined by Posey, Lumpkin and Williams — all four 1,000-point scorers.

"That's another day I won't forget," Brown said. "I have so many memories from Xavier. Once again, my family was there. My oldest son and daughter were there to see me walk across that stage. And my mom, too. She got to see me graduate before she passed."

Brown finished as Xavier's No. 3 all-time leading scorer and held the school record for career steals (242) and career 3-pointers (236).

"That man has ice in his veins," Anderson said. "He was a warrior. He loved to compete. Lenny was a good guy ... (but) he had a lot of baggage. To watch him come out of his shell, it took a lot. Once he found his niche, boy did he find it."

NCAA STRIKES

Lionel Chalmers was all set to begin classes at Xavier in the fall of 1999. He was expected to back up junior point guard McAfee that season.

But in late August, Xavier and the Chalmers family were stunned to learn the NCAA was declaring Chalmers ineligible. The NCAA ruled that when Chalmers had transferred high schools after his junior year, he did not take the courses needed to become eligible — even though Chalmers took the courses and achieved the grades he was told he needed to compete as a college freshman.

Chalmers had good grades in high school and achieved more than the necessary SAT score.

"The first day I got there, they told me I wasn't going to be able to play," Chalmers said. "That was devastating. I didn't understand why. I did everything I needed to do to be able to play in college right away, and they took that away from me."

Xavier appealed to the NCAA and got a minor concession. Chalmers was categorized as a partial qualifier, meaning he still could not play that season but he could practice with the team and remain on scholarship.

"That kind of set me back," Chalmers said. "From there, it was an uphill battle for me."

UC'S NO. 1 AGAIN? PERFECT

When the University of Cincinnati came into Cincinnati Gardens ranked No. 1 on Dec. 18, 1999, it was just more than three years after Brown's last-second jumper knocked off the top-ranked Bearcats at Shoemaker Center.

"It didn't matter because it was a different year, it was different personnel and it was a different situation," McAfee said.

"There was no intimidation factor. I know that we were real pumped and we felt that we had a shot of upsetting the No. 1 team. Studying tape and just watching them play against others, it seemed … a lot of their opponents would be intimidated, but that's one thing that we were not."

This time, Frey emerged as the man of the hour.

He made two free throws with 29.8 seconds left to put Xavier ahead 64-62. He added a breakaway layup with 8.9 seconds on the clock to make it 66-62.

Frey scored Xavier's only points in the last 3½ minutes and scored all 12 of his points in the second half of a 66-64 victory.

PHOTO COURTESY OF XAVIER UNIVERSITY

"Going into every game my freshman year, I was so excited that my emotions and energy took over, and by the end of warmups I was tired," Frey said. "Going into that game, my No. 1 goal was to hold that energy, don't use it all up at the beginning."

Kevin Frey helped the Musketeers upset No. 1 Cincinnati 66-64 at Cincinnati Gardens on Dec. 18, 1999. Frey finished with 12 points, two rebounds and two steals and was the only Musketeer to score in the final 3½ minutes.

Frey recalled that when he was growing up, his father put in a half court in his backyard, complete with lights so Frey could practice at night.

"I can't tell you how many times I was in the backyard shooting against the No. 1 team in the nation," he said. "So basically (the game against UC) was like the moment that you always dream of, you want to be at the line shooting free throws at the end of the game. I felt really confident. You know if you make them, the game's going to be sealed.

"It was definitely the biggest game I played in."

MORE ON THAT NIGHT

The Shootout was only the eighth game of David West's college career and he had the ultimate test: a matchup against Kenyon Martin, who would go on to be the National Player of the Year and the No. 1 pick in the 2000 NBA Draft.

West came to Xavier from Hargrave Military Academy and moved right into Xavier's starting lineup in his first game. In his fourth and fifth games, he scored 21 against Washington and 15 against East Tennessee State.

Now, here he was. His first Crosstown Shootout. Facing the best player in the nation.

"The coaches had me prepared to go in there and compete regardless of who we were facing," West said. "I'm not going to back down regardless of stature or the name or the hype. I just wanted to make sure, above all else, that we won the game. I showed that I wasn't afraid or nervous or anything."

Martin finished with 16 hard-earned points and 10 rebounds. West totaled five points and nine rebounds before fouling out.

"That was the game I thought, *We have something special with David West*," Prosser said. "He gave as good as he got and stood toe to toe with Kenyon Martin and never backed down."

NEW LEADER IN THE LOCKER ROOM

Xavier was in the midst of what would be a four-game losing streak smack in the middle of the A-10 season. On Jan. 15, 2000, the Musketeers lost at Duquesne 85-78. The Dukes had gone 1-15 in the league the year before and had lost to Xavier five straight times.

Before Prosser even got into the locker room after the game, West — the *freshman* — exploded on his teammates.

"He tore the locker room apart," Prosser said. "I just caught the tail end of it."

"I lost it," West said. "It was one of those things where I felt I had to go off. In the locker room after the game everybody was kind of nonchalant. We had a lot of things going on with egos and guys being a little selfish and Coach had been kind of warning us about impending problems."

West remembers walking down the hallway to the locker room and feeling his anger building.

"There were one or two guys in particular that I wanted to say something to and then it just kind of went from that to … I just let it go," he said. "I think that was the role that the coaches wanted me to step into anyway in terms of the next few years. I think the things I said had to be said, not just from the coach but from a player. I had it on my mind and in my heart and it just came out in like a tirade."

Darnell Williams, the team's lone senior starter, didn't mind one bit. He said some players took it well; others didn't. In the end, he knew West was right.

"That was his competitive fire coming out," Williams said. "He wanted to win that game that bad and he just went off. After the game when I saw him again, he said, 'My bad.' I was like, 'No, you prepare for next year now.' "

PRICE IS NOT ALL RIGHT

Lloyd Price came to Xavier in 1998 from prestigious prep school Oak Hill Academy, a basketball powerhouse in Mouth of Wilson, Va. Price was ranked as the 24th-best player in the country by one recruiting service and came in billed as the highest-rated recruit in Xavier history. He also brought a big smile and lots of charisma. He loved to play basketball.

As a freshman, he played in all 36 games, mostly as the first player off the bench. Overall he had an inconsistent season, shooting just 21.7 percent from 3-point range and 64.5 percent from the foul line. He called it a "horrible year for me."

He was moving into the starting lineup as a sophomore, but in October 1999 he suffered a strained left rotator cuff during a preseason practice after colliding with 6-10 Reggie Butler.

For the rest of the season, Price had pain in his shoulder. He averaged 13 points and six rebounds, but inflammation in his shoulder caused rotator cuff tendinitis.

"He had an abnormal boney growth," former Xavier trainer David Fluker said. "That means the shoulder bone tends to grow into the rotator cuff. Therefore every time you raise your arms, you'd get this pain in your shoulders. Lloyd would always talk about having pain in his shoulder. We're doing therapy, rehabilitation, all that, and he still has this pain in his shoulder."

When Xavier was knocked out of the 1999 Atlantic 10 Tournament in the quarterfinals by St. Bonaventure, Price left the Spectrum in Philadelphia and went home to Wilmington, Del. He did not return to Cincinnati with the team and did not return to campus for four days.

"I needed some time to think," he told *The Cincinnati Enquirer* at the time. "It was obvious I was one of the reasons we didn't win the game. ... I know it's all a 'we' thing, but I let myself down, as well as the team."

After the season, Price had arthroscopic surgery on his shoulder to repair a cartilage tear around his shoulder joint.

He was never the same, on or off the court.

"He came back but never really did well after that," Fluker said. "He started getting in trouble, not going to class, having issues on the court and off the court and that's when, I think, he decided to leave. I think after Lenny (Brown) graduated, that was when he started drifting off, doing crazy stuff."

Brown, like Price, was from Wilmington. Brown acted as sort of a mentor to Price, who would leave Xavier in the spring of 2001 and transfer to Fairleigh Dickinson.

"Lloyd was always a guy whose life was way too complicated," Prosser told *The Enquirer's* Dustin Dow in 2004. "We always told him he had to simplify his life. He was the type of guy who, rather than studying two hours for a test, would spend four hours trying to get out of the test. When he left Xavier, I told him I felt badly, but not guilty."

The postscript on Price: In November 2001, he was arrested after robbing a New Jersey convenience store with a starter's pistol. Price was intoxicated at the time, and the store owner eventually would testify on Price's behalf. In September 2002, Price received no jail time, only probation. In 2004, an attempt to transfer to Division II Kentucky Wesleyan fell apart.

"Great athlete," Prosser said. "Probably never realized his potential as a player. Nice kid. It was tragic the way it ended up."

OUT OF AFRICA

Romain Guessagba-Sato came to the United States in January 1999 as a foreign exchange student from the Central African Republic. He could barely speak English. He grew up playing soccer but saw friends playing basketball and gave it a try. A local coach in Africa helped him, and he watched NBA games on satellite TV.

He came to Ohio with the help of the Friends of Africa foundation, was enrolled at Dayton Christian High School and lived with Tom and Tiffany Thompson, his host family.

The story gets only more interesting.

He was not eligible to play that season. But by that spring, word was getting out about Sato's athletic ability.

"You get calls all the time to the office saying, 'Coach, there's a kid you have to take a look at,'" Battle said. "Someone called and said, 'There's this kid who just moved into the Dayton area named Romain Sato, and he can really shoot it. I started calling around to different schools in that area, like Dayton and Miami. They said, 'We heard the same thing.' But some said, 'We heard he really can't shoot but he's an athlete more than a shooter.' Some said they had never seen him play. It was all hearsay."

"Sato was like a legend," Prosser said.

Battle started sending Sato letters. "I was just setting the table in case he ended up being a good player," Battle said. "We had no idea."

The first day of recruiting, Prosser went to see Sato. Afterward, he called Battle. "Jeff, this kid's terrific," Prosser said. "I love him."

By the fall of 1999, one scouting service had Sato rated as the No. 1 high school player in the country.

"He's got to be one of the best, if not the best player, ever to come out of the Dayton area," former Dayton Christian coach Dave Jackson told the *Dayton Daily News*.

In September 1999, Sato verbally committed to attend XU. He signed two months later — before ever playing in high school. In Sato's Dayton Christian debut, he scored 44 points.

"I received my first (recruiting) letter from (assistant) coach Jeff Battle at Xavier, and I couldn't believe it," Sato said. "I had only played one AAU game when I received the letter in the mail. A lot of different schools recruited me. I thought about UD, Miami or Ohio State. I really didn't want to go to a big school after I visited Xavier and talked to Coach Prosser. On a visit to campus I met and talked with Sister Rose Ann Fleming and Coach Prosser. He told me I could play for any coach, but the one thing I could get here was my degree. That's what I was looking for, not just the basketball side. I felt comfortable with the size of the school and felt like they really cared about the students there."

Sato spoke six languages.

"I had to learn English fast — first just to pass the SAT to have a chance to go to college," Sato said. "The first year in college was tough. School, basketball, practice — there was a lot going on. I had to be patient and not get frustrated. My second year was a lot better, but I was still learning."

A NEW ERA

On Nov. 18, 2000, Xavier played its first game in the new Cintas Center, a $46 million, 10,250-seat facility that brought basketball back to Xavier's campus.

"My first college game was a great experience," Sato said. "I couldn't believe I was in college and playing basketball."

Sato had Xavier's first basket in the building, a 3-pointer.

Xavier defeated Miami 68-54.

A CALL FROM JAMAAL?

The night before the Dec. 14, 2000, Crosstown Shootout, Frey returned to his on-campus apartment and listened to his voicemails. When the second one started, he couldn't believe what he was hearing.

It was from Jamaal Davis, one the Bearcats' starting forwards.

"Hey man, this is Jamaal Davis. I'm going to get you tomorrow. I'm going to dunk on you. You're garbage ..."

"He was just going off," Frey said. "So I get fired up. I'm like, *Are you kidding me? I can't believe this.* I go right next door to Reggie Butler and start banging on Reggie's door. He comes out, and he's on the phone. 'Reggie, man, you got to come over and listen to this.' He comes over and I play it for him and he's like, *No way. This is crazy.*

"Then he leaves and I'm still kind of fired up."

Butler gave Frey the phone. Posey was on the line, and he shared Frey's outrage. Posey was then playing in the NBA.

Frey could not sleep that night and could not wait for the game to start the next day.

Xavier ended up upsetting the No. 17-ranked Bearcats 69-67. Frey had 15 points and seven rebounds.

"The whole game, I am so fired up at Jamaal," Frey said. "I'm going at him as hard as I can. I'm even talking to him. I hit a 3 and he got chewed out from (UC coach Bob) Huggins. He came back out and I remember walking by and saying, 'Yeah, that's what you get for leaving a message on my voicemail.' He looked at me like, *What are you talking about?* But it didn't register because I was so pumped up and into the game.

"I think it was Reggie after the game who came up and told me the truth. Apparently it was James Posey who called and left that message on my voicemail."

THE ACC CALLS

Xavier finished the 2000–01 season 21-8 and lost to Notre Dame in the first round of the NCAA Tournament. Roughly five weeks later, Wake Forest University — an Atlantic Coast

Conference school — was pursuing Prosser as its next coach. He met with athletic director Ron Wellman. He was offered the job — before he ever set foot on WFU's campus.

Prosser and his wife, Nancy, went to Winton-Salem, N.C., on a Sunday. Wake Forest wanted an answer after meetings that Monday. Prosser said he first had to talk with Xavier officials.

On Tuesday morning, he went to Mass at Bellarmine Chapel and prayed about the decision to take the job. Shortly after that, he told Xavier officials he was leaving for Wake.

"I guess a lot of it was the allure of the ACC," Prosser said. "For someone who started out as a ninth-grade coach and never thought about becoming a (college) coach, the chance to coach in that league ..."

Prosser's XU teams went 148-65 in seven years as head coach. He had been an assistant under Gillen for eight years.

"In the seven years I was there (as head coach), I never felt unappreciated at Xavier," Prosser said.

"Someone asked me as I was leaving, what do I want people to remember? It would make me happy if they thought I stood for what Xavier stands for. That was my challenge and my charge all the time, to stand for what Xavier stands for."

After meeting with his players, Prosser held an impromptu news conference at Cintas Center during which he got choked up. The goodbyes were not easy. Players were visibly upset. West said he briefly contemplated transferring.

"I sat down with (athletic director) Mike Bobinski and I talked to him a couple days after Coach officially took the job," West said, "and he said, 'Look, David, I'm telling you we're going to get somebody in here that's going to be the best person for this job.' I trusted that. I trusted that Xavier would do the right thing by the guys there. And they did."

12

THAD MATTA
(2001–04)

XAVIER ATHLETIC DIRECTOR Mike Bobinski kept a piece of paper on which he wrote names of coaches who — for one reason or another — caught his eye over the years. The day after Skip Prosser accepted the Wake Forest job, Bobinski pulled that paper out of a file in his office and went to work on finding a new coach. He looked over the 10 or so names and started making calls.

He was getting plenty of phone calls, too. Kansas coach Roy Williams recommended his assistant Neil Dougherty. Michigan State coach Tom Izzo was pushing assistant Brian Gregory, who eventually would become Dayton's coach.

Also on Bobinski's mind was Thad Matta, who had led Butler to a 24-8 record in his first year as a head coach.

Bobinski remembered this about Matta: During the 2001 NCAA Tournament, when Xavier was playing Notre Dame in Kansas City, Bobinski went to dinner with friends the night before the game.

"All of a sudden, I see a bunch of young men walk in, and I'm struck by what a good-looking bunch of guys they were and how well they handled themselves," Bobinski said. "They were really impressive. And then I come to figure out that it's the Butler team.

"The next day Butler plays Wake Forest in their first-round game and proceeds to just take them apart. I think they ended up winning the game by 33. I was at the arena watching the game, and I was amazed at those same guys that I had seen eating dinner the night before."

Bobinski mentally filed all that away.

"As I got into the (search) process, I had that fairly recent and distinct impression of Thad and the work that he was doing at Butler, the way his team carried itself, just their whole approach was something that looked like, to me, would be completely at home in our environment at Xavier," Bobinski said.

Bobinski asked around and heard Matta was a good person, a Midwest kind of guy. But Matta was coaching at his alma mater, and Bobinski didn't even know if he could lure him away.

"I was living the dream at Butler," Matta said.

When Bobinski called to see whether he might be interested in the Xavier job, Matta didn't even know Prosser had left. He remembers asking, "What happened to Skip?"

"I had an appreciation for Xavier because when I was a player (at Butler), that was when Byron (Larkin) and Tyrone (Hill) and Derek (Strong) and all those guys were there and they always kicked our butts," Matta said. "I can remember as a senior in college going up to Pete Gillen and telling him I'd love to be a graduate assistant if he ever had anything open. I went over and worked Xavier's camp one summer.

"When Mike called me, it was like, 'Wow, Xavier!' I knew the winning tradition that was there and viewed it as a unique situation."

Bobinski narrowed his list to North Carolina-Greensboro coach Fran McCafferty, Dougherty and Matta, and set out on a three-city tour. Matta was first up.

They met at the Omni Hotel in Indianapolis. They were supposed to talk for three hours but ended up spending 5½ hours together.

"I think we both left there kind of saying, 'This is pretty good.' We were on the same wavelength on a lot of different things," Bobinski said. "I thought: *If this is the worst guy that I see, I can live with this right here.*"

PHOTO COURTESY OF XAVIER UNIVERSITY

Thad Matta won more games in his first year at Xavier (26) than any other first-year coach in school history.

"From the second we met, it just kind of flowed," Matta said. "It was a very unique meeting. I was being interviewed, but I felt like I was talking to a great friend. It was fun. I was supposed to be at a function earlier in the day and obviously I missed it. I came home and (his wife) Barb said, 'Did you get the job?' I said, 'I can't get the job. It's too good of a job.'"

Bobinski went on to meet with Dougherty in Kansas City, then McCafferty in North Carolina. Matta, meanwhile, had a meeting with his athletic director that he did not think went particularly well.

When he got back to his office after that meeting, he had a message from Bobinski, who had returned to Cincinnati. Bobinski wanted to get together again in Indianapolis.

"Thad had an energy about him," Bobinski said. "He had a

passion about our situation and what could be accomplished and a way of articulating that vision that was so on target and resonated with me so much. I wanted to make sure I hadn't seen a mirage and that I was really as sure as I thought about what I wanted to recommend when I got back to school."

He was sure. The next morning he recommended hiring Matta.

Two days later, Matta came to campus for a visit. By the end of the day, he was the Musketeers' new coach.

"It happened so quickly," Matta said.

ANOTHER IMPORTANT HIRE

One of Matta's first orders of business was to bring in an associate head coach who would be his second in command.

He had shared an office as an assistant coach at Miami University with fellow assistant Sean Miller, who had become the top assistant at North Carolina State under Herb Sendek.

"Thad and Sean had a great friendship," Bobinski said. "We did some things financially that we hadn't done before for an assistant coach. Thad himself through camps and other things … aggressively supplemented what Sean was making to try and make it an attractive enough offer for him.

"One of the things that I think people are forgetting that was extremely important to our success, not only when Thad was here but the success that we're enjoying now and we're going to enjoy for some time, has a whole lot to do with his efforts to bring Sean here to be on our staff that very first year."

GETTING TO KNOW YOU

Matta hadn't seen Xavier play much during the 2000–01 season, but he did know that junior David West was supposed to be a pretty good player. Matta was eager to get to know him better.

The first time they met, Matta said, he was "mesmerized" by the size of West's hands and fingers. West immediately told Matta he planned to return for his junior year and that he had many things to work on. Matta noticed West had attempted only one 3-point shot as a sophomore and told him he liked his big men to get out on the perimeter, handle the ball and shoot some 3s.

West replied: "Coach, no offense to your system. But I like to make shots. And I know the closer I am to the basket, the better chance they have of going in."

"David, if you ever want to go into coaching, you've got a job," Matta told him.

Matta first saw West play in person that summer when West participated in USA Basketball Men's National Team tryouts in Colorado. Matta called his staff and asked: "Fellas, have you ever coached a great big man? Well, we've got one."

"We knew where he was really good," Matta said. "We thought the big thing was going to be getting him out away from the basket and handling the ball better, which ironically, is what he does a lot of now in the NBA.

"I had to feel my way with David and figure out who he was. The biggest thing I wanted to do at the beginning was earn his trust. David wasn't a guy you yelled or screamed at. I talked to him. His mind for the game of basketball is one of the most incredible things I've ever seen. He really understood every aspect of the game, from scouting and preparation to drill work.

"I don't know if I've ever coached a more consistent player. I walked out every night at Cintas Center and looked at the scoreboard and thought, *I know I've got 22 and 12.*"

West wasn't easily won over. He was coming off a season in which he averaged 17.8 points and 10.9 rebounds — both team highs — and he was close to Prosser.

"It took me awhile to trust what Coach Matta wanted to do," West said. "I remember me and Lionel (Chalmers) sat and talked about Coach Matta. He made us buy in first because he knew that if we bought into what he had to bring to the table, then the other guys would kind of follow behind us. And they did.

"He brought that passion. We had our doubts because we're like, 'Man, he's coming from Butler, a smaller school.'"

Following the press conference when he was hired, Matta went to the practice gym in Cintas Center and started introducing himself to the players.

"I want to win," he told them. "I understand what you have at stake. Your interests are mine and my interests are yours. You guys have got to believe that I'm going to do what I can to benefit you."

GONE BUT STILL HELPING

In what has to be considered an unusual circumstance, Prosser made himself available to Matta 24 hours a day. Though he was at Wake Forest, Prosser took the time to go through each returning player with Matta, telling him whatever he needed to know about the guys on and off the court. Prosser talked to Matta about key people in the community and throughout the university.

"He mentored me through my three years at Xavier," Matta said. "It says a lot about the man Skip was. I honestly believe a lot of times when a guy leaves somewhere, they probably want the next guy to fail. He was not that way. He really pointed me in the right direction. I don't know how many people get that."

HOMETOWN HERO

Keith Jackson knew he wanted to stay close to home, and coming out of Purcell Marian High School he had two good choices to remain in town.

Xavier and Cincinnati both were recruiting him. He met Prosser and Bob Huggins.

"It just seemed like Skip was the more loyal guy, so I decided to go with Skip," Jackson said. "That's pretty much how I ended up at Xavier. School-wise I knew it was a great decision just because all their players graduate; so I didn't really even have to worry about that. I just looked at the basketball program and decided that that's my style of play and that's where I wanted to go."

Prosser left for Wake Forest before Jackson's freshman year, and he was definitely nervous about playing for a coach who did not recruit him.

"I was really disappointed because I thought I would play for (Prosser)," Jackson said. "We won a lot of games and Thad was a great coach, so it worked out for me."

ANKLES AWAY

Kevin Frey played much of his junior year in pain. He had bone chips in his ankle and had developed an inflammation of the lining tissue in the joint. He had surgery in April 2001, less than a month after Matta arrived.

For much of his career, Frey battled through pain in his ankle. He started his senior season, but his scoring and rebounding averages were down from the previous year.

"I'd go through a practice and my ankle would be huge and I'd have to spend the whole night icing it," he said. "I pretty much lived in the training room. My freshman year I kept turning it in practice over and over again. I'd tape it and had a brace and it still hurt. Then the MRIs, X-rays, the whole nine yards ... showed bone spurs on the outside of my ankle, and so they cleaned off my whole ankle. After that I developed bone spurs on the front of my ankle, so every time I'd run and my foot would flex, I would have shooting pains up my leg."

He didn't pick up a basketball during the summer before his last season until it was time for practices to begin officially. He said Matta was good about not pressuring him to do more than he could.

"It took me awhile to get back in the flow of things," Frey said. "I remember we played Coastal Carolina in an exhibition game and I was like 2-for-14. I was missing layups and everything. I didn't feel comfortable, I had no flow whatsoever. I remember thinking, *What am I going to do? How am I going to make this work?*"

Every day after practice, Miller would ride a stationary bike next to Frey and encourage him to find different ways to help the team.

"He was just trying to support me, keep me company," Frey said. "That was really cool.

"We'd sit there and talk about practice, talk about plays and ways I could get open and stuff. He knew I was busting my butt to try and help the team. At the time, I really thought I was hurting the team."

Frey averaged 8.5 points and 5.7 rebounds as a senior and finished his career with 1,102 points and 710 rebounds.

PRACTICAL JOKER

West wasn't just a fabulous player, he was also a world-class prankster.

A few examples:

• Teammate Anthony Coleman was shooting around by himself in the gym one night, then went to the locker room to take a shower. When he did, West and Chalmers took his clothes. "We were kind of up by the cafeteria when he came out, and we saw him dart across the parking lot into the dorm," West said. "We left him like a pair of shorts, but mind you, it was February, and it was 20 degrees outside. He ended up transferring." Presumably not because of that incident.

• Another time teammate Andre Johnson left his car running when he parked it outside of an apartment building and ran in to see a friend. West saw this, ran to the car and drove it around the corner. Johnson came back and freaked out that his car was taken. West couldn't keep a straight face for long.

"On the court, I've got my mom's attitude," West said in a 2002 *Eastern Basketball* magazine story. "She's real strong-willed. She doesn't hold anything back. I kind of picked that up from her. My dad, that's who I am off the court. Easy, just a goofball. He loves to laugh."

LESSON LEARNED

Matta's first Crosstown Shootout in December 2001 was a painful lesson.

"I didn't understand the magnitude of the game until I walked out on the court and that ball got tossed up," he said. "At that point I understood this rivalry is for real."

The underdog Bearcats crushed Xavier 75-55 at Cintas Center — the most lopsided XU-UC game in more than

35 years. It didn't help Xavier that West went down with a sprained ankle and played just 23 minutes. He scored only nine points, ending a streak of 30 consecutive games in double figures.

After that night, Matta realized he had to "make sure you know when this game is next year because this one is an important one." Sure enough, he beat the Bearcats in his next two tries.

West even made some headlines in the days after the 2001 game, saying Xavier would have won if he hadn't been injured.

West had sprained his ankle with 1:03 left in the first half and was helped off the court. He came back 4:19 into the second half, but lasted only a minute. He argued with Matta to re-enter the game, which he did. But with 8:45 remaining, he went to the bench for good.

"If I played my normal amount of minutes, we win the game," West said five days after the game. "Hands down. I feel we'd win."

On the other side of town, when he heard of those remarks, UC forward Jamaal Davis told *The Enquirer*: "The game's over. You can't turn back the hands of time. That's a big excuse to me. We're not even thinking about Xavier anymore. Xavier's done. ... We're on to bigger and better things."

Well, so was Xavier. The Musketeers won 21 of their next 23 games after that loss.

PLEASANT SURPRISE

After his junior season ended, West had a decision to make. He had averaged 18.2 points and 9.8 rebounds and thought he could be an NBA Draft pick. No Xavier player had ever declared early for the NBA.

"I was so worried about the things that could happen, all the stories that you hear about guys not taking the opportunity when it was there," West said.

A few weeks after the season ended, he went into Matta's office.

"You could tell he was really nervous," Matta said. "He never looked up."

"Coach, I just want to let you know I'm going to put my name in for the NBA Draft," West said.

PHOTO COURTESY OF XAVIER UNIVERSITY

David West set a Xavier single-game record with eight blocked shots against Coastal Carolina on Nov. 17, 2001. West twice had seven blocks in a game.

"Great," Matta said. "Congratulations."

"I knew it was a dream of his," Matta said. "I hugged him — and he was gone. I knew he was uncomfortable. Once he left, I cried for about four hours."

Matta pledged his support and said he'd help gather any information that might help West on his next steps.

West had long talks with his father, his close friend Chalmers and some other teammates.

Everyone was supportive. It was an emotional time, a tough choice to make.

A press release had been prepared to announce West's decision. The coaches were set to tell the players. Matta was figuring out how to reshape the team without West.

Then came the team's postseason banquet April 9. As usual, the seniors all spoke. Just as Matta was getting up for some closing remarks, West beat him to the microphone. Matta sat back down, thinking it was a classy move by West to announce his departure to the Xavier fans.

"I'm staying," he told the crowd between tears. "I feel like we can do some damage nationally next year; I really believe that."

"I had no idea," Matta said. "And I will tell you, there wasn't one happier person in that building than me."

West had told Chalmers earlier that day that he changed his mind.

"I did know," Chalmers said. "But from what I remember, he really wasn't sure what he wanted to do. It was a hard decision for him."

West said: "I kind of went from leaving to saying, 'Well, there's no sense in rushing into this thing.' I thought if I hung on another year, I could have another year with my friend and have another opportunity to try and do something special."

QUITE A PAIR

It was no surprise West had confided in Chalmers. The two had become close friends since arriving on campus together.

They were roommates from the beginning.

"It didn't hurt that he was a point guard," West said with a laugh. "If you're going to have a friend, it might as well be the guy who's going to get you the ball, you know?"

"You know what?" Chalmers said. "I knew that he would get the rebounds and he had to give it to me, too. It works both ways."

You can see why they remained friends.

"We lived our first two years together in the dorms," West said. "My junior and senior years we were over at the Manor House; he lived upstairs and I lived down. We used to wake one another up for practice. We did everything together ... we were in as many classes together as we possibly could be."

When Chalmers was ineligible to play as a freshman, West listened. When West pondered going to the NBA, Chalmers was there. When Chalmers broke his foot (in 2002–03), West was by his side.

"We understood each other," Chalmers said. "We respected each other. Everything we did, we did together. It just became a good friendship. ... He was a person who was willing to work hard to get what he wanted. I think we both have that."

PHOTO COURTESY OF XAVIER UNIVERSITY

Lionel Chalmers finished his Xavier career with 1,556 points and was picked in the second round of the 2004 NBA Draft by the Los Angeles Clippers.

Their relationship was a factor in West deciding to return for his senior year. It would've been easier to leave, West said, without knowing he was leaving Chalmers behind.

"We grew up together," West said. "It's one thing coming in as 18- or 19-year-olds and then we go through those years where you grow from being a young adult to an adult, and we kind of did that together."

BAD BREAK

Xavier started the 2002–03 season 8-2 and had a New Year's Eve date at home against 15th-ranked Creighton, which came in 10-0.

The No. 19 Musketeers would win the game 75-73 on a short bank shot by West with 4.1 seconds left, but they suffered a potentially devastating blow to their season: Chalmers broke a bone in his right foot.

"I remember they pressed us," Chalmers said. "They inbounded the ball to me, and I was trying to beat the press. Two guys were coming, and I'm making a turn from the right corner to come to get in the middle, and when I turned the corner, that's when I broke my foot. I played maybe 35 seconds longer, but I knew my foot was broken. I called the coaches and said, 'Take me out, I broke it.' "

West finished with 28 points, and Jackson came off the bench and went 7-of-7 from the field, scoring 17. Xavier's only other point guard with any experience was freshman Dedrick Finn.

"I was playing well," Chalmers said. "David (West) was playing well. (Romain) Sato was playing well. I thought that we had a really good team and I felt like it was our year to do well (in the NCAA). I felt like I kind of let the team down. I wasn't 100 percent the rest of the year. That was definitely part of my inspiration the next season."

Doctors put a screw in his foot, which he still has. Chalmers was, remarkably, back in four weeks. At George Washington on Feb. 4, his second game since his return, Chalmers scored a game-high 17 points in 20 minutes. "I was still only about 75-80 percent," he said.

47 BIG ONES

The Musketeers lost their conference opener to Richmond and lost their national ranking, then they rattled off seven straight A-10 victories heading into a home showdown with Dayton on Feb. 8, 2003, at Cintas Center.

The Flyers had won nine straight and were one game ahead in the standings.

"I knew going in that it was a big game for us," West said. "If we lose that game, it's an uphill battle for the rest of the conference season. We just said let's be extra aggressive, extra assertive from the jump ball."

Dayton got off to a fast start, taking a 24-11 lead. West almost single-handedly kept Xavier in the game, scoring 18 of its first 20 points.

"I was able to get some things closer to the basket, so the game opened up for me," he said. "Coach just kept calling my name and calling my name, and it was an opportunity — more than just to score all the baskets, it was a game we had to win.

"I was trying to do much of my work before I caught the ball, just getting myself in a good position where I ... would be able to catch it deep and score.

"I think guys knew every time I touched the ball I was going to be trying to put it in the basket. And I was making free throws, and that didn't hurt. Regardless of how many points I had, we were trailing for most of that game."

Xavier won 85-77. West finished with 47 points, the second-best single-game total in school history (Steve Thomas scored 50 in January 1964). West also had 18 rebounds.

"I just remember they started out the game, no double teams, just single coverage, and Dave scored probably the first three or four times he touched it," Jackson said. "And we're all thinking in our heads, *If they don't start double-teaming him, he's going to go for 40-something.* And they never sent the double team and Dave just kept putting them in; it was like clockwork."

"I could see it in their eyes," Chalmers told *The Enquirer's*

Paul Daugherty. "When he caught the ball, they didn't really want to guard him. Who wants to guard a guy that's on fire?"

West made 15 of 26 field-goal attempts and was 16-of-19 from the foul line.

"I'll never forget it," Matta said. "That was one of the greatest performances I've ever seen. He was special in that game."

THE BEST — NO DOUBT

He was special all season, actually.

West averaged 20.1 points and 11.8 rebounds as a senior and was named the National Player of the Year by The Associated Press, *Basketball Times* and the U.S. Basketball Writers Association. He was a consensus first-team All-American and was named Atlantic 10 Player of the Year for the third straight time.

"It was a culmination of everything," West said. "It was a funny situation, being the guy who wasn't highly recruited. I had to work my way into everything, work my way into the mouths of folks, just kind of kept plugging away and doing things that were going to make people take notice of my abilities.

"Being able to receive an honor like that was huge for me. It was one of the few instances where I felt proud to have done what I had done and kind of see it all come together.

"Nobody expected me to do the things that I did in college, and I think it was a tribute to the environment I was in. I just found a perfect situation for me."

It was a two-way street.

West's Xavier jersey, No. 30, was retired on Senior Day, before his final game at Cintas Center (a 96-65 victory over Temple). West finished as Xavier's No. 2 all-time scorer behind Byron Larkin, No. 3 rebounder behind Tyrone Hill and Bob Pelkington and No. 1 in career blocks, free throws made and free throws attempted.

He also graduated and became the No. 18 selection in the 2003 NBA Draft (by the New Orleans Hornets). In 2008, West was named to the NBA All-Star team.

"Coming into Xavier, I wasn't so much sold on academics, but Sister (Rose Ann Fleming) sold me on that early," West said. "Then, in terms of basketball, Coach Prosser kind of made me buy into wanting to be good, wanting to be better than what people thought I was going to be.

"For the last two years, Coach Matta was the one that kind of brought it all together in terms of his desire to push me and not letting me settle for anything."

EARLY DEPARTURE?

After averaging 18.1 points and 7.1 rebounds as a junior, Sato briefly considered declaring early for the NBA Draft. Like West the year before, Sato decided to stay in school.

"Yes, I was thinking about going pro, but I knew I only needed six months to graduate," Sato said. "I couldn't see myself having come so far to not finish my degree. I talked to my parents, Coach Matta, (assistant) Coach (John) Groce, Coach Prosser and a couple agents. I knew I would play pro eventually, so I wanted to stay and finish my degree. That's what I had come to Xavier for in the first place."

Sato had been to three straight NCAA Tournaments, but his teams had never gotten past the second round. He came back for his senior season hoping to go further.

THE TURNING POINT

The 2003–04 season was one bumpy ride.

The Musketeers were just 5-4 going into Christmas. They

won four straight, then went into a funk.

Xavier was in the midst of its worst losing stretch under Matta when it lost for the fourth time in five games at George Washington on Feb. 28, 2004.

It wasn't just a defeat, it was a shellacking. The Colonials won 81-60, handing the Musketeers their worst loss in three years under Matta. "We kind of gave up," Chalmers said.

Afterward in the locker room, before any of the coaches could speak, Chalmers went off. Nobody stopped him. Nobody said a word.

"I went crazy," he said. "I came in and I let loose. I was really upset. I screamed at everyone — even myself. There were only a few seniors on the team, and I said, 'We're seniors; we can't allow this to happen. This is not the Xavier way. This is not Xavier basketball.' "

"He was so focused after that," Jackson said of Chalmers. "You just had to follow his lead."

Chalmers didn't know what he was going to do until he did it. And it was a little bit out of character.

"It was a natural reaction to how I felt," he said. "I'm a guy who doesn't say much, but when I do say things you can tell that I mean it. That was one of the times that a lot of people were probably surprised.

"It was bothering me, and that's when it came to a head. It was just passion and emotion. I had everyone's attention, even the coaches. We lost the game after that, but that's when we really started to jell together. The identity of the team became strong at that point."

"That was when the rubber hit the road for us," Matta said.

LET THE TURNAROUND BEGIN

It was a season on the brink. That's no exaggeration.

Xavier was 10-9 and had lost five of six entering the Feb. 3, 2004, Crosstown Shootout. The Bearcats were ranked No. 10 in the country.

"I remember leaving my house the morning of the Crosstown Shootout and saying, 'Look, I just want to let you know, tomorrow may possibly be the worst day of my life,' " Matta said.

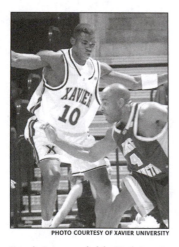

PHOTO COURTESY OF XAVIER UNIVERSITY

Romain Sato never led the Musketeers in scoring during a season but finished as the school's No. 3 all-time scorer with 2,005 points. He has the most career 3-pointers (307). The San Antonio Spurs selected Sato in the second round of the 2004 NBA Draft.

It turned into a typically tight XU-UC game. The Bearcats were ahead 66-61 with 4:15 left. Xavier tied it on a 3-pointer by Chalmers with 2:37 to play.

UC went ahead 69-68 with less than a minute remaining on two Jason Maxiell free throws. Chalmers had the ball in his hands.

"It came down to the last few seconds," Chalmers said. "I love to take that shot, and I knew I could make it. It was my senior year, and there was no better way to go out.

"I just was thinking, get a good shot off if I'm free, but if not, find *someone*. But I was looking to win the game. I came down the court and saw to the right that it was going to be a switch, and their big man switched out on me. I knew if I did my step-back move I could get room and get a good shot off. I got a good look, and I also saw Sato running for the rebound. So I knew if it didn't go in maybe he could get the rebound."

Chalmers nailed a fade-away jumper from just inside the 3-point line with 27 seconds left. UC turned the ball over with 4.9 seconds remaining.

The final score was 71–69.

"That was arguably as big a shot in terms of its lasting impact that's ever been made for us in my time here," Bobinski said.

"I felt like that team needed something big to happen to them," Matta said. "That was the game that really kind of set the stage for the rest of the season."

Chalmers finished with a game-high 20 points.

It was vindication of sorts for the senior point guard, who had taken plenty of heat for Xavier's 10-9 start.

"My senior year, everyone had left and they talked about how we weren't going to be as good with Dave West leaving," Chalmers said. "There was a lot of media talk about how Xavier was going to be down this season.

"I put more pressure on myself than I should have. It took me awhile to loosen up and play the way I knew how to play and to get the team to play the way we knew how to play. That's how we got started slowly. Once we found our rhythm, it was 'sky's the limit' from there."

ON A ROLL

Before the UC victory, Xavier wasn't even considered a team headed for the National Invitation Tournament.

Then the Musketeers won seven straight and finished the regular season having won nine of their last 10 games. Still, going into the Atlantic 10 Tournament, they needed some victories to have any hope for the NCAA Tournament.

"Nobody believed in us," Sato said. "People thought there was no way we were going to make the tournament or NIT. After three years of making the NCAA Tournament, it was going to be a big disappointment, especially for our senior year.

"But we never gave up and we never stopped believing. I remember Coach always said, 'Play every game like it's your last one.' "

Miller called Sato into his office.

"This is your senior year and you should have fun and enjoy this time," Miller said. "Don't worry about losing or winning. Just play hard. If we lose, who cares? We move on and think about the next one."

"In my mind, I knew Chalmers and I had to step up and lead the young guys," Sato said. "We were a young team with only three seniors. We knew we had to finish strong."

ANOTHER (NO.) 1 BITES THE DUST

Xavier knocked off St. Bonaventure in its first game in the 2004 Atlantic 10 Tournament and earned a meeting with No.1-ranked Saint Joseph's in the quarterfinals.

The Hawks had defeated XU by eight points two months earlier at Cintas Center.

There's not a lot of explanation for what happened next: The Musketeers absolutely blasted Saint Joseph's 87-67, the worst an unranked team had ever beaten a top-ranked team.

"I don't think that could ever happen again to be honest," Matta said.

"We kind of shocked them early," Chalmers said. "We made some shots and we played some defense, and the next thing you know we were up 20-something. I think they gave up. I don't think they were prepared for the intensity and the strength that we came with. We were determined, and nothing was going to stop us at that point."

At halftime, the Musketeers were ahead by 22. Matta stressed getting off to a good start in the second half.

Xavier responded with the first eight points of the second half. The lead grew as big as 37.

"They cut it to 30," Matta said. "And (assistant coaches) Sean (Miller) and John (Groce) are screaming to take a time-out. I said, 'Hell no, let's get this thing over with.' That was a great win for us. Even at that point we still had work to do to get into the NCAA Tournament. I think we needed one more win."

They got two.

Xavier defeated George Washington and host Dayton to win four games in four nights and earn an automatic NCAA berth as the conference tournament champion.

UNFORGETTABLE MOMENT

The Musketeers made history in 2004, becoming the first Xavier team to advance to the Elite Eight of the NCAA Tournament — and it was only the second time XU got as far as the Sweet 16.

Xavier defeated Louisville 80-70, Mississippi State 89-74 and Texas 79-71.

Matta won't ever forget a locker room scene after the victory over the Longhorns in Atlanta. The Rev. James E. Hoff, former XU president, had been diagnosed with cancer during the Atlantic 10 Tournament.

"The players didn't know about Father Hoff," Matta said. "I remember seeing him in there with tears in his eyes. Xavier had never been that far, and it was almost fitting that we took it one step further and he was there to see it. I wanted nothing more than for him to see his dream (of a Final Four) come true."

CARRY ON

Xavier lost to Duke 66-63 in the regional final (see Chapter 1) but had completed a stunning turnaround by winning 16 of its last 18 games.

"To be the first in Xavier history in the Elite Eight was amazing," Sato said. "We faced a lot of tough teams, but it was a good run for us. We couldn't worry about our regular season then. It turned out to be one of the best years in my college career."

In his three years as coach, Matta's teams always finished strong. They went 19-3 in February and 19-4 in March, a combined winning percentage of .844.

"I'm most proud of the way we left Xavier — how we upheld the tradition for the fans and everyone that came before us," Chalmers said. "I am very proud that I represented the school well and I left my mark.

"I had a great time. It was a great experience. I wouldn't change anything, not one thing — maybe beating Duke."

HEADING NORTH ON I-71

On June 8, 2004, Ohio State fired coach Jim O'Brien after he admitted giving money to a recruit five years earlier. ESPN.com reported almost immediately that Matta would be a target for the job. New Xavier athletic director Dawn Rogers took notice.

"I think all along we knew that Thad was a Big Ten kind

of guy, and immediately when that job opened I got nervous," she said.

"I remember the day Coach O'Brien was let go and questions started swirling," Matta said. "I hadn't been contacted. I have never made a phone call for a job. The hardest part for me was everybody voicing their opinion on something that hadn't happened. It was difficult to operate."

Xavier had extended Matta's contract through 2013. He talked about how happy he was at Xavier. Matta even told Dustin Dow of *The Enquirer* on June 29: "I'm not a candidate. It's that plain and simple."

OSU athletic director Andy Geiger said later that he called for permission to speak to Matta a week before those comments. Rogers remembers going to see Matta at his summer basketball camp in Cintas Center after the call from Geiger. The two met after camp was over for the day.

"I think we ended up talking for two or three hours in my office," Rogers said. "When he left my office, I didn't really know what his feelings were going to be."

Matta later returned a phone message from Geiger. He recalls the conversation going like this:

"Mr. Geiger, this is Thad Matta from Xavier University."

"Look, I've got a head men's basketball job I'm sure you're aware of. It's open. We have an interest in you. Is this something maybe you have an interest in?"

"Yeah."

"He said, 'Good,' and hung up," Matta said. "That was it. I didn't hear anything for a couple of days, so I never knew what was going on."

On June 28, Geiger flew to Lunken Airport in Cincinnati, where he interviewed Matta, according to newspaper reports.

"We went through the deal and they said they'd get back to me," Matta said.

OSU officials wanted him to come to campus. They told him he was one of three finalists for the job. Matta was scheduled to be in Columbus at 6 a.m. on a Wednesday morning. The night before, he called Geiger and told him, "I'm out."

"I don't want to be disrespectful to our players and to Xavier. This thing is out of hand down here," Matta said

"You need to come up and see Ohio State," Geiger countered.

"Are you offering me the job?" Matta asked.

"I can't do that," Geiger responded. "But if you come here, you're going to like what you see. And if you do a good job, this thing can be done."

Matta thought about it and called Geiger back.

"OK, I'll be there tomorrow morning."

Matta was offered the Ohio State job that next day, July 7.

He took a lot of heat afterward from Xavier fans.

"If (Thad) had never said those famous words — 'I'm not a candidate' — I think it would have been a whole lot different," Bobinski said.

"Thad was really honest with me through the process," Rogers said. His comments, she said, were because he was trying to do what was best for Xavier's program and players in case he did not leave.

"What's unfortunate about it in the end, it hurt everybody," Rogers said. "When we talked about it afterwards, he said, 'I was really trying to protect our program.' I always felt that he did the best that he could."

Matta said it's hard to know how to handle a situation like he was in.

"Everybody thinks about themselves in the deal," he said. "Well, Thad's got to think about himself, too. If this doesn't go right, I will be back and ready to go — or if I get up there and don't like it, I'm going to say no.

"I did what I thought was right for Thad Matta and his family and my goals and dreams and ambitions. Xavier was left in great hands with Sean, and obviously the program has done as well or better than when we were there."

Matta has the best winning percentage of any Xavier coach (.772). He also has the second-shortest tenure as coach of anyone after 1946.

It doesn't help that he's now coaching in-state and only 100 miles from Xavier's campus.

"I think he was tremendous for Xavier basketball," Rogers said. "He came along at a critical juncture. There were so many exciting things going on.

"I don't know to this day if Thad does really understand that it wasn't *that* he left, it was *how* he left. It was not a conversation that I ever had with him, and I don't know if anyone else had it with him. He did an incredible thing for that program. In the three years that he was there, he was a tremendous coach, a tremendous recruiter and it was just too bad that he isn't embraced today like Skip was when he left, that people didn't appreciate what he did."

Matta calls his time with the Musketeers "three of the greatest years of my life."

"I truly enjoyed every aspect of Xavier University — from the people to the fans to the players to the community of Cincinnati," he said. "I think that people don't ever believe this, but Xavier and Butler are my second and third favorite teams. I root for them like crazy."

13

SEAN MILLER
(2004–PRESENT)

JULY IS NOT TYPICALLY A TIME when college basketball jobs change hands. Usually programs are settled and looking ahead to recruiting, scheduling, welcoming new players and the start of the next season.

But when Thad Matta accepted the Ohio State job on July 7, 2004, Xavier was in an unusual position.

"I remember the whole thing made you really uneasy," then-athletic director Dawn Rogers said. "The best thing was having this associate head coach there that I had a tremendous amount of confidence in."

Sean Miller was hopeful he could become Xavier's next coach. He also knew that if not, he could join Matta's staff at Ohio State.

"No one at Xavier ever gave me the wink, so to speak," Miller said. "Thad thought I would have the opportunity to be the next coach, but nobody promised him that either. I just went about my business in hopes that the phone call would come."

Before Rogers knew for certain that Matta was taking the OSU job, she met with the Musketeer players to tell them what she knew. It was just her and the team. She remembers:

"I think it was Brian Thornton who said: 'We just want you to know that we feel really comfortable with Sean Miller and we think he would be a fantastic coach.' I said, 'Hey, I really appreciate that, knowing how you feel about him. He certainly will be a part of the mix.'"

After Matta announced he was leaving, Rogers met that night with Miller at the Marriott Hotel in Mason. Before that, Rogers talked to Rev. Michael J. Graham, Xavier's president. He asked what she was thinking. She said she wanted to sit down with Miller "and if we have a good conversation, then he's the right guy for us." They were in agreement.

Rogers admired the way Miller coached and recruited, but they had never discussed his coaching philosophies. They talked for hours at the Marriott.

Miller remembers Rogers' most important question: Did he believe that Xavier did not have to be a stepping-stone job? He did.

"I was amazed at how prepared he was," Rogers said. "He

PHOTO COURTESY OF XAVIER UNIVERSITY

Xavier coach Sean Miller confers with assistant Chris Mack, right. As a college player, Mack transferred from Evansville to Xavier and was a Musketeers team captain in 1991–92 and 1992–93.

had obviously thought about it at great length. I was just so impressed with everything that he had to say about who he would recruit, what his program would look like, who his coaches would be. I left that meeting, called Father Graham, and we met the next morning. He met with Sean and we offered him the job. We introduced him that morning. It was really quick."

Miller was, in fact, announced as Xavier's 16th head coach July 8, a decision radio analyst and all-time leading scorer Byron Larkin dubbed "a no-brainer." The players were thrilled.

Miller credits former bosses Matta and Herb Sendek (North Carolina State) for preparing him for the opportunity. His experiences under both, Miller said, allowed him to know what he wanted his program to be, from recruiting to scheduling to strength and conditioning.

"Something that I always loved about Sean was he would talk about honoring the jersey," Rogers said. "He'd talk about the fact that when you put on a Xavier basketball jersey, you have to earn that, you have to play hard. One of the things I really appreciate about him is he understands how hard success is and he is so meticulous in his work process. The players respect him and they trust him because he doesn't betray that trust. He's a really sincere, honest guy."

AT ODDS? MAYBE NOT

Keith Jackson was recruited by Skip Prosser and played his first three seasons for Matta. Now he had to start over again.

Jackson had mixed feelings. He was happy Miller got the job, but he wasn't sure Miller was too keen on him. Miller called Jackson to his office soon after he became head coach.

"It's funny," Jackson said. "I always felt like we kind of butted heads my first three years. And then he sat me down and told me how much he respected how hard I worked and he made me a captain, which was totally out of the blue because I thought he didn't like me. He was the guy who always was hard on me."

Jackson had come off the bench for 85 of 95 games in his first three years and had a career scoring average of 3.7 points a game. Miller told Jackson he had talked to members of the team, and they recommended Jackson as a team captain.

"That shocked me, but I was more than happy to accept that role," Jackson said.

FIRST-YEAR BLUES

Miller was Xavier's first head coach without college head coaching experience since Pete Gillen was hired in 1985.

Not only that…

• Miller had a tough act to follow, taking over after Xavier's most successful NCAA Tournament run in program history.

• He came after a coach who won 26 games a year for three seasons and won 77 percent of his games.

• The program had eight straight 20-win seasons and four consecutive NCAA appearances.

• The only senior was Jackson. Miller would end up starting a freshman, two sophomores and two juniors. He had no natural leaders; they were too young.

• The schedule's first six opponents included area rival Miami University, Miami (Fla.), Creighton, Tennessee and No. 20 Mississippi State.

The Musketeers started 2-5, and Miller remembers thinking to himself: *I may break the record for the lowest winning percentage in Xavier history.*

"It's as real as it gets is how I would put it," he said. "There were many times when I would go to bed at night with the sickest feeling in my stomach because whether you want to admit it or not, the elephant in the room, so to speak, was: *Can this guy do it?*"

"There were struggles," Rogers said, "and you'd kind of hear: 'We didn't interview anybody else; why did we hire Sean?' I just don't think the fans know what to do with him. When he wins, they get mad because they think he's going to leave, and if he doesn't win, they rip him to shreds. I would say, 'Guys, you can't have it both ways.' "

As can be expected from such a young team, Xavier had an up-and-down season, finishing 17-12, 10-6 in the Atlantic 10 Conference. The team was not invited to any postseason tournament for the first time since 1996.

That said, the Musketeers won three of their last four games, and four players averaged in double figures for the season.

"The way that season ended gave me great hope," Miller said. "We played our best basketball at the end. I felt good about where we were headed. Having said that, the Xavier fan base is rabid and they're on you. I don't know in my first year as a head coach that they respected me a whole lot — nor did they really need to.

"No one really wanted to hear me talk about how young we were when, in fact, I was still in a sense proving to everyone that I could get the job done."

GOODBYE SEC, HELLO A-10

Thornton had a lot of college options coming out of high school in Louisville. Though heavily recruited by Matta when he was at Butler, Thornton thought he could do better than a Midwestern Collegiate Conference school.

So he chose Vanderbilt from the Southeastern Conference over Purdue, North Carolina State and Tennessee. "It was going to be big-time basketball, and obviously the academic credentials Vanderbilt has kind of speak for themselves," Thornton said.

He liked the city of Nashville and was on the SEC All-Freshman Team. He played well for two years, averaging 7.2

points as a freshman and 11.5 points as a sophomore, but the Commodores were a combined 28–33 during his time there.

"I don't like to lose," Thornton said. "Winning is fun. At that point, I kind of decided that I wanted to make a move."

Because of an existing relationship with Matta, Xavier became an immediate candidate. Thornton said he also considered Michigan and Tennessee.

"Xavier made a lot of sense because my mom and half my family were in Louisville and my dad and the rest of my family were in Indianapolis," Thornton said. "Xavier was a team that just came off of several NCAA appearances and was really on the rise, and Coach Matta was doing a good job up there."

The summer after he transferred from Vanderbilt, Thornton had surgery on both knees. He had to sit out the 2003–04 season anyway; now, he just couldn't play much basketball at all. No practice. Just rehabilitation and running.

"It was great being around guys like Romain Sato, Lionel Chalmers and Anthony Myles, being part of that Elite Eight run and being in Atlanta when we beat Texas and lost to Duke," Thornton said. "I think that experience gave me a lot of motivation to hopefully be part of some success once I had my opportunity to be back on the court."

Even though he had never played a game for Xavier, Thornton was voted one of the team captains for the 2004–05 season.

THIS IS HOW YOU DO IT

Miller was a standout point guard at the University of Pittsburgh from 1987–92. He started four years for the Panthers, finished with 1,282 career points and was the school's all-time assist leader.

The fact he was a successful Big East Conference player

goes a long way with the XU players. Every now and then, Miller even reminds the guys that he was once a player — and a good one, too.

Thornton remembers his coach being frustrated after a loss at Temple when the Xavier guards had a hard time getting the ball inside against the Owls' zone defense.

"I was having a pretty good season at the time, but whenever we played against a zone, it seemed like the zone kind of took me out of the game and I became somewhat ineffective at times," Thornton said.

"Coach Miller got so mad about the fact that we couldn't get the ball into the post — not just to me but the other guys, too — that he ended up suiting up for practice. He played point guard and basically said, 'I'm fat, I'm out of shape, I'm 36 years old, but I'm sure going to be able to get the ball in to Brian and the other post players.'

"He goes out there and practices for 20 or 30 minutes at the point guard position, basically puts our point guards on the bench and is like: 'Watch how I'm going to do this.' And he does exactly what he says and everybody gets excited. The ball gets inside, we score, it works out, and then he's kind of incapacitated for the next day and a half because he was so tired from practicing. ... He coughed for the next hour and a half."

OK, STAN, IT'S TIME

At practice before Xavier's sixth game of the 2004–05 season — against No. 20 Mississippi State on ESPN — Miller told Stanley Burrell he was moving him into the starting lineup.

"I really thought Stan was one of the centerpieces to our future," Miller said. "He was really talented. He loved the game. He played with such passion."

Burrell scored 10 points against Mississippi State and ended up leading the Musketeers in scoring as a freshman, averaging 12.7 points a game. But his lack of defense sometimes drove the coaches crazy.

"All I cared about was offense," Burrell said. "I was young, so I really didn't understand how important defense was. But Coach never really got on me bad because he knew that offensively I had a lot of responsibilities."

"I was confident he would learn and grow," Miller said. "Clearly he did. I was willing to give him more rope early on. Quite frankly, I didn't have a lot of choice. He was our leading scorer as a freshman. Whether it was fair or unfair, he maybe had a bigger role than he was ready for."

RISING TO THE OCCASION

Sometimes Burrell appeared ready for his role.

On Feb. 13, 2005, he produced one of the finest performances ever by a Xavier freshman.

Burrell pumped in 32 points — 22 in the second half — in an 83-72 victory at Duquesne. He made 10 of 13 field-goal attempts, was 4-of-7 from 3-point range and made all eight of his free-throw attempts. Burrell also grabbed eight rebounds.

"It was one of those games where you think you can make every single shot," Burrell said.

Looking back on it, Burrell also recalls that Bryant McAllister, the Dukes player he was defending, scored 20 points.

"I could not defend one bit," Burrell said. "Every time I scored, my man scored on me, too. It was terrible."

Still, Burrell had the second-best scoring total for a freshman in XU history, behind only Darnell Williams' 35 points in February 1996.

OH, SO CLOSE

Thornton had one of the best games of his career with 21 points, six rebounds and three assists in a tough 89-85 loss to 10th-ranked George Washington at Cintas Center on Feb. 2, 2006.

The Musketeers led by as many as 17 in the first half, but it was back and forth for much of the second half. XU was ahead 83-82 when George Washington got a 3-pointer from Maureece Rice. Thornton got leg cramps and was on the ground during the play, leaving the Colonials with a man advantage.

"It was a game we should have won," Thornton said. "We were up by 10 at halftime and we ended up losing because I got cramps ... and I had to come out for the rest of the game."

This was also the first game Burrell did not start since the beginning of his freshman season.

Why? He had missed a practice leading to the game.

After Xavier defeated Dayton at home on Jan. 28 in a game that started at noon, Burrell took a flight late that afternoon to New York City to visit a girlfriend. His plan — which he told Miller — was to return the next day in time for practice.

"I have no problem with you doing it; just make sure you're back," Miller told him. "I'm going out on a limb for you; don't make me look bad."

"I promise I'm not going to let you down," Burrell said.

And then ...

"They ended up having a huge snowstorm and my flight got delayed, so I had to catch another flight," Burrell said. "I shouldn't have taken the chance, even though my flight itinerary would have gotten me back on time. I missed practice and it really cost my team because I didn't start that game and we ended up losing."

Burrell first entered 4:09 into the game. He finished just 4-of-12 shooting with 12 points and three turnovers.

"That's what life is all about — you live and you learn," he said. "I learned from it and it made me a better person."

A BIG INJURY

"It was kind of a freak play," Thornton said.

He's talking about the end of his college career.

Thornton was having a solid senior season, leading Xavier in scoring and rebounding. Then came Xavier's Feb. 11, 2006, game against La Salle at Cintas Center.

"In the first half, it was a two-on-one break with me and Stanley, and he was going for a left-handed layup," Thornton said. "I was on the right side and he missed, and it was kind of a scramble for the ball. I tried to go and pick it up, and a guy from La Salle dove in to try and get the ball away from me and he just ran into my leg. My (right) ankle got caught underneath him and just snapped. It was broken."

PHOTO COURTESY OF XAVIER UNIVERSITY

Brian Thornton earned a master's degree from Xavier and became the school's first Academic All-American. "It's an honor," he said. "It feels good to be recognized on that level, because you have to show success in the classroom at a high level, but you also have to be successful on the court. Having that combination really means a lot to me."

Thornton had surgery the next day.

ESPN analyst Dick Vitale sent him a signed copy of one of his books and told Thornton to keep his head up. Jay Bilas, another ESPN analyst, wrote Thornton a letter about what a great career the player had and how he was going to be successful in life.

"He was like, 'If you ever need anything, references or whatever, please let me know,' " Thornton said. "That meant a lot to me that guys like that, who you see on TV on a daily basis, thought enough of me to extend their arms and to say thank you and good job."

His one regret: Thornton never played in an NCAA Tournament game.

"Obviously there have been lots of times when I wondered what would have happened if I didn't get hurt," he said.

"Probably the hardest thing for me as far as my college career, the biggest disappointment — it's not that I didn't score more points, or I didn't do this or that — it's that I never had the opportunity to be part of 'One Shining Moment.' "

BETTER LATE THAN NEVER

Less than two weeks after Thornton was lost for the season, Miller kicked starting guard Dedrick Finn off the team, prompting yet another adjustment.

After Xavier lost at Dayton on Feb. 21, Miller said, he learned that Finn had violated the team's curfew the night before the game. He added that Finn had been warned several times before.

The next day, Miller called Rogers and asked if she could meet in his office.

"I can't have him on my team anymore," Miller said. "I have to draw the line. We might not win another game, but I can't do this."

"It was a really unfortunate situation," Rogers said. "I don't think anybody felt good about it, but I was glad that Dedrick was able to finish up and graduate. I really in my heart believe

(Dedrick) tried to do the right thing and he would just kind of always get himself in a bad situation."

Finn started 102 career games and was averaging 5.0 points and four assists as a senior.

"Dedrick had been warned, reprimanded, disciplined and talked to probably as much in his first three years as any player I've ever been associated with," Miller said. "We attempted to help him in every conceivable way.

"It was, to me, the greatest decision that I have ever made as a coach to this day. It wasn't easy. I don't necessarily celebrate making it. But if I had to do it all over again, I would've made that same decision, much, much earlier, almost the day that I became the head coach. Just knowing you can't have a set of rules and a way of doing things that's sacred to winning, to have any credibility with the team. It isn't binding; it's just lip service. That's a mistake that I will never make again."

FRESH START

Xavier finished the regular season 17-10, without its starting center and point guard and with no seniors in the starting line-up for the second straight season.

The Musketeers did not have a bye in the 2006 Atlantic 10 Tournament, which was being held at U.S. Bank Arena in downtown Cincinnati. So they would need to win four games to earn an NCAA Tournament bid.

Impossible? Not at all. They had done it two years earlier.

"We were a completely different team; we had lost Brian and Dedrick," Josh Duncan said. "In a sense we had nothing to lose."

"We changed the style even one more notch after Dedrick was gone, playing Stan at point guard and having a short bench,"

Miller said. "What I found was we had unbelievable chemistry. We had guys that were on the same page and seemed to be almost exhilarated, like a fresh beginning."

Miller's motto for the tournament: "Play hard."

That's all he talked about with the team. He wrote those two words on the blackboard before each game. "I said that *ad nauseam*," Miller said.

"If you see a loose ball, dive on the floor," Miller told his team. "If you can get a rebound, go get it. Just play as hard as you can."

Xavier 75, Massachusetts 66. *Play hard!*

Xavier 59, Charlotte 55. *Play hard!*

Xavier 70, Fordham 59. *Play hard!*

"We just wanted it so bad," Duncan said.

"It started in Game 1, just watching our team learning the value of being on the same page," Miller said. "It rekindled how it felt to win. Some of the messages that I think our players have ingrained in them today really started right then and there."

The Musketeers played Saint Joseph's in the final. An NCAA berth was on the line.

Xavier was clinging to a 62-61 lead after two Justin Doellman free throws with 5.1 seconds to play. Saint Joseph's would end up with the ball out of bounds under the Xavier basket with 1.3 seconds left. The inbounds pass went to Dwayne Lee, who attempted a jump shot from the right corner. But Justin Cage blocked the shot and knocked it out of bounds to preserve the XU victory.

"He kind of paused in the air," Cage said. "I went up and I think he expected to jump into me, and I didn't jump off my feet. Then when he tried to shoot it, I was just long enough to block his shot."

Fans rushed onto the court when the buzzer sounded.

For the second time in three years, Xavier had won four games in four days to capture the conference tournament.

"It was awesome to cut the net down," Burrell said. "That's when I first got the feeling of how much goes into winning. It was addicting after that. I wanted to win everything."

One hundred miles away, in an Indianapolis hotel room, in between Big Ten Conference Tournament games, Ohio State's basketball coach was watching the game on TV and got all choked up.

"I remember crying in my room because I was so happy for Sean," Matta said. "I called and left him a message. I couldn't even talk on his voice mail."

THOSE DARNED ZAGS

Miller's first NCAA Tournament as a head coach lasted one game: a 79-75 first-round loss to Gonzaga. Again, Xavier had no seniors. Gonzaga had a national player of the year candidate in Adam Morrison, who would score 35 points and dominate the closing minutes.

Xavier, seeded 14th, was leading until a Morrison 3-pointer put his team ahead 72-71 with 1:56 left. Morrison scored nine points in the last 3½ minutes.

"Morrison just went crazy," Burrell said. "I remember having 22 points and five assists, and I was playing well, just doing everything trying to get us to the next round.

"When they won the game, Coach came on the bus and said: 'Remember this feeling for next year. We want to get back. You have a taste of it now.' "

Burrell was also outspoken after the game, criticizing Morrison's trash-talking and saying he "has no class whatsoever."

Morrison admitted to talking a lot, especially to Cage, who was guarding him, and especially late in the second half.

"I did apologize," Morrison said afterward. "But what I said is not for the public to hear. It's a college basketball game."

I NOW PRONOUNCE YOU ...

In August 2006, Doellman married his fiancée, Meredith, a Xavier soccer player who had just graduated. They met at the end of his freshman year and got engaged in December 2005.

Doellman said he asked Miller to go to lunch so he could get his coach's thoughts before deciding to get married before his senior season.

"I wanted his support," Doellman said. "I didn't want to do anything behind his back. I just have that respect for him and wanted his OK. I was nervous. He's kind of like a father figure, and going to him with that kind of situation you wonder what he's going to say or how he's going to react. And it couldn't have been better.

"He was real calm about it; he didn't really seem surprised. He told me how he and Amy (Miller's wife) were engaged his senior year. He was very supportive."

The fact that Meredith played college sports, too, meant she could relate and empathize to situations Doellman faced.

"(Getting married) was probably one of the best things I could have done for my career," Doellman said. "It made me focus a little bit more, and Meredith kind of helped push me through some ups and downs. I wasn't going back to a dorm room by myself and just having to sit there and be depressed about something. I could come home to her and she would cheer me up. Just being around someone you love that much helps you get through things."

PHOTO BY GREG RUST/XAVIER UNIVERSITY

PHOTO BY GREG RUST/XAVIER UNIVERSITY

Justin Doellman owns the school record for most games played with 132. He scored 1,402 points during his career and is the Musketeers' No. 18 all-time scorer.

Drew Lavender finished his college career with 1,428 points, scoring 769 in two years at Xavier and 659 in two years at Oklahoma. He led Xavier in assists and steals both years he played there.

HERE THEY COME

Throughout the 2005–06 season, Xavier coaches salivated watching Drew Lavender in practice. Ineligible to play that year after transferring from Oklahoma, Lavender could compete in games again in the fall of 2006.

XU did not recruit Lavender out of Columbus Brookhaven High School, where he was a McDonald's All-American. He started two seasons at Oklahoma, averaging 11.3 points and 9.7 points, but decided to leave, he said, because he was not getting along with coach Kelvin Sampson.

Geno Ford, who coached Lavender's brother at Shawnee State University, found out Lavender was leaving Oklahoma and called his friend, Xavier assistant coach James Whitford. That led to a campus visit from Lavender late in the summer of 2005.

"I thought it was a good fit for me," Lavender said.

He practiced against Finn and Johnny Wolf during his year sitting out and tried to stay as much a part of the team as possible.

"It was pretty tough watching us lose some games and feeling like I could help us," Lavender said.

Another key player was sitting out that season, as well.

In the fall of 2005, Xavier coaches approached 6-foot-8 freshman forward Derrick Brown about redshirting. Brown came to Xavier awfully thin, and the Musketeers had solid veteran forwards.

"We didn't think he would get as much out of his freshman year," Miller said. "We thought with five years, he could be a really special player.

"We called his family and high school coach before the season. We needed the help of his family. They really supported me, and to this day I really appreciate that. Derrick was so young and so thin. It's one of the best decisions as a program we made."

STANLEY & DREW

Xavier started the 2006–07 season 7-1 and clearly had more experience and depth than in Miller's first two seasons.

For the first time in his career, Burrell had a backcourt mate in Lavender who also was scoring in double figures. And that took some getting used to.

"I was so used to having the ball in my hands all the time and being the one making the play," Burrell said.

"It took a little while for them to grow and understand each other," Duncan said. "They got better as time went on, just like any relationship would."

Burrell and Lavender did not talk much outside of basketball. They were different personalities on and off the court.

Burrell is 6-3, an emotional player, more prone to ups and downs. He was trying to be a good team leader by doing all the right things.

Lavender is 5-7, steady, focused and rarely showing emotion on the court. He's laid back off the court, and tended to push the limits away from basketball.

"My size is a weakness to some people, but to me, I'm going to use it as an advantage and try to be quicker," Lavender said. "I tried to out-think a lot of players. I had to play harder. Everybody's not blessed to be 6-8, 240."

The two players had this in common: They both were willing to do anything to win.

"My thought process was to go out there and do what I do," Lavender said. "As long as we win, I'm happy; I don't care who's scoring."

"I was one of those guys if I was scoring and I was making my shots, I was helping the team big-time," Burrell said. "But if I was off, I was killing the team because I didn't defend, I didn't rebound, I didn't try to be a good leader, I didn't do anything else besides just shoot the ball.

"Drew coming in allowed me to do so many other things besides scoring. ... So it did make me a better player in the long run. But at first, it was really, really hard."

ROLLER COASTER RIDE

Burrell started his junior season with so much inconsistency it even drove him nuts.

He scored 26 points against Villanova in the semifinals of the Paradise Jam in the Virgin Islands, then came back and scored just four on 1-of-13 shooting against Alabama in the final.

He scored 15 against Miami, followed by three points on 1-of-7 shooting against Western Carolina.

He was averaging 11.6 points and had just scored 12 at Creighton heading into the Dec. 12, 2006, Crosstown Shootout at Cincinnati.

In the heated rivalry, Burrell went *scoreless* for the fourth time in his career, missing all 10 of his field-goal attempts and all four 3-point attempts. He also grabbed just one rebound, though he had six assists.

"I'm coming off the last Shootout where I had 20 points (as a sophomore) and I'm thinking I'm going to go off on them again," Burrell said. "I put too much pressure on myself going into the game. I just couldn't get my shots to fall at all. I had a terrible game. I worked so hard. I didn't understand why things were going bad for me."

The Bearcats won that night 67-57. Burrell thought he was hurting the team more than helping.

"After the game, he started to think bigger picture about doing a lot of different things to be a great player, not just scoring," Miller said.

"One of Stan's greatest strengths is his work ethic, his passion and his caring about everything. It can also be his Achilles heel. Stanley worked hard; that's why he feels tremendous anxiety when things don't go well, especially when it applies to his shot. He feels like he's invested a great deal, why isn't this thing going in?

"To me, the best shooters, the best scorers, they have no anxiety. It's like they couldn't care less how many they miss in a row, and that mind-set works to their advantage."

JUST DO IT

Xavier fell to 5-3 in Atlantic 10 play after a 93-91 loss at Duquesne on Jan. 31, 2007, a defeat that really bothered Miller. When the team returned from Pittsburgh, Miller and Mike Bobinski — who began a second stint as Xavier's athletic director in 2006 — had a lengthy conversation in Bobinski's office.

"He talked to me about believing in who I am and staying the course," Miller said. "He said, 'Don't let anybody on the outside determine our fate or tell us where we're going. You lead the way, do the things you believe in and we're going to be fine.' "

Bobinski stressed how it was just one loss. Xavier was 15-7 with eight regular-season games to go.

The Musketeers went 8-0 the rest of the way. They were regular-season co-champions of the A-10.

"We became a great offensive team," Miller said. "We were a machine."

HURTIN' FOR CERTAIN

Duncan struggled during parts of his junior year because of injuries. He hurt his back before the season started. It tightened up on him in practice and "got worse from there."

His back got better, and he played the first 20 games of the season before injuring his ankle Jan. 24, 2007, at St. Bonaventure.

"Somebody shot a layup," Duncan said. "I went up for a rebound and nobody was even around. I came down and I guess my foot was sideways, and I just rolled my ankle real bad."

He missed four games and averaged just 5.3 points and 1.8 rebounds over the last 10 games.

"I never felt great after that with my ankle," he said. "It got slightly better, but I never was back to my old self. It was frustrating. I think it made me a better person to go through something like that."

THANKS TO THE NCAA ...

Coaches always talk about taking it "one game at a time." But when the 2007 NCAA Tournament field was announced, it was impossible for coaches at Xavier and Ohio State not to notice their potential second-round matchup.

"It was a heckuva storyline," Miller said.

"Unbelievable," said Matta, the Buckeyes' coach. "What I didn't like about the game was we knew they were a bad matchup for us."

Sure enough, both teams advanced in the NCAA and were set to meet in Lexington, Ky. Ohio State was ranked No. 1 in the country and was a top seed in the Tournament. The schools had not played since the 1984 National Invitation Tournament, and this was only the fourth meeting ever between the schools that are separated by roughly 100 miles.

And then there was the fact that Matta, a good friend of Miller's, had left Xavier in 2004 after three years as the Musketeers' coach.

"We weren't in the locker room thinking, *Let's get Coach Matta back and make him feel bad for leaving*," Burrell said. "It was never about that; it was more like, *Let's get to the Sweet 16*."

"It was weird, but it wasn't as big of a deal personally as maybe people would think," Miller said. "The goal for all of us is to guide your team to a championship, to guide your team to a great season, to guide your team to the NCAA Tournament and advance."

It seemed as though the Musketeers were destined to pull

off the upset. They outplayed the Buckeyes most of the way and led by 11 points with seven minutes remaining. Xavier was still up nine with three minutes to play.

"Sean and our staff put together as perfect a plan as they had seen all year long," Bobinski said.

"I remember at one point saying to myself, 'It's been a heckuva season.' It looked like it was out of our grasp," Matta said.

Ohio State went on a 9-3 run to pull within 61-59 with nine seconds left. OSU center Greg Oden fouled Cage hard on a rebound. Xavier fans wanted an intentional foul called; it wasn't.

Cage had a one-and-one free-throw situation. He made the first foul shot for a three-point lead.

The second one bounced twice on the rim — and fell out.

"I wasn't nervous or anything," Cage said. "I wanted those free throws. It just didn't go in."

The next scene forever will be etched into the minds of Xavier players, coaches and fans. Ohio State's Mike Conley gave the ball to teammate Ron Lewis, who raced up the court on the right side. He launched a 3-pointer from about 24 feet.

Swish.

"It was a dagger," Doellman said. "You could feel the air just sucked right out of the building."

"We basically had nothing left after that shot went in," Burrell said. "In overtime they ran away with the game. But it was *our* game, and we let it get away from us."

Indeed, OSU dominated the overtime and won 78-71.

The shame of it was that Cage may have had the best game of his career. He was 8-of-8 from the field, including three 3-pointers, and finished with 25 points and six rebounds.

He also helped defend Oden, one of the top players in the

country, who worked hard for every one of his 14 points.

"We never would have been in that position if (Cage) hadn't had that level of game," Miller said.

"He couldn't have done any more than he did," Doellman said. "He was devastated obviously because we lost, but it wasn't his fault or anything like that. As a team we made sure he knew that."

Cage is OK talking about the game, but it's not always easy.

"It's not that it haunts me," Cage said. "But I think about it a lot. If I had made (the second free throw), we could have gone farther in the Tournament. It was the game of my life. What more could I have done?"

During postgame handshakes, Matta — who had recruited Cage to Xavier — hugged him and muttered, "I'm so sorry."

"He was kind of teary-eyed," Cage said. "The cameras were flashing, and it kind of choked me up for a minute."

"Probably the biggest mistake I made in that game was I downplayed it," Matta said. "I said it was just another game. I probably should've made a bigger deal, knowing what was going on in their locker room.

"I'll never forget the handshake at the end. I've never had an odder feeling. I was elated that we won, but I felt bad for Sean, for Justin (Cage) and Justin (Doellman) and Brandon (Cole). I was as happy as I could be for our players and our program, but why did it have to be them?"

Miller tried to keep perspective. His team had won 25 games. It played great against Ohio State.

"You immerse yourself in the total picture," he said. "I really was at peace. We didn't foul the 3-point shooter; that's not what we did. We lost to a great team. We had to play an incredible game to be in the position we were in. I could live with that."

Bobinski compared it to the loss against Duke in the Elite Eight of the 2004 NCAA Tournament when Xavier also surrendered a lead late in the game.

"I think it was a little worse, amazingly enough, even though the stakes in the Duke game were higher," Bobinski said. "The Ohio State loss seemed to burn a little bit deeper for whatever reason, and I wish I could explain why that is. It wasn't like the Duke loss felt very good."

THREE'S COMPANY

Preparation for the 2007–08 season started immediately after the Ohio State loss.

The players were hungry and determined to advance deeper in the NCAA. Seniors Burrell, Duncan and Lavender got together to talk about their commitment to leading the team.

And in their one-on-one postseason meeting, Miller talked at length with Burrell about becoming Xavier's defensive stopper, like Cage and Romain Sato before him.

"I felt like he could do it," Miller said. "He clearly had showed great progress and promise through his junior year."

Miller asked Burrell: What's more important to you — being one of the top 10 scorers in school history or winning big games and taking the program to places it's never been? That struck a chord with Burrell.

"I wanted to be more the guy that went out as a winner, went out as a champion and not just some guy that scored a bunch of points," Burrell said. "My whole mind-set was: What can I do to help my team win? I thought, *I'm a senior, this is my last go-around, and if we don't win, it's going to be on my head.* I just worked at it every single day."

Burrell took the same work ethic, desire and anxiety he had

as a shooter and applied it toward his defense, Miller said.

"He would review extra film," Miller said. "He knew his assignments inside and outside. He was relentlessness with conditioning and physical toughness."

The team had its stopper.

A LITTLE SETBACK

Xavier surprisingly lost at Miami in its second game of the season. The Musketeers had won six of their last seven games against the RedHawks and held an 11-point halftime lead.

In the end, XU's Jason Love fouled Michael Bramos on a 3-point attempt. Bramos made three free throws to give Miami a 59-57 victory before its largest crowd in Millett Hall in three years (6,140).

The next day in the locker room, Miller got his players' attention.

"We were watching film," Duncan said. "After watching it, he picked up one of the stools and threw it up against the wall. And then he kind of walked out. Everybody was mad that we lost that game."

A STATEMENT GAME

As bad as the Miami loss was, it was evened out 11 days later when the Musketeers knocked off No. 8 Indiana 80-65 in the final of the Chicago Invitational Challenge.

Excluding victories over rival Cincinnati, it was Xavier's first regular-season victory over a top-10 team in 19 years.

It was significant for other reasons:

• Lavender beat his old coach; he played for Indiana's Sampson at Oklahoma (remember, the two did not get along that well). They did speak for a few minutes the day before the game, mostly wishing each other luck. "The whole team was looking forward to it, but I think I was a little more focused for that game than a lot of games," Lavender said. "Just the way that me and Coach Sampson ended our relationship, it was a special game for me. I wanted to do so good and I wanted to win."

• C.J. Anderson, a transfer from Manhattan College, held his coming-out party. He torched the Hoosiers for 19 points and eight rebounds and was named co-MVP of the tournament (with Lavender).

• B.J. Raymond had 19 points and 10 rebounds for his first career double-double.

• Burrell, embracing his role as defensive stopper, battled Indiana's star freshman, Eric Gordon, who came in averaging 28.8 points. Gordon finished with 20, 16 in the second half. "The whole 40 minutes, I didn't care if I scored one point or if I made any good passes; all I cared about was using all my energy on slowing him down," Burrell said. "After that experience against him, I had the confidence that I could guard anybody."

WHAT A RUN

From Dec. 31, 2007, to Jan. 6, 2008, Xavier played three games that indicated it could be a special season.

The Musketeers hammered Kansas State from the Big 12 (103-77), Virginia from the Atlantic Coast Conference (108-70) and Auburn from the Southeastern Conference (80-57).

"We were clearly hitting on all cylinders," Miller said.

During that stretch, they scored an average of 97 points, won by an average of 29 points and showed depth, balance and toughness.

Seven players scored in double figures, six *averaged* in double figures, and as a team Xavier shot a combined 58.5 percent from the field, 59.4 percent from 3-point range and 82.9 percent from the foul line.

"Coach challenged us by putting those games on our schedule in the first place," Burrell said. "He believed in us and when we had to play them, we just took on that challenge."

NOT GOOD NEWS

In the first half of an impressive 62-60 victory at Charlotte on Feb. 13, Lavender turned his ankle. He continued to play but finished 0-of-5 from the field, with zero points, six assists and seven turnovers.

"One guard from Charlotte fell on my ankle," Lavender said. "I pinched two nerves on one side and strained muscle tissue on the other side. Or something like that.

"I had sprained ankles before. I thought I'd be OK in three or four days. It never got that way. Five or six games in, I thought my ankle should be OK. It was frustrating for me."

The status of Lavender's ankle would be a hot topic for weeks. He sat out the March 6 game against Saint Joseph's (XU lost 71-66). Sports talk radio, fans and media debated whether he should play on or sit and rest.

When it came time for postseason play, Lavender was declared ready to go. He played in the NCAA Tournament with extra tape and a brace, and though he claimed to be 100 percent, he said later that wasn't the case.

"I just said I was so it would take a lot of focus off me going into the games," he said. "It never healed all the way. It was a little painful, but for the most part I was OK. I was about 85 percent."

MAKING HEADLINES

Rarely does the announcement of conference postseason honors create any kind of major headlines, but when the Atlantic 10 awards were released, Burrell could not remain silent.

He was the league's Defensive Player of the Year and a third-team all-conference pick. Lavender and Duncan were second-team selections, and Duncan got the Sixth Man Award.

But Burrell did not like that no Musketeers were on the first team and that some of his teammates weren't honored at all. His rant, as reported by Dustin Dow of *The Enquirer*:

PHOTO BY GREG RUST/XAVIER UNIVERSITY

"I'm really upset about how things turned out. I called this after the Dayton game, and no disrespect to Brian Roberts, but I said things like this are going to happen; we're going to be left out. I've got champions in that locker room. B.J. (Raymond), C.J. (Anderson), Derrick (Brown). Those guys shouldn't have been left out like that. No way.

"It's ridiculous. This league is pathetic. We went 14-2, top 10 in the nation. Forget first team,

Stanley Burrell totaled 1,612 career points, which rank 12th on Xavier's all-time scoring list. He is tied with Lionel Chalmers for the third-most 3-point field goals with 235, behind Romain Sato (307) and Lenny Brown (236).

Josh (Duncan) is probably the player of the year. You've got the best team and nobody on the first-team all-conference team? It's ridiculous.

"… I'm sick of people overlooking us. I'm sick of us being labeled as a mid-major; we don't get no respect, man."

A few months later, Burrell was no less passionate about what he perceived as a slight. He said he felt bad for teammates who did not get any recognition and he felt as a team leader it was up to him to speak out.

"I had to stand up for those guys because I would want an older guy to stand up for me," Burrell said. "It would have been easy for me to be quiet. I got my award. But that's not the right thing to do. I was almost in tears. I would do it again in a heartbeat."

TOUGH ROAD AHEAD

The good news on Selection Sunday 2008: Xavier was awarded a No. 3 seed, highest in school history.

The bad news: The Musketeers had a challenging path laid out for them, starting with Georgia, the darling of the country after winning four games — including two in one day — to capture the SEC Tournament title.

The Xavier team was watching the NCAA draw at Miller's house.

"When I saw it come across the screen, it took everything in my power not to say, 'Aw, you've got to be kidding me,'" Miller said.

SAVING THE BEST FOR LAST

Before getting into details of Xavier's 2008 NCAA Tournament run, it has to be noted that Duncan, a former Moeller High School standout, put together a string of fine performances, including what might have been his best.

"I tried to do the same things that I had been doing throughout the year, just being aggressive," Duncan said. "It was in the back of my mind that this is it. It's one and done. I guess I just kind of got into a rhythm. I felt confident and tried to play relaxed and free."

Duncan averaged 18.3 points and 5.3 rebounds in four NCAA games, including a career-high 26 points in the Sweet 16 against West Virginia.

"From February on, statistically, he put it all together," Miller said. "He's one of the biggest reasons we got to the Elite Eight. So many times he was a difference-maker. He was such a unique player in shooting. We wanted him to be tougher around the basket, use his size in rebounding and become a better defender. That's the drum that I beat from Day 1, knowing that if he ever put that together, you would have yourself a terrific player. And that's what he became."

CALLING ALL SENIORS

Xavier came out tight in its first-round game against Georgia and trailed by nine points at halftime.

Miller didn't even wait until he got to the locker room to explode. He met Burrell at midcourt and shadowed him all the way to the locker room, screaming the whole time: *What are you doing? You're scared. You're tentative. What's going on?*

They walked into the locker room, and Miller went right after Lavender and Duncan, too.

"You guys are seniors — is this how you're going to go out?" he yelled. "Is this how you want to leave a legacy? Are you going to go out like this or are you going to fight for it?"

"He was just trying to challenge us and push us," Duncan said. "He's a good coach. He knows what he's doing."

Miller kept thinking that he could not afford to have his top guys playing scared or nervous.

"We were really, to me, hanging by a thread," Miller said.

"I took the position of losing my mind at halftime in hopes that they would either get mad at me or have nothing to lose. Though there wasn't a lot of strategy talk, I think it helped the team come out and refocus."

The Musketeers battled back for a 73-61 victory.

"After the game he came back in and his attitude was completely different," Lavender said. "He was talking about how tough we are. It was kind of funny."

They knocked out Purdue next (85-78) and were headed to the Sweet 16 for only the third time in the program's history.

Then Xavier got past West Virginia (79-75) and a familiar face, former Bearcats coach Bob Huggins, but it took overtime and some clutch shooting.

The Mountaineers were ahead 71-65 with 3:20 left in OT, but XU responded with a 7-1 run and tied it on a 3 by Lavender. West Virginia took the lead one more time, 74-72, then Raymond nailed two 3-pointers in a row. The second one came after a Xavier timeout with two seconds on the shot clock.

Burrell threw a long inbounds pass across the court. Raymond caught it, went up and hit the game-clincher.

"That was the play," Miller said. "Honestly, I don't even know how great of a play it was. It looks good when the shot goes in. My purpose in calling the timeout with two seconds (on the shot clock) with us in the lead was to make sure we didn't turn it over or take a horrendous shot that would lead to an easy West Virginia layup or 3-pointer."

And Miller thought Raymond was the perfect person to take the shot.

"Unlike Stan, he would be the guy you could never talk out of shooting because he thinks it's always going in," Miller said.

Xavier was headed for its second Elite Eight appearance and

a date with No. 1 seed UCLA in Phoenix. The seniors had accomplished a huge goal, but everyone was focused on the chance to get to the Final Four.

That wouldn't happen. UCLA was simply too tough, and Xavier did not play as well as it had earlier in the tournament. The final score was UCLA 76, Xavier 57.

The Musketeers pulled within six early in the second half, but the Bruins built their lead to 20 points.

"UCLA had the home crowd," Miller said. "They were ex-perienced, having been in the (regional final) game the last two years. They were relaxed, calm, confident. They were a better team than we were."

That said, it was a Xavier team that set a school record with 30 victories, won a regu-lar-season conference title, was ranked as high as No. 8 and ad-vanced to the Elite Eight.

"We were a very unselfish team," Duncan said. "Nobody was looking to get the credit. It was all about Xavier winning; it wasn't about any individual player. Everybody on the team bought into that, and that's a huge reason we were successful this year."

PHOTO COURTESY OF XAVIER UNIVERSITY

Josh Duncan averaged in single digits his first three seasons but led Xavier in scor-ing as a senior (12.4 points a game). His scoring average increased each year he played.

STATE OF THE PROGRAM

As soon as the season ended, Miller was asked about going else-where, most specifically Indiana. Without hesitation, Miller said he was not leaving the Musketeers. Period.

"I'll be back at Xavier," he said right after the UCLA loss.

He didn't leave the door open. He didn't say, to quote Pete Gillen, never say never.

"The 48 hours that I remember most in my professional life is the way Xavier treated me, to take me from where I was as an assistant to giving me this job, at a time when the program was in the Elite Eight," Miller said, reflecting on July 2004.

"There are certain things they wanted me to do then ... to make this place not necessarily a steppingstone, but to make this a program you can make your own, and thrive and enjoy and look at as a unique way of competing against the best programs in the country. I want to uphold my end of the bargain.

"How long that period of time is I'm not saying. Twenty years? Fifteen years? Ten? I do know that right now is not the time for me to entertain anything else."

Less than two weeks after those comments, Miller and Xavier agreed on a contract extension through the 2017–18 season.

Miller believes Xavier is poised to be consistently mentioned among the top programs outside of BCS conferences, along with schools like Gonzaga and Memphis.

"I think this program is primed to have more seasons like the one we just had," he said. "It's foolish to say it's going to happen every year. But we can be the very best non-BCS program in college basketball."

POIGNANT MOMENT

A day or two after he was named Xavier's head coach in July 2004, Miller went to visit the Rev. James E. Hoff at his on-campus apartment. Hoff, a former university president, had been diagnosed with terminal cancer that March and by July was living out his final days.

His physical condition had deteriorated, and Miller hadn't seen him much since the team's postseason banquet that April. "I went over and I sat in front of him," Miller said. "I didn't really know what to expect. I had been at Xavier for three years and I had gotten to know Father Hoff as well as I could for the role that I had (as associate head coach). He knew me. He knew every coach. But he didn't know me as the head coach. I didn't even know if he wanted me to be the head coach."

Miller laughed. Then he continued:

"I said to him: 'Father, I just want you to know that I'm going to try to continue the Xavier way of doing things, and I hope that you trust in me that I'm going to be able to carry on this legacy of coaching and do things the right way and we can have another season like we just had.'

"He grabbed my arm. He could barely talk. He looked at me and said, 'This program is in good hands. It's going to keep going, and you are going to make it go ...' And he used his hand and kind of went to the sky, like an airplane taking off.

"At that point, he started crying. He couldn't talk. And he just kept doing it over and over again as I sat there holding his other hand."

Hoff died July 23, 2004.

"It was one of those moments that you feel happened for a reason," Miller said. "I oftentimes think of that, whether it was early when things were hard or whether they're going the very, very best that they've ever gone here recently. That message and that mind-set — it's so reflective of Xavier because that's who he was, always pushing to do better, to do more, to be the best that you can be."

14

LAST WORD:
A TRIBUTE TO SKIP PROSSER

THIS BOOK IS SPECIAL TO ME. It's the reason I saw Skip Prosser for the last time.

We had talked on the phone about this project. When he was in Cincinnati in May 2007, he called me out of the blue and asked whether I wanted to meet him that night at Hap's in Hyde Park, one of his favorite places. We settled in at a table on the patio out back and talked for more than two hours.

We talked about Xavier, Wake Forest, my family, his family, coaches we both knew. He talked to Xavier students at the bar and bought them a round of drinks. He chatted with everyone who approached him. I will always be thankful for that night.

Skip died two and a half months later. The evening before a memorial service at Xavier, several media members — organized by Todd Jones of the *Columbus Dispatch*, a former Xavier beat reporter at the *Cincinnati Post* — gathered at Hap's to toast Skip. A few hours after we arrived, in walked Dino Gaudio, Skip's closest friend, who would take over as Wake Forest's coach. We were all there for the same reason.

Stories were told. A few pints of Guinness were raised in Skip's honor. Tears were shed.

In August 2007, I was asked by *Basketball Times* editor John Akers to write a column about Skip. I had covered his hiring at Xavier in 1994 and was the Xavier beat reporter from 1996–2000 for *The Cincinnati Enquirer*. Here's that column, rerun with Akers' permission.

It seemed fitting to end this book with a tribute to a good man and a good friend.

✶   ✶   ✶

BY MICHAEL PERRY
FOR BASKETBALL TIMES

Skip was different. He just was.

In the aftermath of his sudden, stunning death in July (2007), there were many stories told about George Edward "Skip" Prosser. Here are a few more that help to explain why Skip stood out in the world of college basketball.

• It was the 1997–98 Xavier season, and after one loss, center Torraye Braggs would not talk to *Cincinnati Post* reporter Kathy Orton after the game. I can't recall whether Skip read this in the paper or heard about it from one of the assistant coaches. But the next day before practice, Skip dragged Braggs — all 6 feet 8, 236 pounds of him — out of the locker room at the Cincinnati Gardens and pushed him toward Orton. "If you can talk to her after we win, you can talk to her after we lose," Skip told Braggs. "Now go answer all of her questions." Orton and I stood there in shock.

We talked about this later. Skip believed that learning to work with the media was part of the education process. Whether or not a player would go on to a professional career and have to deal with the media didn't matter. He represented his university at all times, even in dealing with reporters.

• One year, before the much-hyped Crosstown Shootout — the annual city rivalry between Xavier and the University of Cincinnati — all the local TV reporters showed up to practice for interviews. Skip emerged from the locker room, saw the newspaper beat reporters waiting to talk to him on the court, and he waded through the TV cameras to the print reporters. "You guys are here every day," he said. "They're not. You shouldn't be the ones to have to wait."

His practices were open. In the four years I covered Skip's teams at Xavier for *The Cincinnati Enquirer*, I attended almost every practice, heard his pre-practice talks, was invited to listen when guest speakers came and was free to roam into the players lounge and training room. It allowed me to get to know the players better, and to earn the trust of the coaches, players and support staff. Watching practice allowed me a better understanding of what coaches saw and why some players played and others didn't. It helped me be a better reporter.

He respected that I had a job to do — even though it differed at times from what he might prefer my role to be.

Yes, he was different.

Did we occasionally clash? Of course. I was the beat reporter, after all. Skip often didn't like the headlines on stories. He didn't always like questions that were asked of players, nor their answers. He questioned the play of stories in the paper, why we would have to rush to break a story with "negative" news, write about injuries or lineup changes. He was especially bothered if he thought Xavier got second-class treatment compared to the Bearcats across town.

But always we could talk about it. And then it would be

over. No grudges. Later, after I was off the beat and Skip was off to Wake Forest, I considered Skip and his wife, Nancy, friends.

When Skip suffered a heart attack in his office July 26, college basketball lost a man who was good for the sport, good for student-athletes and good for the universities he represented.

I recall an alumni event after a road game for which Skip made players dress in a shirt and tie. "Look people in the eye and call them by name," he said. "Make a good impression. One of the people in that room might have a chance to hire you someday." Always teaching.

Skip Prosser loved U.S. history (his father was a WWII veteran) and Irish history.

He loved the Pittsburgh Steelers, the colors black and gold and Bill Cowher — really everything about the city of Pittsburgh. He'd show video of Jack Lambert's hits to players to fire them up. "*We're* the intimidators," he would tell the guys in a pregame pep talk.

He loved the movie "Dead Poets Society." The only video he owned, he once said.

He loved to read: Basketball books. History books. Didn't matter. I ended up reading "Angela's Ashes" by Frank McCourt after Skip came to practice raving about it.

He loved quoting others, from Thomas Paine to Mike Krzyzewski to "Billy" Shakespeare.

Among some of his favorites: "Carpe diem" — Seize the day (Horace); "Acta, non verba" — Action, not words (from Skip's alma mater, the U.S. Merchant Marine Academy); and "Our chief want is someone who will inspire us to be what we know we could be" (Ralph Waldo Emerson).

He loved giving out nicknames. I was "Michael Dean" (Perry).

He loved his sons Mark and Scott and wife Nancy and called his mother Jo "a saint." Scott, who developed viral encephalitis when he was 7, was his hero. "A tough, tough, tough kid," Skip called him.

Skip took the fall for his team, never blaming players publicly and also hesitating to accept accolades for his team's success. "It's not about me, it's about the kids," he would say.

Nobody took losing harder or more personally. Skip could not stomach defeat. Many around the program used to joke that they couldn't wait until the next game after a loss so Skip could be himself again. Yet even in his worst moments, after some of his toughest losses, he'd see me standing there on deadline with notebook in hand, look up and ask softly: "Michael Dean, you need me?"

Skip had a gift with people. He made everyone feel special. He remembered names, your family members' names, details about your life, and that was as true for a campus maintenance worker as it was for a big-name donor or alum. When we would talk in recent years, conversations always started with: "How's the family?"

Though he rose in the college ranks, he remained humble and never forgot his roots. When Xavier got him a Jaguar to drive, Skip rolled down the window, smiled and said: "Not bad for a high school coach from Wheeling, West Virginia, eh, Michael Dean?"

This story could go on and on. And many others could add to it. Gaudio no doubt could tell stories about Skip ("My guy," he calls him) day and night for weeks on end.

You always wanted Skip to succeed because he was one of the good guys in sports and in life.

He was different. In a very good way.